brightly burning

brightly burning

***

Alexa Donne

TITAN BOOKS

BRIGHTLY BURNING
Print edition ISBN: 9781785659423
E-book edition ISBN: 9781785659430

Published by Titan Books
A division of Titan Publishing Group Ltd
144 Southwark Street, London SE1 0UP

First edition: June 2018
10 9 8 7 6 5 4 3 2 1

A CIP catalogue record for this title is available from the British Library.

Printed and bound by CPI Group (UK) Ltd, Croydon, CR0 4YY

For my mom, my first and most fierce advocate,
and the reason I am a writer

And for all the birds who will not be ensnared

ONE

The gravity stabilizers were failing again. I glanced up from my sketchpad to see globules of liquid dancing up from my drinking glass. They shimmered red, like droplets of blood, though I knew it was just cherry-flavored nutri-drink. *Dammit, that's my protein ration for the day wasted.*

A sigh escaped me, and resignedly I stowed my drawing tablet and stylus in the drawer under my mattress. They would be calling me any minute.

A moment later, right on time: "Stella Ainsley, please report to Area Twelve." The speaker crackled and popped, as it had done for years. I'd tried to fix it, but on a ship as old as the *Stalwart*, there was only so much you could do.

I tucked my long hair as best I could into a bun atop my head—harder than one might think with your hair floating in all directions—then I grabbed my toolkit and headed into the corridor, half bouncing, half floating with each step. Orange lights flickered on and off, rendering the hallway dimmer than usual, quite the feat, considering Ward Z was generally known as Dark Ward. A few small windows were cut in between brushed-chrome walls that hummed with the shudder of the engines, but starlight was insufficient to light the inside of a ship. Ward Z was the domicile of the *Stalwart*'s lowliest; why squander precious electricity on waste specialists and mechanics? Most of the ship's light energy was diverted to the fields. The *Stalwart* was the single largest provider of food in the fleet. I made a note to fix the light later, nonetheless.

It was a short journey to the supply bay, my quarters being conveniently close; I moved quickly from orange flickering over dull chrome down two levels to the antiseptic white glow of the ship's belly. The *Stalwart* was at least clever enough to allocate decent energy reserves to the working parts of the ship; it would do no good to repair essential systems if I couldn't see.

"There you are," Jatinder greeted me, wiping a sweat-slicked hand against an equally sweaty forehead. Small droplets floated up from the tips of his fingers. I could barely hear him above the grind of the engines.

"You couldn't call Karlson?" I asked, bouncing over to the secondary systems panel. "I have to lead class in less than an hour."

"That's more than enough time." Jatinder tsked. "And if it takes longer, Ancient Earth Sciences will wait. I need you and your lovely, tiny hands."

"My hands are perfectly normal sized," I mumbled as I set to work on the machine, which alternately *whooshed* and wheezed. "Did you already try hitting it?" I asked Jatinder, who grunted in the affirmative. Nevertheless, I gave the thing a good smack before resorting to more invasive techniques. But still I floated.

Jatinder attempted small talk as we worked. "You heard about any of your applications?"

"One said no. Two still pending," I said. "It's hard to find engineering positions, as you know." My hand slipped noisily against a pipe.

"Oh, my God," he said in Hindi, one of the few phrases I'd learned by this point, as he said it so much. "You must think me completely naive."

"What?" I played dumb, though heat rose to my cheeks at being caught in my lie. Jatinder knew me too well after more than three years of working together.

"We both know you aren't applying anywhere as an engineer. You hate the job, despite being very good at it— and not at all humble, I might add—and unless someone on another ship dies with no apprentice in place, you're not getting an engineering transfer." I opened my mouth to reply, but he kept going. "I had hoped you'd get over your foolish dreams of being taken on by some miracle ship to teach, but what is this? Your third round of applications?"

My cheeks burned furiously hot, from embarrassment, anger, and just a bit of despair. Jatinder was pessimistic—and pedantic—to a fault, but he wasn't wrong. Yet I clung to hope that I might escape the fate of being stuck in the bowels of an ailing food-supply ship for the rest of my life. Or worse, being jettisoned down to Earth whenever the *Stalwart* inevitably failed, doomed to certain death on the frozen planet below. The last ship that had deorbited over a year ago hadn't been heard from since. Crew probably all froze to death.

"Plenty of ships need teachers," I offered, my voice small.

He threw me a look that dripped with pity. "Stella, you know the good private ships don't take on governesses from the likes of the *Stalwart*. You're even less likely to get off this place as a governess than you are as an engineer. Unless that family of yours wants you back, you're stuck here."

My family? I could hear my aunt Reed's shrill tone in my ear as if she were standing next to me: *You have caused me nothing but grief. I am happy to see the back of you.* Those were her parting words to me. No, I was sure my "family" did not want me back.

I swallowed his harsh truth down like cold tea, pushing it past my throat, into my stomach, where I wouldn't have to think of it. Squaring my shoulders, I set to fixing the gravity stabilizer with extra verve. "I hope your brother gets back soon," I said sharply. Jatinder, barely older than I, was only temporarily in charge until Navid returned from a resource mission. I knew comparisons to his older sibling always chafed. "He said he'd try to get me a new tablet while he was away. Mine has been on the fritz."

"I don't know why you bother. There's nothing to paint but gray walls and billions of stars."

"I use my imagination. You should try it sometime."

It took a solid forty-five minutes, but I managed to remove the extra bounce from everyone's steps by returning the ship's gravity settings to normal.

"See? Just in time to go teach the bright young minds of tomorrow," Jatinder said, tossing me a soiled rag. I found a relatively clean corner and wiped my greasy hands off as best I could.

"I'll see you next shift, Jatinder." I rushed to get up to the school deck in less than fifteen minutes. Considering the *Stalwart* was several miles long and eight levels deep, that was no easy feat.

Having fixed the gravity problem at least, I moved up the decks more efficiently than I had on my way down, zipping through narrow corridors I'd practically memorized during my six years on board. Past residency wards U through Y, where officials long ago stopped caring about the colorful graffiti adorning the walls—some of which was my own. The warm orange and purples of a sunset over Paris, a city I'd studied but was likely now a frozen ruin, blurred by on my left just before I hit the stairwell that would take me up, up, up.

I arrived out of breath but with a minute to spare, my adrenaline rush of joy dissolving with a fizzle as soon as I saw the look on George's face. I knew that look. Someone had died.

"What happened?" I asked, ignoring the little flip my stomach did as George hovered close.

"Arden's mom," he said with a sigh. "It happened fast. Med bay couldn't do anything for her."

Of course they couldn't. On the list of things that were always in short supply: water, air, spare parts, food, medical supplies. I taught Earth History, so I knew people used to live eighty, ninety, even a hundred years. Not anymore. Jatinder's brother, Navid, was considered on the older side at the ripe age of thirty-four. George and I weren't the only orphans on board, though we were two of the only *single* almost-eighteen-year-olds left. Half our class was already married.

George settled a large, warm hand over my shoulder, giving it a squeeze. "See you at dinner later?"

I nodded, and George smiled just a bit, making me melt. I turned, crossing with a slight hesitation over the threshold into the room. It was a morbid location on the best of days—windowless, gray, illuminated by buzzing neon light—and when death came to call, the gloom clung to the walls, seeping through the rivets like motor grease. The kids were quiet, a wholly unnatural state of being for their age, and the pupil who ordinarily would be the happiest to see me met me with red-rimmed eyes and a quivering lower lip.

"Oh, Arden," I said, engulfing her in a hug. She sniffled into the slick fabric of my coat, and I glanced over at my thirty-odd pupils, sitting behind their communal-style desks with eyes politely averted. Enough of them had suffered the loss of a parent or family member that no one would judge a fellow student for crying in class.

What should I say? Surely not the platitudes they'd said

to me, a seven-year-old shocked numb by the passing first of a father—accidental death, on the job—followed swiftly by a grief-stricken mother, by her own hand. Something about God's will, and how at least now there'd be two fewer mouths to feed. While a pragmatic person, I wasn't heartless.

"You can skip today's lesson if you want. You won't get in trouble," I said gently, easing my way out of her grip and toward my desk. She nodded solemnly, retreating to a shadowy corner where the recessed lighting in the ceiling didn't quite reach.

"Good afternoon, class," I began with a deep breath, retrieving my lesson planner from the communal drawer all the student teachers used and flipping to where our last lesson had left off. "Who can tell me how a volcanic explosion can lead to an ice age?"

A hand shot up. Carter, one of my eagerest pupils, always reading ahead for the pleasure of it. Despite the melancholy, I caught more than a few kids rolling their eyes in Carter's direction. I called on him, knowing failure to do so would send him into a tizzy.

"When a supervolcano explodes, all the dust it releases into the air blocks the sunlight," he said. Competent enough for an eleven-year-old.

"That's just one part of it," I said, "but good job. And how long can an ice age last?" Carter's hand flew up again, but this time I waited a beat longer. A boy named Jefferson took the bait.

"Ten thousand years?"

"Not the big one," I said. "I was thinking more of how long this current one is predicted to last." Because there was no point in making a roomful of children panic.

"Two hundred years," a girl in the second row called out.

"That's what we're hoping," I said. "And when it comes time to go back down to the surface, all your farming skills will come in handy." I toed the *Stalwart*'s line perfectly, following the lesson plan they'd given me to a T, even if it made my teeth ache to push out the words. I knew an ice age caused by a supervolcano explosion could last a thousand years, and two hundred was a lowball estimate. "Your assignment for today is to write a short story about your ancestors who left Earth. What do you think they thought about the supervolcano? How did they find out about the evacuation, and what was it like to leave Earth behind and live in spaceships for the first time?"

I pointedly didn't mention all those who had been left behind. It was possible for human beings to survive an ice age; history indicated as much. But the percentage would be paltry; the casualties high. I tried not to think about all who had perished, though it was hundreds of years ago.

The students set to writing—it would be a class with a lot of downtime. I decided to seek out Arden, lest she be left too long to her own thoughts. I found her huddled in the back, crying over a potted plant.

"I don't understand," she sniffled, her voice hoarse.

"I know." I crouched down to her level, laying a comforting hand on her back. "It's not fair."

"But I watered it and everything!" Arden gestured at the plant, which, now that I considered it, was looking a bit droopy.

"If I can't figure out how to make it grow, I'll never get to be a farmer, and what if they stick me with something awful, like engineering?" she let out in a string of breathless words, then snapped a hand over her mouth. "I'm so sorry, Stella, I didn't think—"

"It's okay. Engineering isn't all that bad, but I know it's not for everyone." It was barely for me, but I'd take it over farming, personally. Arden, however, came from a long line of farmers—everyone on the *Stalwart* did—and I understood her angst. Everyone had to pull their weight on board, and working the fields was one of the more stable, fulfilling jobs.

"Did you put it under the sunlamp?" I asked. She nodded in the affirmative. "Okay, then how much did you water it?"

"What do you mean?"

"Well, you can water a plant too much, effectively drowning it," I said gently.

Arden's face fell. "I used my water rations to give it more. I thought it would help."

"Oh, Arden." I sighed. "Drinking your daily water ration is very important. You'll get dehydrated." Especially with all the tears she'd be expending over the coming weeks and months. "Come with me." I directed her to the front of the room and out into the corridor, where I unzipped a stealth pocket in my skirt and handed her my half-drunk day's rations. She greedily sucked it down, offering me her first smile of the day.

"Listen," I began, and her reaction was immediate—she obviously did not want to talk about her mother. So I veered into safer territory. "You're really bright, Arden, one of my best students. I'm sure you'd make a fine farmer, but it's not so bad if you end up doing something else. What don't you like about engineering?"

"It's dirty," she said, eyeing my less-than-pristine hands, then lingering on my face. *Great, I must have a smudge on my face. And George didn't say anything. Jerk.* "And," Arden continued, lowering her voice to a conspiratorial whisper, "I really, really don't like the dark."

"It's actually not that dark down there," I reassured her. "But you shouldn't be afraid of the dark, either. Think of it this way—the dark helps us to better see the stars, so it can't be all bad. Don't you like the stars?"

Arden nodded, glancing over at a large recessed window, through which distant stars could only just be seen. I wandered over, knowing Arden would follow, leaning so close to the thick glass that my breath fogged it up. I cupped my hands on either side of my face to block the haze of light from behind, squinting out at the myriad heavenly bodies.

"After I lost my mum and dad, I started talking to the stars," I said. "Someone told me that when we die, we are released out there, turned into something burning and brilliant. I don't know if it's true, but it brings me comfort. Maybe you can talk to the stars too. They're excellent listeners."

"Thanks, Stella," Arden whispered, leaning heavily against my side. And then she turned and was gone.

The ship shuddered, and I found myself careening backwards, landing hard on my tailbone as all the lights blinked out, leaving the ship in darkness.

two

I blinked against the pitch-black, spots of color dancing across my vision, smarting from the pain radiating through my backside.

"Arden?" I called out, feeling blindly with my fingers across the cool surface of the floor and wall, hoping to find her warm body.

"Stella, I'm scared."

She sounded close. I rose to a crawl, moving toward the sound of her voice until I bumped into what felt like her side. Feeling for her arm, then her hand, I intertwined our fingers.

"Arden, we're going to stand up now, and I'll lead you back to the classroom. It's just a blackout, and there's an emergency light inside. Then I'm going to go fix this." All I heard in return was a soft whimper, but she stood up all the same.

As we gingerly crossed through the hatch door to the

classroom, I said in my calmest, most commanding voice, "Everyone stay where you are and don't panic." I was surprised to find my voice shaky. I needed to maintain my grip so I wouldn't scare them.

This was not an ordinary blackout—that much was clear to me; that shudder preceding lights-out signaled some sort of engine failure, and the lack of emergency lights or any call over the intercom for my services told me we were looking at auxiliary system failure as well. I made quick steps to my desk from memory, and rustled through the large bottom desk drawer for the emergency lantern. As soon as it sprang to life, illuminating the front of the room in a dull orange light, a sigh cascaded from front row to back.

I called on a girl named Kayla to read her story, and then as quietly as possible, I darted back out into the hallway, peering down both ends. My vision had mostly adjusted to where I could make out the general outline of the walls, barely aided by the soft, useless glow from the windows. But no one appeared to be coming to our aid. I could just picture Jatinder down below, cursing up a storm at Karlson while I remained notably absent.

Then, the best sound in the entire world:

"Stella? Are you guys okay?" George's voice echoed down the hallway. He stepped into the classroom and, oh, God, I could tell he was wet—just showered. He smelled amazing, like fresh-cut grass, or what they told us it smelled like, anyway. I realized I was reacting wholly inappropriately—this was an emergency, and I was swooning over a freshly showered boy.

"We're fine," I reassured him. "But can you watch them? I need to get down to engineering."

George nodded, then indicated I should come close. *Yes, please.*

"It's serious, isn't it?" he asked in a low voice.

"It might be," I said. "Just don't tell them that."

He gave me a look. "I may be just a farm boy, but I'm not stupid."

"You are not just a farm boy," I chided. George was always selling himself short, so thankful for a place to belong that he lost sight of his many gifts. Like his ability to put up with a taciturn best friend like me. "If the lights turn back on, you'll know everything is fine," I said, my version of a bad joke. George's mouth remained in a firm line.

I turned back to face the class. "George is going to hang out with you guys—maybe if you're lucky, he'll walk you through some more math drills." I heard several groans. Then I threw a special wave over at Arden and sprinted out the door.

I'd made my way through the ship in the dark enough times to move quickly and efficiently, tripping only a few times—mostly over my own feet. There was a hum in the air, like a machine taking a nap while powered down, which gave me hope that the ship wasn't dead. Something was on, just not the lights. As I skirted past the field levels, I heard chatter, even laughter. The residents of the *Stalwart* didn't seem particularly concerned. The blackouts happened every few weeks now.

Then, as I made the small jump from the bottom of the

ladder taking me to Area 12, the emergency lights zoomed on, a low-intensity blue light lining the ground as far as the eye could see.

"Stella, you layabout, where have you been?" Jatinder greeted me with a frown but very little heat behind his words. A smudge of grease extended from his forehead down to his chin, and he was dripping sweat down his brow. Things were clearly in chaos. Karlson was already there, down on his knees, his upper half disappearing into a mechanical panel. I could hear the muffled clang of his wrench at work. I rushed to grab my kit from my locker.

"What's the situation?" I asked, retrieving my gloves and swapping out my day coat for my work cover.

"Engine Two failed, knocking out most secondary systems, most notably the lights," Jatinder said. "It's salvageable—and luckily the primary engine is fine, but we had to power it down temporarily to access Engine Two's panel without killing ourselves. I've already been in there; got the emergency lights back on, as you can see."

"And just in time," I said. "Any longer, and I would imagine there would be panic."

Jatinder only shrugged. "This ship is used to calamity. And we're not called the *Stalwart* for nothing. Now, you and Karlson, I want you to work on getting Engine Two back up—diagnose the problem, fix it, then file the report. Are you done with the air-filtration issue?"

We heard a grunt and then a bang. Karlson extricated himself from the floor, bringing himself up to his full height, which was a good foot taller than both Jatinder and me. While nepotism had gotten Karlson his initial assignment to the engineering team—it helped when your uncle was the captain—his natural gifts for machine systems far outstripped mine.

"You ready?" he asked, slipping his headlamp on as I did the same. "This might take a few hours, but I promise not to wear you out." He winked, but his dirty sense of humor had zero effect. A few years ago, I would have blushed, stuttered out my reply, but after working in close quarters with Karlson for three years, I just pretended to be amused and moved on.

But he was something nice to look at while I put in hard labor for the next few hours, which was the bright side I comforted myself with as I headed through a heavy metal hatch into the darkness.

I somewhat regretted giving up the remainder of my water rations to Arden. I had sweated out half my body weight, it seemed, getting the engines back online and all systems back up and running. But now they were, so smoothly that none of the hundred or so bodies packed into the mess hall for dinner seemed at all flummoxed by the two-hour blackout.

George was all smiles when I found him at the back of the room at a table surrounded by six girls from our age group: Becca, Cassidy, Eartha, Faith, Joy, and Destiny. Descended from American Midwestern farmers who'd won the lottery to join the *Stalwart*, and perpetually sunny, they found me a bit odd and let me know it—politely, but still. They all wanted a piece of George, one of the better specimens for marriage in our group, and the only one with an adorable *Empire* accent. Never mind that I was also from the *Empire* and had the requisite Old-World British accent myself, but apparently it was only swoon-worthy from a boy.

Dinner was a mush stew with little nutritional value to recommend it (that's what the protein rations were for), and while we ate, the digital message scroll that ran along the top of the wall let residents on board know the news of the day, as well as who had e-post waiting. I found my eyes glued to the screen for the daily "weather" update.

Year 210, day 65. Earth condition:
Change in ice cover minimal. Status: Fleet advised to
remain in orbit until future notice.

I glanced around; no one seemed to be paying much attention. The report rarely changed. We were used to it, the status quo: the ice age seemed to be lasting longer than anticipated, we should stay in space as long as possible, etc. On the nicer ships, this wasn't a problem—ships like the *Empire* or the *Lady Liberty* were kept up in repairs, extending their shelf life beyond what their builders had originally intended. Optimistic estimates said those ships could stay in orbit another twenty, thirty years at least. But the *Stalwart*... she wouldn't last that long. We were already past our expiration date. One of the chief reasons I was desperate to get off. If the fleet was going to cling to space as long as possible, I wanted to as well.

The e-post notification part of the scroll had started; I scanned eagerly for my name. It had been weeks since I'd answered the job advertisements I'd found on the fleet community board; surely the other two would reply soon.

"Stella? Hello?" George snapped his fingers in front of my face to get my attention. "Why are you so spacy today? Was it that bad down there?"

I found all eyes glued on me. Eartha and Faith had the good sense to look scared, so apparently not everyone on board was clueless as to how badly things could go on an old, dying ship. "It was fine," I said. "I'm just waiting for some post."

"Who would write to you?" Destiny said. There was no particular rancor behind it, but it hurt, nonetheless. Indeed, who would write to the orphan with the relatives who hated her?

I had to fess up. I fastidiously avoided looking at George as I did. "I applied to some jobs off-ship. Teaching jobs, that sort of thing."

The silence that followed was awkward. The girls barely concealed their looks of pity—they clearly agreed with Jatinder that a transfer would never happen, that I was wasting my time and burning up hope—and George's mouth formed a straight line, his jaw so tight, I was sure he was clenching his teeth together with all his might. I had gone behind his back, and he was pissed.

Just when I thought it couldn't possibly get worse, Faith,

like a testament to her name, piped up, "Well, you have a message." She pointed to the scroll, and indeed, there was my name. A giddiness I couldn't control spiked from the pit of my stomach up into my heart—what if it was an offer?—only to plummet straight back down, forming a pit of dread at the base of my spine. And what if it wasn't?

"I should go check that," I said, getting up from the table.

My feet carried me from the mess hall to the community room, where most of the desktop tabs were thankfully unoccupied. I logged in, pulling up my message portal, and there it was, right at the top in tantalizingly bold writing.

Application for teaching position on board the *Scandinavian*

I clicked on it, holding my breath as the message loaded. And immediately let it out in a dejected puff. "We regret to inform you..."

It was like a kick in the gut, or being vented out into space without warning. I glanced out the window, and of course, just my luck—there it was. The *Scandinavian* went merrily about its business orbiting the Earth, not caring one whit that it had just dashed my dreams. I could see the *Empire*, too, much farther away, but immediately apparent in its elegance. It wasn't a hunk of barely functioning metal like the *Stalwart*. The *Empire* was constructed as a luxury ship for high-class people. I could just picture my aunt and cousins taking tea at this hour, gazing out upon the dirty countenance of the *Stalwart* and laughing at my expense.

Just as I risked being drowned by the disappointment, George poked his head inside the community room, his red hair like a beacon. Only the look on his face quelled any momentary surge of happiness I felt at seeing him. He'd come to hash it out.

"And?" he asked as he approached, choosing to take a seat in the row in front of me so he was facing me head-on.

"They said no," I said, my voice wobbling against my wishes.

"Who was it?"

"The *Scandinavian*."

"They're crazy not to take you. But I can't say I'm not glad."

"That's an awful thing to say," I bit back.

"No, it's not. You think I want you to go?" George said, a pleading look in his eyes. "I can't believe you didn't tell me. How long have we known each other?"

"Six years," I answered quietly. Guiltily.

"Six frexing years! Team *Empire* Orphans, Stella. I can't believe you would just throw that away."

"You don't understand," I tried to explain. "I'm suffocating here. I just... I don't want to die down there like my father did."

"You won't," he said. "I won't let that happen to you. I promise."

"You can't promise that. People die every day. Today it was Arden's mom; tomorrow... who knows?"

"You can die on another ship as easily as this one, Stel."

"You and I both know that's not true," I scoffed. "The

death rate on the *Stalwart* is triple what it is on the *Empire*. And we're six times more likely to have to attempt reentry within the next two years. And you remember what it was like with the Kebbler outbreak. Not all ships, or the people on them, are created equal."

It was a low blow, reminding him. The Kebbler virus had raged through the fleet six years earlier, disproportionately killing the poorest citizens. There were never enough vaccines to go around, it seemed, and their distribution was notably skewed. From the working-class section of the *Empire*, both of George's parents had died, while my well-to-do relatives—and I, too, luckily—had escaped unharmed. All the rich people on the *Empire* had.

"So your solution is to leave? To leave me behind?"

"It's not like that—"

"Then what is it like?" George snapped. "I'm not as smart as you are, Stella. I'm good at two things. Farming, and being halfway decent at teaching kids numbers. Neither of those is in particularly high demand outside the *Stalwart*. I'm stuck here."

"You'll be fine. You have Becca, Cassidy, Eartha, Faith, Joy, Destiny…"

"They're not you. They're…"

"Pretty? Prospective wives?"

"That's not fair," George said, looking distinctly uncomfortable.

"Listen," I said, backtracking, "it's not about leaving you. I promise. I'll miss you something awful. I just can't stay, not if I have the chance to leave. Which is looking distinctly unlikely now, anyway."

The tears threatened to come, with a vengeance. Two jobs down, just one to go. Odds were I was facing another rejection, and it wasn't often that teaching jobs popped up on the fleet. I'd be turning eighteen soon, which was when I'd be locked into my full-time position as engineer. I was running out of time.

"Hey," George said, reaching past the tab screen to gently nudge my chin up. "It's not the end of the world. You're great. And if they couldn't see that, they're stupid."

"What happened to being glad they rejected me?" I sniffed.

"I can be both. Happy you're staying, and mad at them for being stupid enough to reject you." He leaned back in his chair, rolling into a stretch. I tried my best not to stare at the way the muscles of his stomach went taut under his thin shirt. It should be illegal not to wear your day coat on board. "Where else did you apply?" he asked.

"To the *Shanghai*. They said no weeks ago. And then I applied to this funny little private ship I've never heard of. The *Rochester*?"

George shook his head. "Never heard of it either. Must be on the other side of the orbit order."

"Yeah. So that's my last hope. And of course, it's the one I wanted the least."

"Come back to the mess with me." George hopped up, pulling me toward the door. "They're showing a movie. Apparently there are witches and crazy Earth weather."

I pictured myself sitting in a dark room for two hours with George, watching as the other girls tried to play footsie and sneak hands where they shouldn't go. All while nursing a bruised ego over my failed prospects. I just couldn't muster up the emotional fortitude it would require. "No, that's okay. I'm going to head back to my room. Draw myself into a better mood."

George did not appear convinced this was a good idea, but he let me go without any further chastisement. Ward Z was as dark as I'd left it that afternoon, and my quarters were cramped as always but blissfully quiet. I pulled out my tablet from where I'd stowed it earlier, clicking it on to find the warm glow of the screen and the half-finished landscape I'd been toying with for days.

Using the watercolor setting, I'd dashed an orange smudge against the sky to represent what I thought a sunset looked like, purple-and-white mountains rising in the background, a blue-green lake in the foreground—purple because I'd heard them described as "purple mountain majesties" in an old American anthem once. Orange because books told me that was the color of the sun dipping in the sky. And water was blue-green, the colors of life so rarely found in space.

I sighed, abandoning the fool's errand of trying to capture an imaginary, long-forgotten place, opening a new file, switching to the charcoal setting, and starting a portrait. I always began with the eyes—they were bright, laughing, and kind. Then the line of his nose—strong but fine—then those lips. How many times had I wondered what it would be like to kiss him? To kiss anybody, for that matter?

This wasn't making me feel better. My life was nearly half over, and I was stuck. So many of my peers retreated into romance, companionship, finding solace in the familiar rhythms of family life. But I couldn't ignore our position, and I didn't want to be married off to some boy, like a prize cow. Not that we had any of those on board. Old Earth expressions had a funny way of persisting.

I gave up on representing charcoal George, just like I knew I should give up on flesh-and-blood George. But I'd tackle that challenge tomorrow.

three

A tendril of hair loosed itself from the bun coiled tight atop my head. It teased against my ear and caught Jatinder's disapproving eye.

"You should cut that silly long hair, girl. Or else someday you'll catch it in a gear shift and tear the scalp straight off your head. Won't be pretty."

I grunted a response, the best I could offer him in a conversation we'd had many times over the last three years. We were two hours into the shift; Karlson and I were checking and double-checking the systems that had failed earlier that week, just in case. Thus far, we'd come to the same conclusion repeatedly: the ship was old, and things like this would continue to happen.

What I didn't bother to tell Jatinder: I had considered a haircut, more than once. The dangers of long hair in a machinery environment were very real. But I kept my hair long for the same reason I put up with ship repair: for the tenuous connection it gave me to my parents. To my mother, who used to pull a wide-toothed comb through my long hair fifty, a hundred times until it lay glossy and sleek. To my father, a skilled engineer who took pride in every job, no matter how thankless. They were long dead, and as such, I barely remembered them, but for the tug of that comb; the softness of my mother's voice; my father's strong, weathered hands as they guided mine over a machine part.

"You going to the memorial later?" Karlson asked as he paused to wipe the sweat from his brow. "I hear they're bringing in a DJ after the speeches. Good stuff to dance to."

"I don't know," I said. "I was thinking of turning in early."

"That's so boring," he chided. "We only get a chance to have fun, to dance, maybe three times a year, and you'd actually skip it? We should enjoy it while we can. There won't be any DJs down on Earth."

"Don't get on that stuff again. I don't get why you're so obsessed. We should be trying our hardest to stay up here, not planning on going down there."

"It's just practical," Karlson said for the thousandth time. He was an avid "Earth truther," telling anyone who would listen that Earth was in all probability habitable again, and we were wasting our time, wasting away up here.

"Anyway, it's not like I haven't been to the last five memorials," I said. "The speeches don't change."

"Is this because you're trying to avoid someone whose name rhymes with Morge?"

"No," I answered a bit too quickly. Karlson smirked.

"You should come to drink away your sorrows, then. I'm sneaking in some hooch. It'll help."

"I didn't hear that!" Jatinder mock-shouted.

"I'm happy to share, though I'm sure the adults have their own stash, better than mine."

"Maybe I'll confiscate your stash." Jatinder waggled his eyebrows.

Karlson ignored him, turning back to me, lowering his voice to accommodate greater privacy. "Seriously, Stella, come. We've had too hard a week not to have a little fun. Go with me as friends."

It *had* been one hell of a week. Jon Karlson might not have been my favorite person on board, but spending the evening with him would trump orbiting George and his groupies for the evening. I shrugged and nodded in one movement, drawing from him an all-too-unsettling grin.

The space usually home to transport and cargo planes had been transformed. A platform at the aft end displayed a familiar red-and-black banner emblazoned with the fleet logo and motto: *Survival Through Unity*. Beneath that were the symbols of the fleet's fifteen primary ships representing Earth's wealthiest and most advanced nations that fled at the time of the disaster, plus the logo for the private ship federation.

My eyes traced over the familiar lines of the pitchfork and wheat stalk of the *Stalwart* emblem before moving to the top of the banner, where I found far more beautiful symbols. The elegant fleur-de-lis and Eiffel Tower of the *Versailles*, the lion and vibrant flames of the *Shanghai*, the emerald lady surrounded by stars for the *Lady Liberty*. Technologically advanced, thriving ships I'd never see. Or at least never see again. My eyes locked on the jeweled crown entwined with tea leaves of the *Empire*.

Joy hissed through her teeth, taking me away from unpleasant memories. "They didn't take the *Crusader* off. Awkward."

I wondered if, when we were finally forced to deorbit as they had been, they'd leave our logo on there too. When the *Empire* held its Remembrance Day ceremonies for years to come, would my aunt think of me? Probably not.

I spotted Karlson saving us seats in the third row, but first Joy pulled me toward George and the other girls to show off her handiwork. Against my better judgment, I'd let her dress me and do my make-up. The underlayer—my trusty moisture-wicking bodysuit—was mine, but everything else was clearly Joy's. Bright and showy and wildly impractical. The overdress bodice was laced tight, with a skirt that flared at my hips, swooshing as I walked. The color was bright saffron—a hue that complemented both our brown locks but felt foreign on me, like a second skin that didn't quite fit. My hair was slicked back, gathered into a high ponytail, my eyes lined with dark kohl. I actually felt sort of pretty.

"Stella, you look amazing!" Destiny said, giving me a high-five, which I met a little too enthusiastically. My hand smarted from it, but I didn't care. Joy had plied me with her secret stash of booze, which she called "magic juice," and I had to agree with the term. I might as well have been floating. George gaped in my direction, and I simply smiled back.

"Oh, Stella," Faith piped up, "you left dinner early, so you didn't see you had a message notification on the scroll."

That just figured. It was likely my third and final job rejection. I'd check it later. Tonight I would have fun. But first I had to go sit next to Karlson, who, despite my turning him down for "something more," I was fairly certain still thought this was a date. He stood up from his chair when I approached, nervously complimenting me. Then he offered me more secret alcohol, which I didn't turn down.

Soon Captain Karlson took the stage, introducing Representative Engle and someone named Mason. We knew the drill. Every year, to mark the anniversary of the Kebbler virus outbreak, our elected representative and some other random government wonk from the *Olympus* came over, delivered some pretty speeches, let us dance, and then no one spoke about it for the next year.

Engle's speech was pedestrian, a recounting of the history, peppered with personal anecdotes about how he'd felt watching the *Stalwart*'s population perish from afar. He affected anguish, but you couldn't miss his sense of relief that he'd been spared, having been safely ensconced aboard the *Olympus*. Everyone clapped politely, but no tears were shed. Then Mason spoke.

He was middle-aged, balding, with an unremarkable face, not unlike the parade of bureaucrats I'd seen at the last five memorials. But the man knew how to give a speech.

"Life in space is harsh: life in exile," he began. "Yet we have survived. Persevered. Six years ago, we faced unspeakable tragedy. Many lives—too many lives—were lost to the Kebbler virus. Every ship suffered losses, but none more than the *Stalwart*."

"Liar," Karlson hissed under his breath. Then he leaned over and whispered into my ear. "None of the private ships lost anyone, and no one on the *Olympus* died." I pretended to clear my throat and told him to stop. His uncle, the captain, was glaring at us. Mason continued, oblivious.

"You lost thirty percent of your population. More than three hundred people. Your pain was, and is, immense. But we banded together as a fleet, stopped the virus in its tracks. Survival through unity."

"Survival through unity," the crowd echoed back instinctively. Karlson laughed. I smacked him on the thigh. His response was to pass me the flask. Mason didn't seem to be close to finishing, so I took a sip or three. It was hard to forget how many the *Stalwart* had lost. I hadn't known any of them, as George and I had been imported to the *Stalwart* as part of the Orphan Transfer Program after the outbreak had been contained. But every year as I sat through the speeches, I remembered the panic and grief. Behind us, I was sure George was thinking of his parents.

Finally, a good twenty minutes later, Mason wrapped up

with: "We forge forward, together, but we must never forget."

The room erupted into applause. Karlson took a long drag of drink.

"You're the one who wanted to come to this thing," I said, snatching the flask away so he would take a break.

"My uncle made me." He leaned into me, body warm against mine. "That Mason guy is here for an inspection. He wants to ground us, which I'm all for, but the captain insists on playing nice and begging for a few more years' reprieve."

"Maybe your uncle is right," I said.

"You're my date. You should agree with me." He pouted, a bit drunk.

"We're here as friends, remember? And if I was your date? I wouldn't agree with you just to make you feel better."

I was rewarded with a smile. "That's why I like you, Stella."

His earnestness made my cheeks burn, and thankfully someone shooed us from our chairs so they could clear them away. Date or friends, it would feel good to dance.

He handed off the top-secret bottle to me, since I had several well-placed pockets to store it in. Suddenly I was very popular. The girls were perfunctorily nice on a good day, but never much beyond that. Tonight, we were thick as thieves, dancing en masse on the makeshift dance floor by the stage. Boys whose names I barely knew—several years older than me, and a few younger as well—tucked up close, warm hands on my waist and hot breath in my ear, paying me exaggerated compliments to curry favor. I was an easy target, and shared with everyone.

Then there was Karlson, who at some point insisted I call

him Jon. He oscillated between staying true to his word that we were just here as friends, leaving me to dance for hours with everyone else, and being stubbornly possessive. Toward the end of the night, both of us more than a little drunk, he was all hands, and thankfully recently showered for once. He kept "whispering" in my ear. Only with the booming bass and driving beats, he had to shout for me to hear.

"I heard you're trying to get out of this hunk of metal," he said, close against my eardrum as we held court at the center of the dance floor.

"Probably won't happen," I answered. "I'm stuck here!"

"You should go with me, then. Down to Earth. My uncle may want to keep everyone up here, but I've almost talked him into letting me lead a scouting party."

"That's a death sentence," I said. "It's still too cold."

"It's better than dying up here. You know this ship is rotting from the inside." He got very close to my ear. "We could start fresh down there, eke out a good life."

"You're drunk!"

"Yeah, but I'm right," he replied stubbornly.

"Is he bothering you?" It was him. My George. Pretty, pretty George.

"Hi!" I was practically bouncing. "We're fine! You're fine. We're all just great!"

"Stella, come with me," George said, and suddenly it was like I was floating, following after him, through the crowd, outside into the cool corridor. "What's with you? You've never been like this."

"Like what?" I could feel the bass reverberating in the metal walls and desperately wished to go back inside, but then I realized George had a firm grip on my arm.

"Throwing yourself at guys."

"I'm not throwing myself at anyone," I insisted, trying to dance my way out of his hold. "They're throwing themselves at me! Are you jealous?"

"No, I'm not jealous," George said. It sounded ridiculous to my ears, like the highest notes on the piano—*tink, tink, tink.*

"I don't believe you." I quieted him with a finger pressed over his lips. Lips that looked too inviting, lips I could kiss. So I did.

It was clumsy, wet. A blur. But also bliss. Until it wasn't.

George shoved me away. "Stella! What the frex!" I felt my stomach plummet. "I don't... I don't think about you that way. So please... don't."

Suddenly things were clear. I had laser focus. And I felt like I was going to be sick.

"I'm sorry," I spat out, careening away down the hall to the stairs. Up. I wasn't sure where I was going, but with each level, my head felt a bit more clear. Then I was on the main deck, and I knew where I was headed: the community room. Straight back to the desktop tab in the corner. I logged on, checked my messages. I clicked on the one that called out to me in bold:

Application for teaching position on board the *Rochester*

I read the first line of the response:

Dear Ms. Ainsley,
We were delighted to receive your application and would like to offer you employment aboard the Rochester.

And then I promptly vomited all over my shoes.

four

I woke regretting all my life choices. My body ached, but that pain was secondary to the wretched pounding in my head, as if something had burrowed into my skull with a hammer and was striking it against my temple over and over. Still, I rose from my bed, shuffling to the food port for my day's water and protein rations, gulping down half the water in one go.

My underdress was the worse for wear—more soaked in sweat and grime than usual. I'd had a banner week. At least my chance to steam-clean my clothes was close. It was Friday, so I just had to get to Sunday. I pulled on clothes, thankful my day coat, at least, didn't smell like stale hooch.

For once, the dim of Ward Z was a gift, and I wasn't the only person sleeping in after last night. The corridors were mostly quiet. I trudged, slower than usual, to the community room to ensure I had not imagined the missive from the

Rochester. So much of last night was a blur.

I avoided my favorite station—back corner by the window— lest they connect me to last night's vomit splash. I repeated the fuzzier of the evening's steps: logged in to my account, opened my message portal, clicked on the top missive, no longer bold. And I read it again in the sober light of the morning:

Dear Ms. Ainsley,

We were delighted to receive your application and would like to offer you employment aboard the Rochester. *We were impressed with both your teaching credentials and your experience with ship maintenance. The* Rochester *is a private ship with a small but dedicated crew, and we would request that in addition to tutoring your intended pupil, you also offer auxiliary support to our engineer. We will provide you with a monthly stipend of two hundred digicoin, as well as room and board, of course.*

While we did already appeal to your ship captain for permission to take you on aboard the Rochester, *please be sure to speak with your placement head as well prior to departure. We will require you to bring your citizenry papers along with you. We've arranged for a shuttle to pick you up in two days. I am very much looking forward to making your acquaintance in person. Welcome aboard the* Rochester, *Stella.*

In Salutation,
Iris Xiao
First Officer, the Rochester

Wait. Two days? They'd sent this yesterday, which meant the shuttle would arrive *tomorrow*. Frex. Suddenly it was all real, and panic rushed me. I'd have to say goodbye to everything I had known for six years: Jatinder, Karlson too, the children—Arden!—even the girls from my age group. I'd miss them all. And George most of all. Oh, God, I had kissed George. Heat rushed into my cheeks, and the hammer in my head started going again. For a brief moment, I worried I'd vomit, anointing yet another corner of the community room. But thankfully it passed.

I hadn't anticipated the crying children.

"But who will teach us about Earth history?" Carter wailed to a background chorus of sniffles and moans from the others.

"And art," Arden chimed in. It was her favorite subject—a useless bonus class I snuck into other lessons when I could. Even Jefferson, the resident smart-ass, seemed upset.

"You always taught us the weird death stuff that no one else did, Miss Stella. I'll miss you," he said.

"I'll miss you, too," I said honestly, drawing as many of the kids as I could into a big group hug. "Now you'll have someone offship to talk to—isn't that exciting?" A murmur of consideration went around. It left the worst of the criers in slightly better spirits, enabling me to extricate myself from the hug and head for the door with a final wave. But Arden wasn't ready to let me go.

"Stella!" She jogged after me, catching me halfway down

the corridor. She grabbed hold of my hand. "I've been talking to the stars, like you said. I think my mom got my messages."

"Good!" I said, crouching down and blowing out a steadying breath, willing myself not to cry. "I'll miss you a lot, Arden. Just send me a message through the tabs instead of the stars. George can help you until you're old enough for your own account."

George. I sighed at the reminder, then put a smile back on for Arden. "And don't stop drawing. Or give up on that plant." I drew her into a hug before saying a final, solemn goodbye.

Luckily there was no risk of tears with Jatinder.

"You can officially count me as surprised and impressed, Stella," he conceded, shaking my hand. "We'll miss you here— and those tiny hands—but I wish you the best of luck."

"I'm sad I won't get to say goodbye to Navid." *Or get my new drawing tablet,* I kept to myself. "And I'll miss you, too."

"I'll be sure to pass on your best wishes to him," he said. We shared an awkward embrace—the kind where neither person really wants to touch, but a handshake would seem too formal—then I turned to Karlson. Him, I offered my hand.

"Transferring off-ship just to get away from me, eh?" Karlson said. "Bold move, Ainsley."

"It was that or do something drastic, like parachute down to Earth."

I ignored how attractive he looked when he laughed at my joke.

I couldn't find George. I wandered the ship for hours, and upon arriving at each successive location with no George to be found, I developed a hollow feeling in the pit of my stomach. I had less than twelve hours left on board, and my best friend was making himself scarce. Avoiding me. Eventually, lights-out and curfew caught up with me, and I was forced to retreat to my quarters on Ward Z. I packed in the dark, my meager belongings fitting easily into the small carry bag I'd brought with me to the *Stalwart* all those years ago from the *Empire*.

My hand touched something fuzzy, tucked away in the back of my wardrobe—worn to the point of no longer being soft. Even if I couldn't see it properly, I knew what I had found. Earl Grey, my old stuffed elephant. When Aunt Reed handed me over to the orphan export board, I'd clung fast to him, even though I was far too old for stuffed animals. The other kids made fun of me—*Baby Stella needs her bestie, Mr. Elephant*—but not George. He'd stood up for me, told everyone he wished he still had his childhood stuffed toy, only his had been thrown away during quarantine, and that I was lucky to have a piece of home—they were all just jealous. We'd been friends ever since.

And now we wouldn't be anymore. The thought made me want to cry, so I forced myself to sleep. When the lights came on the next morning, I did one last sweep of the room, making sure I'd grabbed everything I needed, especially my drawing tablet and stylus, and my water and protein rations for the day. I would save them for the journey. Earl Grey went in last. Then I pulled on my gray overcoat, put on my regulation boots, and sat down on the bed.

This was it. Something flickered inside me, tickling up from the bottom of my spine. Hope. I wouldn't die on the *Stalwart*, or plummet down to Earth against my wishes. Who knew what awaited me on the *Rochester*? But I knew this much: It was new. And it was mine. With the spark heating the soles of my boots, I hefted my bag over my shoulder and stepped out into Ward Z for the last time. "Goodbye, dark, cold, sad place," I whispered to no one but the stars in the sky.

The transport bay was cold and I was early, so I dropped my bag on the ground, fashioning it into a makeshift chair, and sat down to wait. I pulled out my drawing tab and clicked it on, finding my last work in progress staring up at me. George. Or half of him, at least. He was missing his jawline, hair, cheeks; his smile. A fresh wave of grief washed over me. I'd never see his smile again. I imagined I could hear him, calling my name.

"Stella! Stella!"

Wait, that wasn't in my head. I turned around and there he was—breaking his jog to skid to a stop in front of me, chest heaving. "I've been looking everywhere for you!" he said breathlessly.

"You?" I said, rising to my feet. "I searched the whole ship for you yesterday, but you were clearly avoiding me!"

"I…" George at least had the good sense to look ashamed. "Yeah, I kind of was. But I didn't know you were leaving! Destiny told me this morning, who heard it from Joy, who heard it from Karlson… What happened?"

"I got that last job. Totally unexpectedly. And they're sending a private transport for me, so I couldn't exactly change the date. I tried to find you…"

"Listen, I'm sorry. I didn't mean to—" He stopped himself before he could rehash the details, for which I was thankful.

"I know," I said. "All that matters is you're still my friend. I'm going to miss you."

"I'm going to miss you, too. So much. You don't even know." His voice broke on the last bit, and I couldn't help but crack a smile.

"Are you going to cry, George?" I chided. "I have Earl Grey in my bag, if you need him," I joked, but my heart was fit to bursting. Mending my friendship with George meant everything.

"*Empire* orphans forever," he said with a smile.

I recited it back, feeling the prick of tears behind my eyes. "I'm going to hug you now," I warned, not bothering to wait for permission. George was stiff at first but soon melted into it, and suddenly we were like we'd been in old times. George and Stella, *Empire* orphans forever.

The screech of metal and an airlock venting behind us alerted us to the arrival of the transport. George held me tighter. It was like I was home. But home wasn't forever. Sometimes you had to leave. I knew that in my heart. I broke away, wiping a stray tear with a callused index finger. Crying was no way to start an adventure.

"Write to me," I said. "Whenever you can. And help the kids send messages too. I promised Arden you'd help." George nodded, pursing his lips together hard. "Tell me which of those silly girls you choose. For the record, Joy's my favorite. Team Brunette, all the way." It was an attempt at levity. I glanced back. The ship had settled, and an attendant emerged, approaching to pick up my bag. Two men scurried to load several food crates; this was clearly a stop with dual missions.

"I'll see you later, okay?" I made a promise I couldn't keep, but it seemed to make George feel better. He nodded.

"Bye, Stella. Check your messages tonight. There'll be one from me."

"Thanks," I said, turning to board the shuttle before I could do something rash, like change my mind.

The attendant, it turned out, was also the captain, and the shuttle was tiny. He pointed me toward a seat—it looked comfortable, at least—that was only feet from the food crates, now secured with ropes and netting for the journey. The hatch door shut, I peered out the window, and there was George— he'd changed positions for one last chance to wave goodbye, which he did, and I returned the wave. It was now or never.

"Strap yourself in, then," the captain said, voice gruff and accented. I couldn't quite place it.

"Where are you from?" I asked as I took my seat. The chair was indeed comfy—padded better than a bed, and it seemed to recline, too. I could catch a nap if I wanted.

"The *Saint Petersburg*. You know it?"

"A little," I said. The *Saint Petersburg* had held orbit neighboring the *Empire*, and many aboard specialized in private transports, like this one. An *SP* transport had taken the *Empire* orphans to the *Stalwart* six years ago, too.

"I am Sergei Orlov," he introduced himself. "You strapped in? Good. We must depart right away while traffic is clear. We'll talk later."

He disappeared into the cockpit, hidden past a short, dark corridor. I took a deep breath. In, out. The engine shuddered on with a kick-start that sent my heart racing, the small ship lifting up, hovering. I pictured George on the platform outside, watching us go. I imagined he looked sad.

We started moving, slowly at first—into the airlock, I presumed. Then the engine roared, g-forces pushing me back into my chair until I felt glued to its padded surface. I could see out the adjacent window, barely. Gray turned to black as the ship faded behind us, giving way to the stars. I realized I was gripping the hand rests and willed myself to stop. We zoomed through space, the engine working itself up to a frenzy for a good ten minutes. And then it stopped. The pressure on my body eased. Sergei stepped out from the cockpit, looking very pleased with himself.

"Perfect takeoff. Good momentum for the trip. Here, I have food and water for you." He tried to hand me a small rucksack—overkill for daily rations, if you asked me.

"Oh, no, that's okay," I said. "I brought along my day's rations, as I figured when we arrive tonight I'll be fresh out of luck for food and water on the *Rochester*." I unclipped my safety belts and moved to go to my bag. "It should tide me over well."

He scoffed. "We're not arriving anywhere tonight, let alone the *Rochester,* my young traveler. And I've seen what those aboard the *Stalwart* get—you'd best take what I'm offering. I promise you these rations are heartier than anything they give you on that death bucket." He shoved the bag into my lap.

"What do you mean, we're not arriving tonight?" I asked, trying to contain the alarm in my voice.

"It'll take two days at least to get to the *Rochester*. Didn't they tell you?"

"Tell me what?"

"The *Rochester* is in orbit around the moon."

five

couldn't help it. I laughed.

"I'm sorry," I said, "but I thought you said the *Rochester* was orbiting the moon. But that's crazy."

"*Nyet*, not so crazy. She orbits the moon, I promise. It's odd, but they are loyal customers and pay me handsomely for my services, so I go. Four to five days, round trip. I make them pay for fuel." Sergei chuckled to himself and didn't bother to try to convince me further. He proceeded to make himself a cup of tea.

"Pour me one too," I said, feeling bold. I made my way to the hatch window and could see the fleet growing smaller behind us. What had I signed up for? "Wh-why would a ship orbit the moon?" I asked, hating the way my voice cracked. Like I was scared.

"That, you can ask them when I deliver you. It's none of my

business why some fancy private ship would do such a crazy thing." He handed over my tea, the smell making my mouth water. Tea was a rarity on the *Stalwart*. It smelled heavenly, and the first sip fulfilled the promise of its aroma.

"Shouldn't you be flying the shuttle?"

"Autopilot. It'll be a smooth ride. Hope you have something to read."

I didn't, but I had my drawing tab. Reluctantly I set down my tea, though only after taking another hearty sip, and retrieved my tab.

"When you are ready to sleep, you let me know. I have a special drink for that. You'll sleep much better, longer."

I nodded, waving him away, and turned on my tablet. And there was George again, half-formed eyes twinkling up at me. I swiped it away. Time to draw something new.

I took Sergei up on his sleep aid and awoke who-knew-how-many hours later. A quick look out the window and seeing nothing but space cartwheeling into infinity told me we were far from the fleet, and Earth. The moon had to be close.

"Good morning," Sergei said as he emerged from the cockpit. "Or evening, rather. We will be there soon. We've made good time." He looked me up and down. "Do you wish to change? I can give you some privacy."

"Oh, no," I said, looking down at my sad state of affairs. My underclothes had turned pungent. "These are all I have. I'm fine," I said in a quiet voice.

Sergei tsked under his breath. "At least you're going to a better place. The *Rochester* imports the best clothing. I bring it to them. You'll see."

I doubted part of my stipend would include clothing, but I nodded at him, hoping he'd drop the subject. Instead, he decided making conversation was the order of the day. "What do you know about the *Rochester*? Why are you going there?"

"I don't know much," I said. *Like, you know, that the ship is orbiting the moon.* "Only that it's a small, private ship that needed a teacher. The ad said one pupil, age ten."

Sergei looked pleased, like he knew a secret he could let me in on. "They say it is haunted. Lots of spooky goings-on on board. I never stay longer than I must."

"What do you mean, it's haunted?"

He shrugged. "I've heard reports of strange sounds, sabotage, people disappearing. More than a few personnel have left. I have transported them happily away."

"Can I have another cup of tea?" I needed something to warm the chill that was settling in my bones. Sergei grunted in the affirmative and went to heat some water. I moved back to the window, but the view was the same as before. "How close are we to the moon?" I asked. "Can I see it from the cockpit?"

Sergei eyed me while plucking two tea bags out of a colorful box whose emblem I did not recognize. "If you are very careful, and promise not to touch anything."

I was enthusiastic and emphatic in my reply, immediately bouncing forward through the cramped galley way and into a gallery of glass and blinking blue screens. The view beyond the front window screens was breathtaking. The moon shone white, its smooth surface mottled dark in a scattershot pattern like a bruised peach. I couldn't help but compare it to the only other heavenly body I had glimpsed so close; its beauty was mesmerizing, but in a sad, melancholy way. The surface held no life, no swirling cumulus masking the teeming ecosystem below, like Earth. Yet it called to me, a hunk of rock slipping solitarily through the skies.

But she wasn't alone—I had decided the moon was female—no, just off to her left side, if I squinted, I could see a ship. Or, more accurately, I could see the glint of moonlight refracting off the sleek metal surface of a craft. We'd have to fly closer for me to make out any detail.

"You see her, yes?" Sergei came in behind me, teacups in hand. It seemed he favored the feminine as well, but he was referring to the *Rochester*. I nodded. "Another few hours, at most; then we will dock." He handed me my tea and, to my surprise, invited me to sit. With bated breath, I lowered myself into what would have been the First Officer's chair and got a view of the nose of a ship from a whole new perspective. In the foreground blinked screens scrolling ship data—speed, fuel measures, etc.—and beyond that, the unbroken vista of space.

"I should have been a pilot," I let out breathlessly.

Sergei smirked into his teacup. "Yes, it is a very good life. But, not always so safe. And very lonely. You're better off as a teacher, you can trust me."

I didn't have the heart to tell him that being a teacher could be just as lonely as drifting out in space. Sometimes the loneliest you could be was surrounded by people who didn't understand you.

We docked with the *Rochester* at three in the morning. Despite my daylong sleep, my internal body clock vehemently protested the late hour; as the ship door lifted open, I found myself yawning. The airlock was small, barely large enough to hold the transport ship, and through the reinforced glass doors at the far end, I could see the shadowy figure of a woman there to greet me. Sergei led the way, not bothering to unload the food crates—he'd already told me he would do it in the morning before he departed—with me trailing behind, dragging my bag along the grated floor in my weary state.

The glass door slid open to reveal the figure, a petite woman in a well-fitted uniform jacket, which tapered into a dress, its form-fitting black fabric covering her short legs. Did they not wear wicking underdresses aboard the *Rochester*? I'd never seen such a fine coat. The woman in it smiled, the corners of her eyes crinkling with wrinkles of a severity I'd rarely seen.

"Welcome aboard, Stella. I am Officer Xiao, though you may call me Iris." She offered me a hand, which dutifully I shook, all the while thinking there was no way I'd be so informal as to call her by her first name. Sergei had no such compunction.

"Iris, my old friend," he greeted her, pulling her into a

bruising hug that featured more backslapping than I felt strictly necessary. His choice of adjective was apt—Officer Xiao had to be at least forty. Old by fleet standards, though the judgment was not meant as a slight on her appearance. I found her age made me think her more sophisticated, someone I immediately felt I could trust.

"Sergei, always a pleasure," Officer Xiao said with genuine warmth and maybe a hint of flirtation. "You know where to find your temporary quarters, and feel free to help yourself to something in the kitchens. This is a late one for you."

"Made excellent time," Sergei said before waving us off and disappearing down the shadowy corridor.

"Please forgive the dark conditions," Officer Xiao said once we were alone, gesturing for me to follow closely behind her as we made our own way. "We were expecting you first thing in the morning. The ship's lighting systems are on a sleep timer, and it didn't seem necessary to tamper with them when I could show you to your quarters myself."

"Dark" was a relative description. The *Rochester*'s night setting was brighter than Ward Z on its best day; cool blue lighting piped along the floors and ceilings, casting the corridor in an eerie glow. Even in shades of dusky blue, it was apparent that the *Rochester* was the nicest ship I had ever set foot on. There was not an exposed rivet to be seen, and no brushed-chrome finishing—when I ran my fingers against the wall as we moved briskly into the heart of the ship, I felt only smooth coating and tapered edges. I couldn't wait to see it with the full complement of lights on.

"Here we are," Officer Xiao announced as we arrived at a depression in the corridor, which I realized was a door. "I have it key-coded at the moment, but we can reset it with your bio scan tomorrow." She tapped and swiped at a panel set at chest level by the door, punching in a four-digit number code. The two interlocking panels that comprised the door whished open with near-silent precision, revealing quarters four times the size of mine aboard the *Stalwart*.

"Welcome home," she said with a flourish. My mouth hung agape.

"This is all for me?" I stepped carefully over the small rise at the bottom of the hatch, through the doorway, and into the room, which could best be described as pristine.

"Of course it is. We wouldn't ask you to share. Anyway, we have more rooms than crew on board. Jessa has two rooms dedicated to her use. We thought three might be pushing it."

"Jessa? Is that my pupil?"

"Yes. You'll meet her later today. But for now, try to get some rest. Morning lights are on at seven, and breakfast is served at eight. I am up at six, should you need anything. Sleep well, and we are very glad to have you here." Officer Xiao bent slightly, dipping her head to me in a formal bow. Clumsily, I returned the gesture. Then she left me.

It took me five minutes to find the button that shut the door. Then I was faced with a new problem: standing in the pitch-black with no idea where anything was. There was no blue-piped lighting in here. Fumbling in the dark from memory, I unzipped my bag and found my tablet, using its meager illumination to search the room. There was no light switch.

I closed my eyes, breathing heavily, inhaling and exhaling to the same rhythm as the low hum of the ship's machinery. Willing myself to calm. To think. This was a ship, not unlike the other three ships I'd been on in my life. They couldn't be too dissimilar.

A sound, high-pitched and bloodcurdling, jolted me out of my Zen moment. It was like a laugh. But that couldn't be. I was spooking myself in the dark.

"How do I turn the lights on?" I mumbled to myself, then jumped again as the lights flicked to life, like magic. Maybe Sergei was onto something, and this ship was haunted. Or maybe…

"Lights off," I tried, and, voilà, they were off. Voice-activated asset control, like aboard the *Empire*. Only in my aunt Reed's quarters, none of us children had our voices authorized by the control system, so only she could use them. "Lights on," I said one more time, convincing myself I'd entirely imagined that eerie laugh.

I investigated the bed, which was three times the size of my old one, testing a hand on it and finding it firm but springy, the charcoal-colored sheets soft instead of slick. On the *Stalwart*, everything was designed to wick moisture and require less-frequent washing. I considered for a moment that I shouldn't lie down on the covers in my filthy clothes, but a childish giddiness bubbled up inside me, overpowering my practical side, and I flung myself backwards onto the pillowed surface. Bliss.

I lifted my head to survey the room from this angle, then cocked it to the side, curious. There appeared to be another hatch door directly across from me. I got up, taking two, four, six, eight steps across the room—it was insanely large—and tentatively pressed the square-shaped button I found next to it. *Whoosh*, the panels parted, and I literally gasped. I had my own bathroom.

At this rate, *I* should be paying *them* to live here. This was more luxury than I could handle. Even the *Empire* wasn't this well appointed.

Stepping inside, I waved my hand in front of the sink faucet, and just like the lights, it spouted water like magic. I gazed longingly at the shower, but who knew how water was rationed here, so I didn't dare use it. Instead, I retreated from the bathroom and set to peeling off as many layers as I could so I could try to get some sleep.

I left my bag on the floor, as I didn't see any obvious areas for storage. I'd have to ask about that when the household was awake. I got down to my underdress, then slipped under the covers, sighing as my whole body sank into the plush of the mattress. I tried not to think about the laugh as I requested the lights be turned off. Thankfully, my mind and body were wearier than my conscious brain could battle, and before I knew it, I had drifted off to sleep.

SIX

I awoke to Officer Xiao bustling about at the foot of my bed, folding linens.

"Oh, good, you're awake!" she said, then frowned. "We've got to get you out of that underdress, though. Did you shower?"

"No, but I will whenever I get my shower rations for the week."

"Stella, we don't ration the water on board the *Rochester*," she said, her tone somewhat flabbergasted. "You can shower whenever you like. Everything's on a Kolburg recycling system. You'll also see you have your own personal desk-tab unit over there." She pointed to a desk to the left of the door. "And I've got some new clothes for you."

She indicated the drawer that appeared at the foot of my bed when she pressed a hidden spring hinge and walked to the left of the bed. Then, placing a hand against one of the wall alcoves and pressing inward, she revealed a closet full to the brim with dresses and jackets.

What *was* this place?

"Oh, and whenever you're feeling a bit stir-crazy, there's always the window."

"Window?" I asked, peering around. I didn't see a window. She moved to the other side of the bed, pressing another stealth button. And then half the wall opened to reveal a black canvas of stars. That got me out of bed.

"I've never had a window this big," I said stupidly, letting the view engulf my comparatively tiny body.

"Hope you don't mind that we put you on the star-facing side. We had one or two rooms that face the moon, but they weren't quite as spacious."

"It's perfect," I breathed.

"I'll leave you to shower and get dressed, and then I'll come back in about an hour to show you where the dining quarters are."

I searched the room for a rations tube and found none. "We don't get our daily rations delivered to our quarters?" I asked.

"No, not on a ship of this size. The captain prefers we dine together." She cast a kind smile in my direction. "I know you'll have a lot of new routines to adjust to on board. I'm confident you'll do well." The door closed with a *whoosh* behind her.

Excitedly, I peeled off my underclothes and stepped inside the bathroom, eyeing the shower again. I extricated a hair tie from the end of my greasy braid, tossing it onto the floor and looking for an on switch. But—I wasn't crazy, was I?—I didn't see one.

"Shower on," I said, and immediately water spouted from all directions. Unfortunately, it was freezing cold. "Too cold!" I shrieked, squirming with hands protecting my most sensitive bits from the onslaught. But quickly the water turned warm. I sighed, letting the pulsating rhythm of the jets of water massage my aching muscles, savoring the feel of water sluicing down my back, wetting my thick hair thoroughly.

"Please close your eyes," a flat, feminine voice intoned, shocking me within an inch of my life.

"Wh-why?" I asked, sure this was a trick.

"I am going to provide soap now," the voice continued. "I don't want you to get any in your eyes."

Of course. You talked to the ship. The ship talked back. I closed my eyes, then smelled the sharp aroma of soap. I found a rough sponge on a ledge in front of me when I opened my eyes.

"What about my hair?" I asked the shower. On the *Stalwart*, there was a special soap for washing hair.

"One moment."

I felt the pressure of something squirt against my skull. I worked the gel into my hair until it foamed satisfyingly, sighing as the water washed away the last week. Death. Dancing. Saying goodbye to George.

"What is your name?" the voice asked.

"Stella," I answered reluctantly. "And, uh, what's your name?"

"Thank you for asking," she intoned. "My name is Rori. Or *Rochester* Onboard Roving Intelligence."

"Nice to properly meet you, Rori," I said.

"Likewise, Stella. Please close your eyes again. I am preparing some conditioner." I didn't know what conditioner was, but I obeyed. This time, it didn't foam.

And then, after another minute, it was over.

"There is a towel to your right. Have a nice day, Stella."

My shower was so polite! I dried off, finding a new toothbrush and toothpaste by the sink, so I happily brushed my teeth as well. With water, even. Now to figure out those new clothes.

"Stella, you look lovely," Officer Xiao said when she came to fetch me, and despite her compliments, her gaze made me self-conscious. I tugged at the black fitted sleeves of my bodysuit, then adjusted my dress, fashioned on top like a uniform—stiff fabric, squared shoulders, a taut, half-neck collar—much like what Officer Xiao wore. I wasn't accustomed to such luxe, tailored clothes. And so few pockets.

My new boots pinched my feet as I followed Xiao down the now properly lit corridor, recessed lighting in the ceiling panels revealing details the previous night had obscured. Where the *Stalwart*'s overwhelming geometric theme was squares, the *Rochester* favored the soft, rounded countenance of circles. Every twenty feet, between breaks in the bulkhead, were circular doorways, giving the corridor the feel of gliding down a tube. Our rooms may have been white, but the dominant color scheme in the gangways was black, offset with gray so dark, it might as well have been black. It was like walking through shadows.

"Officer Xiao?" I asked as we walked, remembering my query from the early hours of the morning. "Last night I thought I heard someone laughing outside my room. Do you know what that might have been?"

"Someone laughing? Don't be ridiculous," she scoffed. "I'm sure if you heard anything, it was just one of the cats or something."

"I'm sorry, did you say cats?"

We turned right, down a shorter hallway, then left. "Oh, yes," Xiao said. "Call it a quirk of the Fairfax family. The first generation aboard this ship brought their cats, and we've had them ever since. They're harmless, I assure you. Friendly, even, if you're their sort of person."

It had been many years since I'd encountered a housecat, but I was sure they couldn't laugh.

We arrived at a hatch door that looked no different from any other—how would I ever find my way around this place?—but when Officer Xiao pressed the button to open it, its function was clear. It was the ship's mess hall, writ small. A table about eight feet in length and several feet across was bolted to the floor in the center of the room, with ten swiveling, padded seats lining each side and bookending the heads of the table. Directly across from the door was another magnificent window, the moon blooming in the panel's right-hand corner. We were so close, I could make out details of individual craters.

If my eyes were overwhelmed, it was nothing compared to the onslaught my other senses faced. I breathed in the scent of food, practically tasting it on my tongue. My mouth watered. There was oatmeal, real buttered toast, soy bacon, sautéed tomatoes, baked beans, and my beloved tea, to cap it all off. We had had spreads like this on the *Empire,* but I never imagined I'd see one again. I didn't wait for Officer Xiao's permission to grab a plate, and she didn't object. Indeed, she took a seat at the head of the table and nibbled on some toast.

"Jessa likes to sleep in, and we don't press her about it, given her age," she said. "You'll meet her a bit later. Otherwise, the captain prefers we all keep to a strict schedule as outlined to you last night. Lights are out and everyone must be in their private quarters at twenty-two hundred hours."

"Will I meet the captain later too?" I asked between mouthfuls of beans and toast. I imagined a man Xiao's age, with a weathered face and imposing manner. My new boss.

"Oh, no, he's currently off-ship. You'll find he spends a good amount of time away."

The dining room door slid open, making me jump. In limped a middle-aged woman with messy, graying hair stubbornly curling out of a tight bun atop her head. Her clothes were less formal than mine and Officer Xiao's, more akin to what I had worn aboard the *Stalwart,* black and gray slick fabrics with many hidden zips and pockets. Following close behind her was a tall, dark-skinned man in a navy uniform who peered quizzically at me from behind rectangular spectacles.

"Good morning," Xiao greeted them. "This is Stella Ainsley, the new governess and auxiliary engineering support." She turned to me, first indicating the woman. "Lieutenant Poole is our primary engineer, so you'll be assisting her on occasion with ship repairs."

Lieutenant Poole grunted a response, looking me up and down and seeming to find me inadequate. She pawed four slices of toast onto a plate, spooned a heap of beans beside it, stuck two pieces of soy bacon in her mouth, and left.

The man laughed, taking a seat to my left and extending his hand to me. "I'm Orion Carmichael, *Rochester*'s Chief Technical Officer. Grace can be a bit... brisk," he said by way of explanation.

"But you'll find she's excellent at her job," Xiao interjected. "Give her a wide berth, and she'll give you the same."

"How many crew are there on board?" I asked.

"We run a small, tight ship," she said. "We have seven crew members, including you, plus Jessa, our sole civilian on board. So eight, total."

"All this food is just for eight people?" I said incredulously, surveying no fewer than four platters of food, enough to feed four dozen aboard the *Stalwart*.

"Albert heard it was your inaugural breakfast and pulled out all the stops. The better for all of us," Orion said, reaching for the platter of soy bacon and pushing several onto his plate. "Plus we have Sergei as a guest, right, Iris?"

I thought I saw spots of color rise to her cheeks, but when Xiao spoke, she was cool as a cucumber. "Orion, do you have Stella's comms unit ready?"

"Incidentally, I have it right here." He produced from his pocket the oddest piece of jewelry I'd ever clapped eyes on. The front piece was brushed chrome and shaped like a gently sloping letter *S*, with a long, curved plastic back. "It goes over your ear," he explained, then helped me fit it on. The *S* part rested just inside my eardrum, while the back part molded comfortably to the slope of my skull.

"When I point to you, just say your name." He recited a long string of numbers, then pointed, and I did as I was told. Two tones chirped in my ear. "Voice activation is all set."

"We wear our comms at all times while on duty," Officer Xiao said. "It's the easiest way to communicate with one another while on board. Just use the 'on' and 'off' voice commands to speak to someone. For example: 'Comms on. Paging Stella Ainsley.'"

There were two more chirps in my car, followed by Rori's voice announcing Officer Xiao. The *ping* repeated at intervals every five seconds.

"You have to accept the page," Xiao said. "Respond with 'Accept.'"

I did so, and next thing I knew, I was hearing her in my ear, like she was standing right next to me. Even though, of course, she was.

"Now our comm connection is open, and will remain so until one of us cuts the connection. Just say 'Comms off' to do so." Her voice in my ear cut out. "You can page anyone on the ship this way, apart from the captain. He doesn't accept comm hails from anyone except for me and Lieutenant Poole, though he can page any one of us as he pleases. If you have any issues, please contact me before speaking to the captain."

"Is it true he's coming back soon?" Orion asked.

"Yes, that is what he tells me, though he did not specify a timeline. He could be back in two days or two weeks. Who knows?"

"Have you told Jessa?"

"No, but I was going to, after I introduced Stella. If you're done, I'll take you down."

I hastily finished chewing a piece of toast and sucked down a second glass of orange juice before following Xiao on our way.

"That's the bridge to your right," she said as we reached the front of the ship. I was starting to get a sense of the *Rochester*'s layout; like the bulkheads, it was circular. All points led either to the bridge or to the transport bay at the aft end of the ship. I peered through a wide doorway to a room not unlike Sergei's cockpit but about four times its size. We stopped at a double-sided stairway and headed down on the left into a space likely originally intended as a crew recreation area. Now, however, it was a playroom-*cum*-schoolhouse. A girl of approximately ten with dark curly hair cropped short, framing her pale face, stood in the center of the room, hands held politely behind her back.

"You must be my new teacher," she said, crossing the space

between us and extending a hand to me.

"You must be Jessa."

She gave a small nod. "So pleased to meet you."

Uncanny. Even my best charges on board the *Stalwart* had never been so polite. Jessa bit her lip and looked to Xiao for approval. "Very good, Jessa," she said. "Now Miss Ainsley won't know what hit her when you transform into the handful that you are." Xiao turned to me. "I've been teaching her since the last governess left, so there have been some gaps in her recent education, though I daresay her math and science have improved markedly."

"Will I be watching her outside of school as well?" I asked. "Or do her parents do that? Her mother?" Though Xiao had mentioned only one civilian—Jessa—perhaps her mother was counted among the crew, like her father, the captain.

"My mother is dead," Jessa informed me so matter-of-factly, I was taken aback.

"I'm so sorry," I stuttered out, mentally kicking myself. I loathed meaningless platitudes like that myself, so why was I offering them to her? Jessa was unfazed.

"That's okay; she died a long time ago. And I don't need a babysitter anyway."

Xiao expressed her disagreement on that point with a look, then said, "Orion and I take it in turns looking after Jessa after-hours. Orion gets her up in the morning, and I usually put her to bed. We'll add you to our rotation."

I nodded, concealing how sad I found it. A girl being raised by officers.

"Jessa's a very quick study," Xiao said, not missing a beat, and I caught a brief second of my charge looking inordinately pleased with herself. "With your experience, I'm sure you'll know how best to catch her up and acclimate her."

I felt a tug on my hand. "I've only ever been on the *Rochester*," Jessa said. "Will you tell me about your other ships?"

"With that, I'll leave you," Xiao said, heading for the stairs. "Formal lessons start tomorrow. Stella, you'll find your timetables on your personal tab in your quarters."

I spent the day getting to know my pupil.

Jessa was, more precisely, ten and three-quarters. Her favorite subject was literature, followed by science. She excitedly asked me a thousand questions about the "rest of the world," which I answered with as much detail and color as I could, sugarcoating more than a few things about the *Empire* and *Stalwart*, however. Jessa was rapt.

"How many people are aboard the *Stalwart*?" she asked, her eyes going wide when I told her over seven hundred.

"Most ships don't have that many, though some, like the *Mumbai*, have far more," I explained.

"The *Rochester* is boring," Jessa said. "It's the same five people all the time, plus Hugo when he's here." Her expression left *Not enough* unsaid.

"I've met Xiao, Poole, and Orion, but who are the other two?"

"Albert and Mari," she said.

I remembered Albert was the cook. "Who's Mari?"

"She's our medical officer. She hates me."

"I can't imagine anyone hating you."

"She didn't like my last governess, either." Jessa's expression turned dark. "Mari's weird. She never comes to meals, so you probably won't see her much either."

I didn't push it, even though I really wanted to know more. Not just about this Mari character, but about Jessa's last governess. Why had she left?

Discussing the other ships in the fleet led to an impromptu Earth geography lesson. Jessa knew some of the basics— she, in fact, informed me that the *Rochester*'s origin was the United States of America, and she was accordingly familiar with its place on the map. I pointed out the farm belt of the U.S., where most of the *Stalwart*'s ancestors had come from. She pointed to the northern end of the state of California and told me her ancestors came from someplace called Silicon Valley. We couldn't find it on the map.

By the time Orion appeared with a dinner tray, exhaustion had caught up with me. A quick mental calculation reminded me I'd gotten only about four hours of sleep since I arrived. I didn't even have the energy to be impressed by dinner, which was a far cry from the mush I was used to. I dipped large chunks of bread into hot, buttery butternut squash soup, taking bites between yawns.

After relying on Orion to show me the way back to my quarters, I peeled off my clothes and changed into my new nightdress, then collapsed into bed. My first day aboard the *Rochester* faded into sleep.

I awoke with a start the next morning to Rori informing me that it was seven a.m. and time for me to get up. She was very nice about it, but still I groaned, pulling myself out of bed. I surveyed my closet of new clothes, reminding myself that I could now wear a fresh bodysuit each day, if I wanted. Laundry was every Sunday, and there were seven to choose from. It felt weird, so I put on the same one as yesterday instead.

For my overdress, I chose one of the numerous black numbers, thumbing right past three alarmingly bright options of magenta, turquoise, and azure that I was sure I would never have occasion to wear. It took me a minute of turning my safe black choice over and inside out to figure out how it went on. On top, it was cut like a jacket, formfitting but not corseted. Once I slipped my arms through the sleeves, I had to pull the stiff panel of cloth across my chest to fasten it nearly under the other arm. Simple and not too fussy, just as I liked it. But then it had a flaring, mostly decorative skirt that jutted from my hips, accentuating my curves. I found it curious to wear a dress meant more for fashion than form, as there was only one set of pockets sewn between the bodice and the skirt lining. Then I pulled my hair into a bun and put on my comm piece, sitting on the edge of the bed and wondering how to kill time.

My desktop tab caught my eye. Several new icons greeted me. Clicking on one, I found the *Rochester* ship schematic. Another showed me my teaching subject schedule for Jessa, with corresponding links to the required textbooks. A pop-up said they would be synced to my private reader tab, which I found after searching the desk's drawers. On the *Stalwart,* we had shared readers preloaded with textbooks and a few children's stories—none of the great literature or history books I had come to love on my aunt's ship. But this one was stocked with hundreds of fiction titles, not just textbooks, and it was mine. I held it tight to my chest and hugged it like an old friend.

The message app on the desk tab blinked, and I found I had not one message, but three. All from George. Warmth flicked at my insides. I started with the oldest message first, the one he'd promised me in the shuttle bay that he'd go and write immediately upon my departure. It was brief and earnest, i.e., quintessential George.

Hey, Stella—
You just shot off into space, and here I am writing to you, as promised. I'll miss you, Stel, you can be sure of that. Don't be a stranger, and, well… I'm sorry about the other night. I was a jerk.
Fly safe,
George

The next message he transposed on behalf of my Ancient Earth Sciences class—one line per pupil, so it was a tedious read, but one that made me smile. And then the third was from George again, worrying about my lack of reply. I fired off a quick missive letting him know that I was okay, briefly mentioning things like the lack of water rations, the smorgasbord for breakfast. The tiniest part of me maybe wanted him to feel a bit jealous, but then guilt burned in my gut and I deleted the unlimited-water-rations part, just to be nice. I sent it off and left my quarters with fifteen minutes to spare before breakfast.

Within three days, I had the ship layout down pat. At least the parts I traversed most often. It was clear from the schematics that there was a lot more to the ship than I had seen, including a top level only accessible via a locked elevator by the bridge and a staircase with a no entry sign taped beside it. When I asked Xiao about it, she calmly explained that the captain preferred we keep out of certain spaces while he was away, and much of the upper and lower decks consisted merely of cold storage, nothing to concern myself about. When I asked Rori about this so-called storage, because of course I regularly conversed with her now, she intoned that I was not authorized to access such information.

Quickly we fell into a comfortable routine and rapport. I shared breakfast with Xiao, often but not always interrupted by a nonverbal Lieutenant Poole lumbering in and absconding with enough food to feed three, then spent my day teaching Jessa, and afterward ate dinner with the whole crew. The mysterious Mari never appeared, and when I asked Xiao about her, she waved me off.

"Officer Hanada likes to keep to herself. Why do you ask?" Her voice edged up in pitch just slightly.

"I'm just surprised I haven't met her yet. And I guess I'm curious what she does all day, when no one needs medical care."

"That is neither here nor there. It's not my job to police Officer Hanada's time, nor is it yours." Xiao pursed her lips and looked me over. Then she seemed to soften. "You're new, so I understand the questions, but there's a hierarchy of both command and information on board. It's best to just accept things for how they are and focus on your job." Xiao offered a smile and patted me on the shoulder. "We're very glad you're here, and I for one hope you stay for quite some time."

I was left with more questions, not fewer, but her parting words had seemed genuine. No one on board wanted to answer my questions, but at least I had George as a sounding board. We wrote to each other every day.

Dear Stella,

It is a bit odd that you haven't seen this woman, and I agree that she can't possibly have that much medical work with such a small crew on board, but I doubt it's a conspiracy.

She's probably just a loner, a lot like someone I know who shall remain nameless.

Or, here's a thought: maybe she's the captain's mistress? Would explain why she's off by herself and they don't want you to ask about her.

You've stepped into some real drama, Stel... maybe
you should come home? Joking. Or am I?
    Cheers,
    George

Dear George,
    Not funny. I'm sticking it out here. I finally get to do
something I love, and I've mentioned all the perks, right?
The food alone is worth putting up with loner mistresses
and mysterious cargo. I just can't imagine what they
would need to keep in cargo on a tiny private ship all the
way out here by the moon.
    Let me know what the next movie night is. I can see if
Jessa has it and watch it out here. It'll be like I never left!
Now I must go shower. Another reason I'm staying here.
(Don't hate me.)
    Best,
    Stella

I was far too keyed up to sleep, so I pulled out my reader, opened my wall-length window for the view, and settled down with Elizabeth Bennet and Fitzwilliam Darcy. Hours later, and Darcy had written Elizabeth a love letter, but she was having none of it, and then Lydia went and made a mess of things. My eyes drooped, and I mumbled for the lights to go out. I drifted, sleepy, blinking slowly, trying to hold the stars in my sights.

With a jolt, I was awake. Laughter, in the corridor again.

I sat bolt upright in the dark, clutching my sheets, like they would protect me. I listened. There was something outside my door. With my breath held tight, I crept out of bed, across to the door, until my ear lay flush against the metal. All I heard was a mechanical hum, the hollow sound of air moving through machinery. Then *scritch, scritch, scritch.* I wasn't crazy—there was someone outside my door. My heart pounded in my chest. Cats. It had to be cats, right? Wasn't that what Xiao said?

Nothing to worry about. That's what they always said. So no harm in checking.

I waited. Counted to ten. Then I opened the door.

seven

Large amber eyes glinted in the dark of the corridor. They were round; definitely not human. I blew out a long, low breath. Cat.

It slunk out from the shadows, revealing itself to be the largest cat I had ever seen, body and tail stretching almost as far as my arm span. He was black all over, except for a pink nose and those amber eyes, his fur copious and, I imagined, soft. He mewled, requesting an invitation, which I granted. I couldn't shake the feeling there was something else out there, someone watching, so I let my new feline friend inside and closed the door quickly behind him.

"Lights on; dim," I requested, and they turned on in time for me to witness the cat settle himself at the foot of my bed. "What should I call you?" I pondered, scratching under his chin, eliciting a loud, guttural purr. Then he yawned, and as if it were contagious, I did too. "Well, I'll figure it out in the morning," I said with a shrug, getting back into bed. The cat resettled himself against my feet, and I commanded the lights off, willing myself to forget the shrill sound in the corridor. The one I was sure had been a human laugh.

I dreamed of the stars. I was swimming in them, on my back, doing a backstroke through black and gold. There was no sound, no air, and yet somehow I was breathing. Laughing, though I could not hear my own voice. I flipped onto my stomach, revealing the moon before me, the *Rochester* flanking her left side. The ship was a beauty, sleek and silver, her nose full of windows and her arms flung back behind her like folded wings. She flared, something bright sparking in her aft end, and with a panic, I realized she was leaving me. "No!" I screamed, but no sound left my lips. The universe echoed my panic, my fast-beating heart, Klaxons blaring in time with my breath. As the *Rochester* kicked away from me, the sirens sounded on, and all I could think was *Why can I hear them out in the vacuum of space?*

And then I woke up and realized the sirens were real. As soon as I opened my eyes and sat up, they stopped.

"Stella, I am sorry to disturb you, but you have an urgent call on comms." Rori's voice seemed to come from everywhere and nowhere. It was strange hearing her outside my shower or my earpiece. I retrieved my comms from my bedside table and put it on, immediately receiving a page from Officer Xiao.

"Stella, I apologize for the early hour, but you are urgently needed," she said while I checked the time—it was just past six a.m. "There's an issue in the airlock in the shuttle bay, and I need you to repair it as soon as possible. We're expecting the captain today, so it must be fixed immediately."

"What about Lieutenant Poole?" I asked, though I'd already hopped out of bed and started pulling on my underdress.

"Tied up in equally urgent matters, I'm afraid," she answered. "You'll find all the tools you need, as well as a spacesuit in the room next to the loading deck. Your bio scan will open it."

"And Jessa's lessons?" I selected the outfit clearly meant for engineering work—a simple black frock with no flouncy skirts but plenty of pockets.

"Don't worry about it. I'll have breakfast brought to you at half past seven."

I retraced my steps from a vague memory of a week ago, until the familiar sight of the transport bay bloomed into view, doors fitted with triple-reinforced glass giving me a view into the now-empty airlock beyond. Nothing looked out of place, but a glaring red light above the door separating the inner and outer bays—the outer one being where the airlock was essential—confirmed Xiao's report. *Alert, alert, danger, danger.*

A wave of cold washed down my back as a memory popped into my mind. Another airlock, a different ship, my cousin Charles threatening to lock me inside so I'd be vented out into space when the next cargo ship came along. I swore I heard his cruel laugh behind me; I whipped around, expecting to see him and his friends, who followed him like lemmings around the *Empire* all those years ago. But I was alone. I hadn't seen Charles in seven years, and no one here would throw me in an airlock to die. I took a deep breath to steady my nerves, reminding myself I was safe now. But the captain wouldn't be if he arrived before I fixed whatever was causing the alarm.

To the right of the transport bay, I found the maintenance hold Xiao mentioned, where there was a spacesuit of my approximate proportions and a kit of tools. The suit was stiff and unforgiving, with a detachable helmet unit that would make it airtight. I climbed into the body of the suit, hauling a zipper attached to an extended wire over my shoulder and pulling with all my might. Eventually sealed up tight, I breathed in cycled air and fidgeted with thick, gloved fingers for my toolkit. I trudged with heavy steps to the holding bay, slapped open the doors and stepped inside. Engulfed by the muffled yet still earsplittingly loud alarm, I flipped open an electrical panel in the wall and silenced the wail. I needed to be able to concentrate.

A tab unit next to the panel gave me the diagnostic picture that I needed. Separate oxygen and nitrogen units supplied the airlock with breathable air, normally cycled together in perfect proportion. The oxygen unit was malfunctioning. The holding bay was pure nitrogen. Any ship that tried to dock would read a proper pressure seal—and "air" present—but it wasn't breathable. Not by humans.

A diagram and blinking red diagnostic lights showed me

where the tanks were inside the landing bay. I grabbed the tab from the wall, and even though I was sealed into my suit, I paused before the door. How old was this suit? One leak and I'd drop like a stone, suffocating to death. When I couldn't put it off any longer, I keyed in an override code and pushed the button releasing the door.

I followed the blinking red light on the tab, making slow, clumsy progress to the right, where I found the sleek panel that hid the massive tanks. The problem was immediately apparent once I'd unscrewed the offending panel. Someone had wrested a bundle of wires out of their proper sockets, disconnecting the oxygen tank from the ship's system. I frowned, talking to no one. "It's like someone reached in and yanked as hard as they could..."

I estimated it would take at least a few hours, maybe more, to fix it. It wasn't as simple as reslotting the wires—I needed to go in deep, where essentially connections were now loose and severed, and possibly redo the wiring from scratch.

Breakfast came and went. Albert delivered into the outer bay a tray with tea, toast, and soy patties, which I took a short break to cram into my mouth. Back out I went, belly sloshing with tea, but with a bit more energy. After another hour, I had sorted the worst of the problem, it seemed, though when I tested the system, the light persistently flashed red.

I hailed Xiao again on comms. "Officer Xiao, I'm having trouble getting the oxygen back online. Is there any way Lieutenant Poole might be free now? I could use a second opinion."

"Lieutenant Poole is still indisposed, Miss Ainsley. Just do the best you can, and I will have her report to the landing bay as soon as possible."

Her answer did nothing to settle my nerves. Who knew how long it would be until Lieutenant Poole would come? I had a thought.

"Rori, are you in here too?" I asked, taking a gamble.

"Yes, Stella, I am everywhere."

Putting aside the fact that Rori's seeming omnipresence was a bit creepy, I felt relief. "Rori, is there any information on the air filtration for the loading bay that you might be able to send to my diagnostic tab? I think I need to do a bit of secondary reading."

"Of course, Stella. Please give me a moment."

True to her promise, Rori complied a moment later with a *ping* to the tab, and I retreated to the corner to read, starting with a schematic overview, then moving on to a detailed troubleshooting manual. I became so engrossed, my head filling with ideas that would hopefully solve this problem, that I didn't notice the outermost hatch door opening.

A small ship cruised inside, making a smooth, practiced landing. Everything went as it should: the ship docked; the outside hatch door closed behind it. I grabbed the tab and confirmed it one more time for good measure: there was no oxygen. If the people in that ship stepped out sans protective gear, they could die.

I screamed from my helmet, "Stop! Do not get out!" Then I realized there was no way they could hear me, and I couldn't take off my gear so that they *could* hear me—I'd choke and suffocate as quickly as I could shout. "Rori!" I yelled. "Can you connect me to that ship's comms? We have to warn them."

"His network comms are turned off, Stella. I can announce the issue once he steps off the spacecraft."

"He'll be gasping for air before he hears you," I said, trying to think of a secondary solution. If I couldn't stop the passenger from getting off the ship, then I had to save him. I moved to the other side of the craft just as the doors slung open and a lanky figure stepped out. Not wearing protective gear, as I feared. I had only a few seconds. I darted a glance at the door connecting us to the outer bay and the passenger, and cast another down at my heavy suit, which made me slow. I would have to push with all my might and hope for the best.

Each step was like sinking through a stew. I counted the seconds in my head. *Five, six, seven*—he'd surely tried breathing by now. He could; he would even think everything was completely normal, until his lungs burned and everything went black.

Ten, eleven, twelve—I rounded the corner of the craft and found him on his side, still as death. My suit was like lead, weighing my limbs and slowing my steps. I grabbed him by both arms and dragged him to the door. It took all of fifteen, twenty seconds but felt like five minutes, me drag-shuffling him, throwing my left shoulder against the hatch button, waiting for it to open. And then it didn't.

Frex! The stupid override command via the tab. There was no time for it! "Rori! Let us in!" And bless her, Rori ignored every single protocol there was and did it. I dragged the man's heavy, near-lifeless body into the next room, the door sliding shut behind us. "How are the oxygen levels in here?" I asked.

"Oxygen is good, Stella," Rori said, as calm as ever.

I wrenched off my helmet and zipped out of the cumbersome suit so I could attend to the man, who was barely breathing. I started mouth-to-mouth resuscitation—which thankfully they'd taught all the teachers aboard the *Stalwart*—forcing oxygen back into his lungs.

"Please don't be dead..."

I breathed into his mouth, pumped his chest, repeated. I checked his pulse—it was thready but present. Then, suddenly, he gasped. Coughed.

He sat up, searching my face, blinking at the unfamiliarity. I found myself taken aback, really looking at him now that the panic had dissipated. He was young, close to my age, with strong features you might call handsome.

"Buy me a drink first, at least." He wiped the back of his hand against his mouth, as if I'd just bestowed upon him an unwanted kiss.

"Excuse me?" I stammered, heat from my cheeks spreading like wildfire throughout my body. "I was trying to resuscitate you. You nearly died."

He squinted at me. "And who exactly are you?"

"I'm Stella Ainsley, sir," I answered. "The new governess."

"And why is the new governess bouncing around the ship bay in a spacesuit, trying to kill me? Or save me? I'm a bit unclear."

"I'm the auxiliary engineer to Lieutenant Poole, who was indisposed," I continued shakily. He wouldn't stop staring at me. "Someone tampered with the oxygen, so I was trying to fix it. I turned off the warning sirens—they were very loud. But I didn't try to kill you."

"Did you say *tampered* with?" he asked, insistent, grabbing my wrist with such enthusiasm, it hurt.

"Yes, but I'm not certain. It was probably just an accident," I fibbed. Something told me that suggesting a sabotage conspiracy, along with tall tales of human laughs in the corridor at night, might cause the captain and Officer Xiao alike to think me unhinged and send me away.

The captain seemed unfazed. He nodded solemnly, released my wrist, and moved on. "I'm going to have to ask you to help me up."

"Of course," I said with more composure than I felt as I assisted him and he swung an arm over my shoulder. I'd never touched a boy for so long. Where was I supposed to put my hands? Hip? Back? Oh, no, that was way too close to his—

I forced myself to concentrate on the task at hand. I supported him to the outer door, into the corridor, the heft of his weight against mine making me slow. I calculated how long it would take us to get to the bridge at this rate—twenty minutes at least. Torture.

But the captain stopped only a minute later, outside the aft elevator. "That should do it," he said, breaking away from me to lean against the wall. "I'd advise you to go fix the oxygen, and I'll make my way back on my own." His tone was resolute;

the look he threw me was cool. Like I wasn't very good at my job, now, was I?

I nodded, willing my racing heart to calm so I could go finish my job. It was a challenge, adrenaline and fear coursing through my veins like fire as I turned, watching the captain retreat, and I headed back in the opposite direction. Once I was strapped back into my spacesuit, tools at the ready, an overwhelming sense of dread replaced my earlier panic. I'd just almost killed the captain of the ship. I was definitely getting fired.

eight

Two more hours of trial and error, aided by supplementary materials kindly provided by Rori, and the oxygen issue was fixed. Relief and triumph took a backseat to my sense of dread as I returned to my quarters and changed out of my now-sweat-drenched clothes and into my best dress, the better to be dismissed in. I marched back to the bridge with my head held high, however, determined to face my sanctions like an adult, a professional. But when I reached the bridge, neither the captain nor Xiao was there. Perhaps the former was in the medical bay, finally putting it to good use. But I had expected Xiao to be here, ready to deal with me.

"Oh, hey, Stella," Orion greeted me from his desk. "Jessa's been watching a movie, if you want to go down there now."

I expected a reprimand, but it seemed things were business as usual. I was at a loss. But I wasn't one to pass up good fortune, so I descended below deck to attend to my pupil. If that axe, indeed, was to still fall on my head later that evening—perhaps the captain was waiting to do it personally—I would face it then. For now, Jessa and I had the fall of the Roman Empire to discuss.

It became immediately apparent at dinner that the status quo was sufficiently more luxe when the captain was on board. I smelled it as soon as I walked in. Meat. I took a deep whiff, searching within my mental catalog. Roast chicken with herbs. Meat was in short supply on the fleet, as farming animals took up more resources than could be justified for wide consumption, so there was just one vessel dedicated to animal farming, and only the richest ships were in the habit of purchasing its limited supply of goods. Even the *Empire*, one of the nicest ships in the fleet, rarely served meat. I recalled having it only a handful of times in my entire life, and only on holidays like Christmas and Evacuation Day.

"I love it when Hugo's home!" Jessa squealed, going right for the steaming platter of chicken and forking three slices onto her plate. Though I suspected eating the meat would make me ill in a few hours, I greedily claimed four slices for myself, along with a healthy dollop of mashed potatoes. It smelled so good, my mouth watered.

"Is the captain joining us for dinner?" I asked as we sat down in our usual spots—Orion and Albert facing the door, Jessa and I facing the stars, with a spot next to me where Xiao normally was. But she'd not yet appeared.

"He's a huge grump and likes to eat alone in his study,"

Jessa said between bites of chicken.

"Don't be rude, Jessa," Orion scolded halfheartedly.

"But it's true!"

"Even so…"

We devolved into a companionable silence, each of us digging into our chicken like it was the Last Supper. I reminded myself that for me, it still might be. Xiao's absence was concerning. Was she coordinating my return shuttle? I helped myself to a second serving, just in case.

"Has anyone seen Lieutenant Poole?" Orion asked. "Chicken's her favorite. Odd she hasn't come in to steal the rest of the platter."

"Xiao told me she was sick," Albert said, stopping me cold, a forkful of chicken poised before my lips. Which was it? Had Lieutenant Poole been on urgent business all day, or was she sick? It occurred to me: the one person aboard this ship with the mechanical knowledge to sabotage the airlock would be the only other engineer on board.

"What's her story?" I asked, doing my best to keep my tone even.

"She's been here longer than anyone," Orion said. "Born on the *Rochester*—one of the few—grew up on board. Trained by her father the engineer to take over the family business. The usual."

Her origin sounded no different from hundreds of others I'd known. In fact, it was similar enough to mine, had my parents not died. I'd still be on board the *Empire*, continuing in the family business of repairing ships. Why would she want to destroy her home, I wondered? I couldn't dwell on the matter any longer—Officer Xiao finally joined us, looking a bit more harried than usual.

"How is he?" Orion asked, his expression oddly grave.

"As good as can be expected after the long journey," Xiao replied, making herself a plate and sitting down beside me. "Jessa, he'd like to see you after dinner," she said, to Jessa's immediate squeal of delight. "You as well, Stella."

My heart jumped into my throat. I swallowed down the lump of my nerves. "What for?" I asked. Xiao cast an incredulous look my way.

"He'd like to meet his newest crew member. Why else do you think?"

I was confused and hesitantly hopeful—but kept my feelings close to the vest. "Of course," I said with a nod. "We'll go as soon as we finish eating."

"Give him until half past eight," Xiao corrected. "He likes to unwind with a glass of spirits after dinner."

Of course, the *Rochester* had liquor on board, too. The place was practically a pleasure cruise ship under the captain's watch.

Once we'd had our fill, I led Jessa back down to her quarters, where I coaxed her into taking a shower, lest she go to greet the captain with chicken grease down her front. She was bouncing, replete with energy despite her full belly, making it a trial getting her dressed. The bodysuit went on after a frustrating five minutes, but when it came to the pretty yellow pinafore I picked out, Jessa wrinkled her nose in distaste and refused to raise her arms over her head to get it on.

"I'm sick of dressing like a baby. If I have to wear a dress, I want one like yours." She fingered the stiff bodice of my dark gray overdress, which I'd specially picked out for my second meeting with the captain. I liked the high collar, cap sleeves, and the fact that this one actually had pockets, despite not being a work dress. I was comfortable—a must, given that I was about to be very uncomfortable in every other sense of the word—but dressed as formally as my station required.

"These are the clothes that you have, alas," I said, nudging her in the shoulder with a pointedly raised eyebrow. With a sigh, she acquiesced, and I pulled her pinafore on. "Mine wouldn't fit you. And don't be in a rush to grow up. Frankly, I'd rather wear your pinafore than half the things in my wardrobe."

With that, I led Jessa up to Deck Two. Just as I realized I had no idea where to go next, Jessa grabbed my hand and nearly dragged me along, stopping before we reached the dining quarters.

"This is it," she announced. We stood before a door that looked like any other, yet somehow it seemed statelier than the rest. "We have to knock," Jessa instructed. She deferred to me, so I did. Three short raps. Tentative.

"Enter!" came a muffled bark from the other side, so I hit the button that controlled the door.

The room beyond was decadent. Tapestries that I

suspected were of ancient Earth origin covered two of the walls, which were composed of a wood-like finish—a warm brownish red. It was purely cosmetic, given that the entire ship was made of metal, and there was no need for wood anything on board. And I was gobsmacked to find shelves filled with actual paper-and-ink books. I'd beheld them only once in my lifetime, contained under glass at the *Empire*'s onboard library.

And then there was the captain, who sat in a plush armchair with a book in one hand, a glass of liquor in the other. The lights were set to their dimmest setting without being off. I recognized my fluffy cat friend napping on the rug beside him. As we stepped closer, I got a much better look at the captain now, my senses no longer buzzing with adrenaline, his face no longer drained of color. My initial assessment was correct—he was young, with dark, unruly hair like Jessa's and features no less striking. She would surely grow into a beauty. He, however, was severe-looking. Bridge of the nose too strong, lips quirked in judgment, thick eyebrows adorning pensive eyes.

"Hugo!" Jessa shrieked, rushing forward to be met in an enthusiastic hug.

"Jessa-Bear," the captain greeted her warmly. "How have you been? I've missed you!"

"Then maybe you shouldn't go away so often and for so long," Jessa replied with a pout.

"Hmm," he hummed in response. "Is that you, Miss Ainsley?" He beckoned me forward and didn't seem angry, so with careful steps, I moved out of the shadows. Would he fire me in front of Jessa? It would be unnecessarily bold. "Jessa, how do you like your new teacher?" he asked.

"I like her," Jessa said. "We're learning about the Romans, and reading Shakespeare, and she promised she'd show me some ship mechanics when I'm older!"

"Did she, then?" In the dim light, I saw a single eyebrow perk with interest. Or judgment. I couldn't tell.

"It was just a thought, sir," I said. "I shouldn't have—"

"No, no, I think it's a great idea," he cut me off. "Jessa could use some hands-on experience. When she's older." Captain Fairfax sat back in his chair, patting his knee, to which Jessa responded by eagerly settling herself on his lap. "Have a seat, Miss Ainsley," he said, "while Jessa and I catch up. You and I can have a proper conversation when bedtime comes."

"Can't I stay up late? Since you just got back?" Jessa begged, but to no avail. The captain shook his head no.

"I'm exhausted. We'll make a long day of it tomorrow instead." It seemed to appease her, and she settled in to fill him in on the minutiae of the last two months he'd been away.

I sat in a chair made of a smooth material I'd never encountered, busying myself by taking in every inch of the room. First I studied the tableau on the tapestries, knights and unicorns and ladies in fine dresses represented on fading threads of red, gold, and green. Then I spent some time with what had to be a Fairfax family portrait—there was a woman, a man, and two children, a boy and a girl. I saw echoes of Jessa and the captain in the structure of their jaws, the thick dark hair, the blue eyes with cutting expressions.

And finally, I took in the books. Their worn spines with faded lettering called to me, but it would have been rude to wander around the room, touching Captain Fairfax's books, so I glued myself to the chair, settling my hands on my knees as a reminder to stay put.

Soon, Jessa and Captain Fairfax were all caught up, and at twenty-one hundred hours on the nose, Xiao appeared to ferry Jessa to bed. They left me sitting in shadows, dreading being alone in this odd slice of old Earth with the off-putting captain. As he took his seat again, he smiled, but on him, with his strong brow and shadows obscuring half his face, it appeared insincere. I waited for him to speak, but he only watched me, expression loaded yet unreadable.

"I'm doing very well," he finally said. "Thanks for asking." It was brusque yet playful.

"I'm glad to hear it," I stammered, taken off-guard. I didn't know what else to say, so I just... didn't.

"I can tell by your accent that you're from the *Empire*, Miss Ainsley. I've visited many times. Excellent tea. What was it like growing up there?"

"It was fine," I replied.

"Merely 'fine'?" the captain parroted back at me. "From your expression saying it, you'd think it was a torture ship. You should feel lucky it wasn't the *Stalwart*. I've visited that ship as well, though I wouldn't call anything about it excellent."

He chuckled, clearly thinking himself clever. A spark of self-righteousness, masking wounded pride, straightened my spine and made my tongue sharp. "That's where I'm from, actually," I said. "I transferred there when I was eleven."

"Oh." He had the good sense to appear contrite. "And how old are you now?"

"Seventeen."

"Well, that's only six years, at least? More than half spent on the well-appointed *Empire*..."

He was lousy at apologizing.

"I was orphaned at seven, so I'm afraid my memories of the *Empire* aren't entirely pleasant. I thought you would have known some of this from my résumé?"

"Oh, I didn't read it," he said with total nonchalance. "I trust Xiao to sort out these things. Well. She sends them to me, but I don't really pay attention. I did note your name and figured you'd be simple enough. Not too full of yourself."

"What does that mean?" My tone came out shriller than I would have liked. I dug my fingers into the chair's cushion to steady myself.

"Your parents named you Stella. Literally 'star'... I reckon they were practical, simple folk."

"I like my name," I said through clenched teeth. I'd wear my teeth to points, at this rate. "And what does Hugo mean? 'Rude'?"

Infuriatingly, he laughed, bright and full, and when our eyes locked, his reflected approval. "I have no clue what it means, but you might be close. I like your fire. You'll do well with Jessa."

"You're not firing me?"

"No. Why would I do that?"

"It's just, I thought, seeing as I turned off the warning beacon... I flagrantly defied safety protocols, and you nearly died."

He waved me off. "It's not the first time that has happened, I assure you. I am disconcertingly prone to... tampering." His voice fell to a low growl, brows knitting together darkly. Then quickly, his dour mood passed. "I do hope you'll like it here. The previous governesses found it... boring, and none stayed long. Are you easily bored, Miss Ainsley?"

"It's Stella," I said, finding myself squirming at each "Miss Ainsley" he uttered. It was too formal.

"Stella," he said quietly, almost to himself, feeling out the sound of it in his mouth. "Then you must call me Hugo," he declared after some consideration.

"Hugo," I tested for myself. The name made him seem more approachable, certainly. Too sophisticated to mean "rude," at least. But it also brought back to mind the thought that had been niggling at me ever since he arrived, and especially as I watched him and Jessa interact. I just couldn't make the math work. "How old are you, sir? It's just that I can't figure how you could have had Jessa and yet look so close in age to me."

"'Had Jessa'?" he repeated back, confusion apparent. "Wait, do you think..." Then he laughed, but it came out more like a bark. "Jessa is my sister," he said. "I'm nineteen, and no father. You wound me with accusations that I look old enough to have fathered a ten-year-old."

"I said you didn't look old enough," I mumbled, feeling my

whole body go hot. Still, I did the mental math and came up short. "How old were you when you became captain, then? And what happened to your parents?"

"You're very good at asking difficult questions, aren't you?" he said. "I was fourteen when I became captain, after my parents' deaths."

"It must have been especially difficult becoming captain at so young an age," I hedged, avoiding the orphan-shaped elephant now in the room. "I can't imagine commanding an entire vessel, or being left to raise your sister at just fourteen." I was rambling, possibly getting too personal, but the captain— no, Hugo, I reminded myself—set me ill at ease, with the way he lounged back in his chair, studying me, leaving silence between us until I was forced to fill the space. "And who decorated in here? It's amazing. I can't believe you have real books."

"Do you like books?" he asked, perking up.

"Of course. I didn't have much to read on the *Stalwart,* but now that I'm here, I have a new reader and tons of options. Jessa mentioned it, but we're reading Shakespeare. I also just started making my way through the Jane Austen collection. And I like history books a lot. But of course, they're not made of paper like these. Why don't you preserve them?" I finished my ramble, mortified, but found Hugo nonplussed.

"Books are meant for reading. At least, that's what my father always said," Hugo replied. "They may be ratty and fading, but they're fulfilling their purpose. You can look, if you like."

I didn't second-guess his invitation, jumping to my feet

and heading for the nearest shelf. I could barely read the words on the spines, not only because the lettering was fading—and the binding falling apart, in some cases—but because the lighting was so low. "Rori, can you turn the lights up a bit?" I asked without thinking. She obliged, and I heard Hugo snort behind me.

"Have you bewitched my AI while I've been away? On a first-name basis with her and everything."

I turned, confused. "What do you mean?"

"No one else calls her Rori. She must like you if she told you her name. And she obeyed your instruction without checking with me first. Unusual indeed."

I shrugged off his bemusement and turned back to the books, running my fingers over the spines of several, until one caught my eye. "Have you read this one?" I asked, gently nudging a half-broken paperback from the shelf, turning it over in my hands, then showing it to him. The title was barely visible, but the cover image was striking. A mountain obscured by clouds, with a name that was familiar to me: Everest.

"I haven't, but I recall seeing my father read it more than once. All the books in here were favorites of his. I'm still getting around to reading them all."

"May I borrow it?" I asked.

"You may," Hugo replied slowly. "On one condition."

I braced myself. This was where the other shoe dropped, I was sure. He was going to say something rude. *Buy me a drink first, at least.* I flushed at the memory.

"This room has temperature and humidity controls, so I prefer to keep the books in here. If you'd like to read it, join me in the evenings and read here. Consider it our standing appointment."

"Um, sure," I stammered in my surprise.

"Excellent," he said, pulling himself up from his chair. "Now, I was serious about being tired, so if you'll excuse me, I will bid you good night."

I set the book on a side table next to my chair, and as it seemed uncouth to camp out in his study, I followed him out and started for my quarters. Only the captain seemed to be following me. I glanced back over my shoulder, and indeed, Hugo was about ten steps behind.

"It seems we are going the same way," he said, jogging to catch up. "I didn't mean to rush you to bed."

"That's okay," I said. "I'm honestly exhausted. I had a six-a.m. wakeup call and a rough morning."

"That goes for two of us," he said, reminding me of our auspicious beginnings just over twelve hours before. "On that topic, I'd prefer we keep everything that happened with the transport bay just between you and me, if you don't mind." I readily agreed, not exactly keen to have everyone know how badly I had messed up. He stopped in front of a door one down from mine.

"Looks like we're neighbors," I said, continuing to my own door.

"I'll try not to snore too loudly," Hugo called out, voice echoing down the corridor. The sound was followed by a curious meow, the fluffy black cat sidling into view. He marched a few steps past Hugo, sitting down halfway between us.

"What's his name?" I asked.

"He wasn't quite as friendly and forthcoming as Rori, I'm guessing," Hugo quipped. I cast him a steady glare. "His name is Luna," he finally supplied. "And I know what you're thinking, but don't worry, he's very secure in his masculinity." Explanation came after a beat. "Jessa named him. She was four. Luna here also has a sister named Jupiter somewhere on board, and another brother named Sunny."

"How have I not seen all these cats on board? I only just met Luna last night."

"Sunny likes Officer Xiao better than anyone, so he's probably in her quarters. Jupiter's a rogue, so who knows where she is?"

"Well," I said, pressing my fingers to the bio-scan lockpad next to my door, "the *Rochester* certainly has a lot of mysteries." Three cats, one inhuman laugh, and a possible saboteur, to name just a few. And now the captain. Young and odd and unpredictable.

"That it does, Stella." Hugo moved to open his own door. Luna stretched to standing and trotted merrily into his room. *Traitor.* "Have a good night."

"You too," I said in return, but he was already gone, his chamber door sliding shut behind him.

ninE

The gentle chime of the alarm woke me, a welcome shift from the angry siren of the morning before.

"Good morning, Stella," Rori said as I roused. "You have unread messages. I did not wish to bother you yesterday but thought you would like to know."

"Thanks," I said, getting out of bed and padding over to my desk tab. In the chaos of the previous day, I hadn't even thought to check my messages, the first day in a week that I'd skipped writing to George. But the top message in my inbox wasn't from him. It was from Karlson, of all people.

Hey, Stella!

Hope it's okay that I'm writing to you. George said it would be fine, though even if he hadn't, I would have messaged anyway.

Engineering isn't the same without you. They replaced you with a thirteen-year-old apprentice, another boy, so now it's testosterone overload all the time. I lobbied for a girl, like you, but Jatinder called me a pervert. It's his mind that went there, though, not mine.

George says you're living like a princess now, with tons of food and no water rations, and I'll admit I'm more than a little jealous. I know you think I enjoy not showering, but it's not true. I'm curious—what kind of vegetables do you guys have out there? How do food deliveries work?

Let me know how you're doing.

Jon

The best way I could think to describe it was weird. That Karlson was writing to me; that he was so friendly and casual; his questions about food supply. How was I supposed to respond to that? So I didn't, instead eagerly digesting George's latest message.

Dear Stella,

You missed a movie last night that I think you would have liked. It was about a terrible nun who becomes a governess for this captain, though she has to care for seven children instead of just one, and there's lots of singing. I didn't really care for said singing, but Joy and Cassidy just loved it. Anyway, it made me think of you and how everything is going. You still like the kid you're teaching, or is she annoying you yet? The kids have been driving

*me crazy—Jefferson's been especially insufferable since
you left—and honestly I'm kind of looking forward to
turning eighteen and transferring full-time to the fields.*

Miss you,

George

Even though George hadn't asked me how I was doing,
I was itching to share my latest news, so I dove into a reply
before breakfast.

Dear George,

*That film does sound interesting, and I'm glad I don't
have to care for seven children. It's been a relief just being
Jessa's teacher, as opposed to full-time caretaker. I know
I mentioned to you that I thought it was really odd that
her dad, the captain, stayed away for such long periods of
time, and I couldn't imagine why. Well, get this—he's not
her dad; he's her brother! And he's not much older than
we are. I think that rules out your Mari mistress theory. I
still haven't met her, by the way.*

*He's... interesting. I was expecting someone kind of
terrible, to be honest, given what some of the crew had
said. He spends months away from his ship, leaving his
baby sister in the care of his employees. Plus, the luxuries
on board are mind-blowing—as soon as he arrived, meat
was back on the menu. I had chicken for the first time in
six years, and it was incredible. I guess I thought he'd be
like my aunt Reed—spoiled, selfish, and cold. But he was*

kind of nice to me. He's lending me a book. Like, a real one. This place is weird.

It's also pretty creepy. I've been hearing things, and yesterday I had to fix a ship problem that I could swear was the result of deliberate tampering. I didn't say anything, though, because they'll probably think I'm paranoid and send me home if I do. Let's just hope nothing else breaks and this was just a fluke.

Miss you too,

Stella

At breakfast, I found *real bacon.*

"This is the best thing I have ever tasted in my life," I said, cramming two more slices into my mouth before anyone else could arrive to judge me. There was no risk with Lieutenant Poole, who had consumed no fewer than six slices in the last five minutes herself.

"Hmm," she hummed while chewing. "Captain's home, so the menu's changed. Always better when he's here."

"You don't usually eat here for breakfast," I said. "It's nice to have a chance to talk to you."

Lieutenant Poole shrugged. "Considering the finer spread, I thought it would be opportune to dine in. I hear you repaired the airlock yesterday all on your own. Good job."

"Thanks," I said, going a bit warm at her praise. She offered it more readily than Jatinder ever did. But it seemed she wasn't done.

"It's lucky you are a quick study. Imagine if the captain had returned and the oxygen malfunction hadn't been fixed. Or if someone turned off the warning alarm."

She knew. I didn't know how, but she did. Lieutenant Poole didn't seem upset; on the contrary, this seemed more like a test. But the captain had told me to keep things between us, so I did.

"I had good teachers aboard the *Stalwart*," I volleyed back. "And Rori helped supplement with ship manuals and troubleshooting guides."

Poole smiled, the first time I'd seen her do more than grimace. "Well, I am happy to have you on board. Have a good day."

She sidled off, a to-go plate of bacon in hand. I got the message loud and clear: I had kept the secret. *Good job.* Like ships passing in the night, a moment later Xiao appeared, though I noted she took no bacon. Come to think of it, she hadn't had any chicken last night either. "No bacon for you?" I asked.

"No, I prefer to remain vegetarian," Xiao said. "The conditions aboard the meat ship *EntenGEN* are questionable at best, and I'd rather not spend my evening chained to the lavatory." She took a seat next to me. "Besides, soon enough the captain will be gone again and meals will be back to normal. And how did your chat go last night?"

"Well, I think." I chose not to mention that I'd accused the captain of being a teenage father, after he'd insulted me. Twice. "We talked about books, mostly."

"Oh, that's good. Nice, safe topic. Listen, Stella," she said, sounding just a touch nervous, contrite. "I should have briefed you about the captain before he arrived, but yesterday everything came so fast, and I neglected to do so, and for that, I apologize."

"There's no need to apologize, Officer Xiao," I reassured her. "Everything went fine."

"Yes, that was fortuitous. You must have caught him in a good mood. But the captain has bad days too, and there are topics you should never broach. Such as his parents."

Was this a good time to tell her I had already done that very thing? Hugo hadn't seemed *that* upset, though, so I kept quiet. It's not like any of us liked talking about our dead parents, but maybe it was different because I'd asked him orphan-to-orphan.

"Just remain professional, and circumspect," Xiao continued, not missing a beat. "When in doubt, tell him how Jessa is doing. Because if there's one constant about the captain, it's that he loves his sister dearly." She paused, checking her tab for the time. "Where is that girl? She's never late for breakfast." Xiao tried her comms, first attempting to hail Jessa, then asking Orion to run down to her quarters and look for her. The persistent frown on Xiao's face told me Orion hadn't been successful.

"Do you want me to go find her?" I found myself volunteering.

Xiao hesitated. "I suppose that could work." She did not sound entirely convinced. "There're only so many places she could be, at least."

With that vote of confidence, she sent me off with

instructions to search the lower deck, new territory for me. A thrill ran down my spine as I stepped into an elevator and pressed the button for the lower level. The doors opened to near darkness. I stepped out into a hallway, blinking until my eyes adjusted to the dim. A chill skittered across my shoulders. It was colder down here as well.

Xiao had said to check the old crew quarters, instructing me to head down and left, so left I went. A draft pushed against my back, a hollow whirring sound accompanying it; I hurried my pace so I could find Jessa quickly and get back up to the light and warmth. I kept my eyes focused on my feet, ignored the eerie sound in favor of the click of my heels on metal flooring.

"Jessa?" I called out to a sea of closed doors on my left. Nothing.

Then, under my boot, I caught a slick of black and nearly slipped. When I leaned closer and touched tentative fingertips to the liquid, I saw its true color: red. The metallic tang that hit my nose completed the equation. It was blood.

"Jessa!" I called out again, this time more urgently. I walked faster, doing my best not to step in any more blood, and trying to shake away all the worst-case scenarios as they popped into my head. I came to a dead stop. There was something on the floor. I squinted down at it. It was a rat.

"Bad kitty!"

I nearly jumped out of my skin, the voice, singsongy yet cold, seeming to come out of nowhere. But then the woman it belonged to slunk out of the shadows, as did the cat she'd been scolding. She was petite but muscular, dressed in a stark white lab coat, and looked to be in her midtwenties. The cat I assumed to be Luna's sister, Jupiter, trotted over to me, licking her chops and seeming to smile at the dead rat.

"You must be the new governess," the woman said, eyeing me up and down, her summary judgment reduced to the single quirk of an eyebrow.

I swallowed hard and willed my voice not to wobble. "You must be Officer Hanada."

"My reputation precedes me." She scooped up the rat carcass with her bare hands, its fur white, a bright blue number 119 branded on its side. The same blue coloring the tips of Hanada's coal-black hair.

She caught me looking at the number. "I like to keep track of my pets. They can be difficult to tell apart."

"You keep rats as pets?"

"The cats don't like me," she said. "The rats are less picky."

I couldn't tell whether she was joking.

"What brings you down here? Governesses don't belong below decks."

"I'm looking for Jessa. Xiao sent me."

"I thought I heard some high-pitched shrieking. Try the old crew quarters. Keep going down the hall. You can't miss it." She deposited the dead rat into a plastic bag with a cool smile. "Better find her quick. Don't want to lose your charge in only week two."

"Are you keeping track of how long I've been here?" Another chill ran across my back, this one not strictly because of the temperature.

She shrugged. "Just a little game I play. You're already ahead. The record for shortest stay is twenty-four hours."

"And the longest?" I found myself asking, though I wasn't sure I wanted to know the answer.

"Two years. -Ish. Don't worry, I'm taking the long odds on you."

"What do you mean?"

"The crew always takes bets on how long you guys will last. I've got you pegged at a year at least. But having met you, perhaps you'll break the record."

She turned and sauntered down a hallway to our right that I hadn't seen before. The dead rat had distracted me. I stepped with care over the bloody patch on the ground and continued on my way until the hallway widened. A communal bathroom on the right, disused but door wide open, signaled that I'd found the old crew quarters. There was light spilling out from a nook at the very end of the corridor, and I could hear Jessa shouting.

"I've got a bogey on my left! Ready the missiles!"

"Um, Jessa?" I caught her kneeling on top of a round table in an old mess hall, pointing at an imaginary sky.

She was embarrassed for approximately ten seconds, then ordered me to join her. Captain Jessa needed a crew. First, I called Xiao on comms to let her know I'd found my charge. Talking to her, I couldn't help but wonder—what odds had she taken on how long I would stay? And why had all the previous governesses left?

Maybe because they were no good at combat jargon.

I found myself thoroughly schooled by Jessa, who cut no corners on authenticity in make-believe play.

"No, Stella! When I give you an order, you say 'Roger wilco,'" she scolded when I missed a beat.

"Still an absolute taskmaster, I see." Hugo appeared in the entranceway with arms crossed over a crisp waistcoat and a glance in my direction that made my cheeks burn. I scooted off the table, smoothing my skirt and checking my hair. Surreptitiously I applied some saliva to the curls that had sprung lose as I'd loaded a missile chute.

"Don't be mean, Hugo." Jessa stuck out her tongue at him. "But I'm glad you found us. You can take over as First Officer. Sorry, Stella."

"No problem," I said, offering a little salute. I was happy to be demoted, and made my way to the exit. Hugo had other ideas.

"Where are you going? Jessa needs a full crew to stop the enemy force."

Blue eyes focused on me. Hugo wanted me to do something, and I found it easy to say yes.

I caught his eyes on me many times more as we took part in Jessa's role-play, Hugo mouthing to me the terms I was supposed to use and, more than once, simply laughing at my ineptitude. Except when I played the part of ship engineer. I did brilliantly at that. When Jessa tired of make-believe, she led the charge back to the mid-deck, Hugo and I trailing behind her.

"There must have been a lot of crew before," I said, indicating the doors as we passed them.

Hugo shrugged. "Way back when, yeah. We haven't been at full capacity since before I was born. My parents moved the crew to the mid-deck at least ten years ago. Except Mari." He indicated a door on our left, labeled with a brushed-metal placard that said FIRST OFFICER. It took me a second to place the name. Hanada. The rat enthusiast.

"But she's not the First Officer," I said.

"Xiao doesn't mind her taking the old FO quarters. They're the nicest down here, and closest to the medical bay."

"Jessa, watch out for the—" I was about to say blood, but it was gone. Someone had cleaned up.

"Watch out for the what?" Hugo asked.

"Nothing." It was strange. The blood gone, Jessa skipping in front of us, and Hugo by my side, I no longer felt ill at ease. It didn't seem as dark or cold. Still, I was happy to return to mid-deck and proper lighting.

"Sorry to monopolize your morning," Hugo said as we exited the elevator. "You can take the rest of the day for yourself. Except for this evening. Our reading appointment stands."

I felt scolded, though Hugo's tone held no malice. I had been considering ways to get out of our arrangement, and now I felt guilty.

"You weren't going to come, were you?"

I thought of making excuses, but any decent one would be a lie, which I was loath to do. "I wasn't sure if you meant it. The invitation."

"Of course I meant it. Why wouldn't I mean it?"

"I just didn't think the captain of a ship would have any real interest in spending time with a crew member." Or someone from the *Stalwart,* for that matter, with such a basic name like Stella. I felt my cheeks burn at the memory of his slights.

Hugo stopped in his tracks, rounding on me with arms crossed over his chest. Jessa was oblivious and skipped on ahead. "You think I'm a total jerk," Hugo stated, as opposed to asked, catching me off-guard.

Suddenly it was far too warm. "I just thought—"

"That I care more about status than people."

I couldn't lie, and I was sure my face said it all.

"I get it," he said. "Especially after my abominable behavior last night. I'll admit with the time I spend on other ships that follow more… traditional social conventions, I can lose sight of myself a bit. But on this ship, there's only eight of us. If I refused to socialize with anyone 'below my station,' I'd only ever talk to Xiao and Poole, and most of the time they still treat me like I'm twelve."

He started walking again, gesturing for me to fall into step beside him. I found myself confused. Unlike last night, today he was easy, playful. Nice.

"Do you like poker? We have a weekly game on Sundays. Everyone plays, though only Mari and Grace offer any real competition. But I suspect books and conversation are more up your alley."

We stopped in front of my room, and he hit me with those blue eyes again.

"Will I see you tonight? It's your choice. But know that my invitation is genuine."

I nodded, unsure I could manage coherent speech. I was discovering I had a habit of always saying the wrong thing to the captain.

I arrived that evening at promptly half past eight, inhaling and releasing a deep breath to calm the butterflies that had taken up residence in my rib cage. As I smoothed a hand over my hair and checked that the dark gray dress I'd chosen was as spotless as it had been ten minutes ago, I realized I was acting like this was some kind of date. I scolded myself and knocked on the door to Hugo's study. And when he barked "Enter" and I stepped through the door, it already felt completely routine.

"I'm glad you're here," Hugo said. "I was worried you'd skip out on me. Though if you had, I'd have hailed you on comms and talked your ear off until you relented."

I frowned as I took my seat across from him, noting my book was ready for me, sitting on the table that bridged the space between our two chairs. Next to it was a glass of spirits. "Shouldn't you want me to come willingly, and not because you pestered me until I gave in?"

His eyes held my gaze, winking curiosity. "Yes, of course. I was joking."

Except I didn't think he was. I got the sense Hugo was used to getting exactly what he wanted, all the time. I picked up my book and carefully opened to the first page. The type was faded in places but still readable. I made it no further than the second paragraph.

"Do you normally prefer nonfiction?"

My gaze flicked up to find Hugo sitting cross-legged in his oversized armchair, hands folded in his lap as he peered over at me. He looked like an overgrown boy. He hadn't even touched his book.

"I love fiction as much as anything else, but I do have a fondness for history and science. Those were the categories available in abundance on board the *Stalwart*."

"I'm surprised such a basic ship would tend toward those subjects."

"Basic?" I bristled. "You think because we grow your food, that makes us bumpkins?"

"No, no, no," Hugo said. "I just… imagined fiction would offer an attractive escape on a ship like the *Stalwart*. I meant no offense, I promise."

I nodded in acceptance of his apology, though I remained wary. "Fiction is an incredible escape, yes, but reader tabs and an abundant library are luxuries we couldn't afford."

"You keep saying 'we.' But you live here now. I'll give you any book you want."

"And which one are you reading? Or not reading, as the case may be?" I pointed to the book that was being ignored on his own side table. Anything to get us away from the topic of where I belonged. Finally, he picked it up, the pages falling open to a spot where I could see a ribbon tucked between the pages.

"*Anna Karenina*," he said. "It's Russian. And depressing and beautiful." He frowned down at the page. "But it's been two months, and I'm fuzzy on what I last read. Might have to start over."

He flipped to the front of the book, and I happily returned to mine. This time, I at least got past the introduction.

"Do you like it on board? So far?"

"Of course. I like it very much." I looked to his book, then down at mine. I longed to return to it. "Do you actually intend to read, or was this an excuse to interview me?"

Hugo made a sound halfway between a grunt and a laugh. "You like to say whatever comes into your head, don't you?"

"On the contrary." I sat up straighter, tilting my chin high. "I usually never say what I'm thinking, but..." *But.*

"But what?" Hugo prodded.

You annoy me, I didn't say. *I feel oddly at ease with you,* I didn't say. Finally, I settled on: "You're persistent."

"That I am." He grinned. "I'll promise not to speak for the next hour. We'll read. But then I get to talk to you until bedtime."

"Are you negotiating to make me talk to you?"

He didn't answer. Instead, he pointed to the table. "Don't you want your drink?"

"I didn't realize it was for me."

"Well, it is. So, do you want it?" I shook my head. He gladly availed himself of it instead.

Hugo kept his promise, and for the next hour, the only sounds I heard from him were periodic sips of his—and my—glass, and the turning of pages. And then, picking up exactly where he'd left off: "Did you leave many friends behind? On the *Stalwart*?"

I gave up on my book with a sigh, looking around for something to mark my place. Hugo came to my rescue, opening a hidden drawer in the table to produce a piece of paper I could tuck between the pages.

"Thank you," I said. "And, yes, I did leave behind some friends." I indulged myself with a plural but immediately felt false. "Well, one friend. George. We message a lot now."

"You're blushing. Is he your boyfriend?"

I laughed so suddenly and loudly that Hugo jumped in his chair. *Great.* Now he likely thought me a loon. A sad, single loon. "Do you realize how inappropriate it is to ask that?" I deflected.

"Oh?"

He was clueless. I sighed. "Yes. You are my employer. And you've only just met me. And it's private."

Hugo shrugged. "Well, you can ask me anything you want. Be as invasive as you want. Consider it payback and my apology."

What possible way could I navigate this without causing trouble? Hugo was playing the equal, but I was all too aware of the power he held over me.

"Where do you go when you're off-ship? And why do you stay away so long?"

There. I punted with both a harmless and a sharp-toothed question, leaving it to him to answer truthfully or not. I was sure there was a story behind his frequent absences. But would he wish to tell me?

"There's a lot to attend to, both on- and off-ship," he started, tone measured. "But with our position out here, I find that to be most efficient with managing my family's affairs, I have to be with the main fleet."

My confusion must have been evident on my face, because quickly Hugo moved to clarify.

"My family also owns the *Lady Liberty*, so you can imagine..."

I sucked in a breath. The *Lady Liberty* was the hub of the fleet, a massive, elegant American ship said to have every luxury available to every soul on board. And as the owner of one of the big five ships, that meant Hugo had a role in government. Like, actually got to vote on essential measures. Suddenly I felt small and, indeed, simple.

"So, what is your book about?" I changed the subject.

Hugo launched into a passionate, if convoluted, explanation of *Anna Karenina*, which easily took us to twenty-two hundred hours, and curfew.

"See you tomorrow night?" Hugo asked as I left him at his door.

I called out over my shoulder playfully, "Sure. I want to finish my book."

"I know you're using me for my library," he shot back.

"Good night." I retreated to my room before he could see how wide my smile was.

ten

I kept my word, returning the next night to finish my book, which turned out to be a riveting account of a mountaineering disaster that happened on the world's tallest peak at the tail end of the twentieth century. As I became immersed in a pursuit as unfathomable to me as breathing in space, my nightly reading sessions with Hugo turned routine. When I finished that book, I found another on the shelf, this one a tense drama about Old World British and Russian spies.

We read together every night, allotting the last half-hour before bed for Hugo's chatter, by which point he was always more than a little drunk. It became second nature to parry his too-personal questions with lighter fare, usually updates on Jessa or recounting the book I was reading. Still, too often Hugo got past my defenses, disarming me with a well-timed question. Like: "Stella, are you lonely?"

All the sound was sucked out of the room, leaving nothing but the loud timpani of my panicking heart in my ears.

"Of course not," I replied, well-practiced in answering dishonestly to put others at ease. "I see you every day. Jessa, Xiao. Everyone else." Of course, I didn't feel close to any of them. Not truly. Jessa was a child, and everyone else was either my employer or too wrapped up in their own life. The more things changed, the more they stayed the same.

"Hmm," Hugo hummed. "But you don't seem really connected to anyone. Close."

His keen gaze, his on-the-nose assessment, rendered me naked; hot from collar to boots, fighting a squirm that tempted me to flee the room.

"I might throw the same accusation back at you," I said, my cool rapidly slipping. And then he smiled! As if I'd pleased him.

"That's fair," he replied. "Everyone on board this ship is a bit like a solitary planet. We orbit the same sun, but on lonely tracks. At least we all have that in common."

"Wouldn't you say we orbit the moon?"

"Was that a joke?" He laughed. "I'm impressed."

A new warmth overcame me, like when my parents used to envelop me in their arms, whispering comforts into my hair. I felt acceptance and the freedom to be myself. And a hint of something else, not familial at all. A flame of desire, which I tamped down but feared I could not extinguish, now that it had been lit.

I found myself counting down the hours of each day until I could join Hugo in the evening. I even started allowing myself a drink occasionally, liking the way it made me all floaty and warm and comfortable during our conversations.

"You know you've been here two months," Hugo said one night.

"Are you in on the betting pool?" Hugo looked at me with confusion, so I elaborated. "For how long I'll make it on board. Hanada told me about it."

He rolled his eyes. "Mari was messing with you. She has a strange sense of humor."

"So it's not true that there were a bunch of governesses before me, most of whom didn't stay long?"

"Perhaps it was a mistake to let you drink." Hugo played as if to take away my glass. I couldn't miss the edge to his voice. "Come on, you know this place isn't for everyone. Isolated from the rest of the fleet and all."

"True," I said, thinking perhaps that Sergei had spun a yarn to keep me entertained.

"Anyway, if there was a betting pool, which there isn't, I'd advise you to stay at least fourteen months." He winked, and I threw my book at him.

"Ha! Now you can't read!" he taunted. "So you have no choice but to talk to me for the next two hours."

"If I can't read, I'll draw. So, alas, you'll have to push through on that Dickens."

Hugo perked up. "How come I've not seen you with a drawing tab?"

I shrugged. "My old tab isn't in the best of shape. The colors are shot; the stylus has totally lost sensitivity. And mostly I've been devouring all your books instead of drawing."

"Go get your tab, then. I want to see your work."

I glanced at a masterpiece on the wall behind Hugo's head, a Degas. "Why would you want to see my scribbling when you have the stuff of the masters at hand?"

"None of the masters live on my ship. If it makes you feel any better, I'll play the piano for you. I'm completely out of practice, but it's the closest skill I have that you might consider an artistic talent."

"I didn't even know there was a piano on board."

Hugo nodded. "There's a drawing room next to the dining quarters. Just give me a week or two to practice. I'm rusty. But you have to show me now."

I took a swig of drink for courage. "Fine."

Within five minutes, I'd fetched my drawing tab from my quarters and Hugo was pulling me over to the love seat at the window. My heart sped up as Hugo arranged himself nearly on top of me. My head knew the alcohol made him extra friendly, but my other senses hadn't gotten the memo. I wiped a sweaty palm on my dress so I wouldn't smudge the tab screen, and I pulled up an old landscape. He leaned close under the guise of seeing the screen better, settling a hand on top of my thigh in the process, and took it upon himself to swipe and flick through the next few images.

"You're really good," he said. "Do you draw people?" I nodded, and he didn't hesitate, navigating his way to my portrait subfolder, albeit slowly. "You weren't kidding about this being old…"

"I've had it since I was eleven, and it was my cousin's before me. It's likely older than Jessa at this point." I took a moment to realize Hugo wasn't listening. His gaze was locked on the tab. He was looking at a picture of George.

"Who is this?" he asked, tracing the crinkles at the corners of his eyes.

"That's George," I said, swiping the image away. Then the next three of George, my cheeks burning. The next, one of Karlson, reminded me I owed him a message. I'd finally relented after five messages and started telling him about the *Rochester*'s vegetable slate. *Weirdo.*

"Are these all boys from the *Stalwart*?" Hugo asked, flicking to the next portrait, thankfully one of Arden, followed by Joy. Then another of George, the one I'd started before I came here.

"All two of them? Yes."

"It's a wonder you wanted to leave."

For a brief second, I wondered if he was jealous, and I allowed myself the flutter of hope that spread warmth throughout my body. But then he wrested himself away, his expression turned sour.

"I'm too drunk to read. I'm going to bed early."

He left me speechless and alone, feeling as uneven as George's half-finished portrait.

"I wish these old books came with reference manuals. Or footnotes. And pictures." I put down the latest in my spy series, trying and failing to envision twentieth-century Berlin.

"Hmm?" Hugo hummed, barely looking up from his own book. Four nights later, and he was still powering through his Dickens—*Great Expectations*. And he'd been nothing but pleasant since our last encounter. Neither of us mentioned his mini-tantrum and walkout.

"I'm having trouble picturing some of these places," I said. I sighed back into my chair. "I asked Rori if she had anything to supplement me, but she came up empty. Said something about not having authorization."

Hugo finally set down his book.

"Come with me," he said, getting up from his chair and not bothering to check that I followed. Which I did. Of course.

He led me down the corridor toward the aft end of the ship, into the elevator, and down to the lower level. Instead of going left, Hugo turned right, to parts unknown. I checked the location markers on each bulkhead we passed. Deck Three, Ward O, Ward N, Ward M... until he stopped at a bulkhead labeled Ward K and opened a door with his fingerprints. We stepped into a room packed to the gills with circuitry, row after row of eight-foot-tall server bays spanning the room.

"Welcome to the library," he said, much to my confusion. There were no books here; how could it be a library?

"My family was concerned about the mass loss of culture

the ice age would bring, so they made an arrangement with the Library of Congress," Hugo explained, leading me farther into the room, which pulsed hot and cold simultaneously. "What you see here is the most extensive digital archive of documents, maps, books, and the old Earth Internet in the fleet."

I gawked at the towering vessels of knowledge around me, which hummed and whirred and wheezed. "Why are you showing me this?" I asked.

"Because I'm giving it to you," Hugo said. "Rori doesn't have access to most of it for performance reasons. It's a vast archive, and I don't want it clogging up her programming. Or having her morph into an evil supercomputer."

"Very funny, sir," Rori chimed in, reminding me she was always present, always listening.

"But there is a way to search through everything, view files, transfer books and documents to your reader." Hugo led me through the maze of servers to the back of the room, where I found a desk tab the size of a window. "This is connected to the servers in this room, so you can search by category, historical period, document type, keyword... and it's a bit antiquated, but all you have to do is connect your reader to the desk tab and manually drag-and-drop any books you want onto it."

He turned the tab on so he could show me. It was slow to start up, and the interface that greeted us seemed ancient—boxy graphics and busy colors—but parsing through it seemed easy enough. I started by popping the term *MI5* into a search box, and hundreds of results came up, sorted by which category they fell under. I clicked into the nonfiction folder and found dozens of historical accounts of British intelligence.

"I'll add your bio markers to the door scan," Hugo said, "so you can come down here whenever you want."

Tightness seized my insides, shock and awe and gratitude bubbling up, making me warm all over. "This is the nicest thing anyone has ever done for me," I croaked out, surprised to find myself on the verge of tears. It would be too mortifying to cry in front of Hugo; I faked a cough so I could wipe my eyes, compose myself.

"It's not a big deal." Hugo shrugged, like he'd just given me a handkerchief.

"But it is," I insisted. "You've given me access to something precious. Something few other humans will get to touch in their lifetime." *Books. History. Art. Hugo's trust.* The weight of the last bit brought heat to my cheeks that I was glad he couldn't easily see. I cleared my throat. "Is this what Xiao and the others keep referring to when they say most of what's down here is cold storage?"

"Oh," Hugo said, clearly taken aback. "Yes, I suppose so." Now *he* was the one clearing his throat. "I hadn't realized Xiao or anyone would have talked with you about it."

"Oh, well, I asked was what down here, and above decks. I was curious."

"You are a rather curious sort of person, aren't you?" Hugo stated. I couldn't tell if he thought this was a good or bad thing, however. "Anyway, it's getting late."

It was all Hugo had to say; I followed him up to our quarters and made with hasty goodbyes. I had a sudden urge to draw. I turned on my tablet to find the last project I'd been working on—that portrait of George. It was funny. I missed him—he was my closest friend without a doubt—but I no longer felt the harsh pangs of unrequited love. They'd diminished into a gentle hum, barely present unless I purposely tried to tap into my angst. It had been a silly, misplaced crush.

I opened a new document, began to sketch a new face. Strong nose. Heavy eyebrows, usually furrowed in thought. Lips quirked in judgment—or interest? Blue eyes that burned like cold fire. I stayed up far past bedtime finishing him, blackening the page with the charcoal brush, capturing all his shadows and light. Eventually I was too weary to go on, but the portrait was nearly done. I fell into an exhausted sleep, Hugo's face flashing against my closed eyelids.

eleven

I woke to a different Hugo. Or, more accurately, I met him at dinner.

"Thank you for joining us, everyone," he said, standing up from his chair and addressing us like an assembly. "Very rarely do we all gather in one place to break bread. Mari actually left her dungeon!"

All eyes turned to Mari, who grimaced and tilted her head in acknowledgment.

"Albert has prepared quite the spread," Hugo went on, "and everyone should help themselves to some wine." He topped off his glass and then passed the decanter to his left. "Except you, Jessa." The table obliged him with polite laughter. Then we dug in to the food, which included pot roast and mashed potatoes. We ate in silence until Hugo started speechifying again.

"I thought we might engage in some thanksgiving," he said. "Each of us say what we're thankful for. I'll start by saying how grateful I am for each and every one of you. I know without a doubt that the *Rochester* has the best crew in the galaxy." I was used to Hugo being chatty, even a bit flirty, but this was sappy in a way Hugo wasn't.

Then I realized that Hugo's eyes were glassy, his brow lined with perspiration. I glanced around the table to find others had noticed it too. Hugo was intoxicated. Well… more than he usually was. Xiao shifted uncomfortably in her chair, sitting straight-backed as if ready to spring into action, should it be required. Orion stifled a laugh, as if drunk and effusive Hugo was the most hilarious thing in the world. Jessa was, thankfully, clueless in the way only a ten-year-old can be. And Lieutenant Poole's expression was dark, concern radiating off her in waves. It was a look I'd not seen on her. Maternal.

We went around the table in turn to appease Hugo, rattling off things we were thankful for, while he clapped enthusiastically for each one. That got Jessa's attention.

"Hugo, why are you acting like such a weirdo?" she asked.

"Jessa, don't be rude," I scolded.

"I'm fine!" Hugo slurred, taking a swig from his glass. "Just happy to be home," he said. No one pointed out he'd been home for weeks. "And we have wonderful new crew, like Stella!" He leaned over conspiratorially and failed at whispering to Officer Xiao. "She likes books."

My face burned hot, and I averted my gaze from meeting anyone else's by fully engrossing myself in my food. Everyone who wasn't Hugo united in an unspoken agreement to eat as quickly as possible, with Orion bravely being first to make a break for freedom.

"I should be putting Jessa to bed now," Orion said, and for once Jessa didn't protest. Hugo had oscillated from buoyant to dour by that point, frowning at them as they went. Albert and Mari quickly followed suit, but when I tried to stand, making excuses to turn in to bed early, Hugo was having none of it.

"Noooo." He stood up from his chair, stumbling a step and grabbing onto the table for support. "We have a standing reading appointment. I still expect to see you in my study in ten minutes! Xiao, see that she makes it." Making sure to take his glass with him, Hugo strode as confidently as he could out of the dining room, wobbling just slightly at the door.

"What's going on?" I asked, dazed as I watched him go. Xiao threw a meaningful look at Lieutenant Poole, who shrugged.

"You might as well tell her," Poole said. "She'll have to dance around it for the next two hours. And with that," she said, taking a serving of pot roast for the road, "I am off to see if I can find any of that liquor stash the captain's obviously got himself into. Good night."

Xiao took a minute before explaining. "The captain's behavior... I'm not excusing it. But today is a difficult day for him. For all of us. Today is the fifth anniversary of the day Hugo's father died. I'm sure you'll understand."

I did, with a cutting clarity.

"Following my previous brief, please refrain from topics

related to the captain's parents, today especially. And stop him from drinking much more, if you can."

I trudged with hesitant feet to the study, unsure which brand of Hugo I would find there. Bright and zippy, or grumpy and morose? I caught him on an upswing.

"Stella!" he exclaimed as soon as I walked through the door. "My little sleuth. I have a book for you!" He bounded over to a bookshelf in the far corner of the room, extracting a hardbound volume and gleefully handing it over.

"*And Then There Were None* by Agatha Christie," I read off the cover.

"She's my mother's favorite author," he said. I couldn't help but feel sorry for him, referring to his mom in the present tense.

"Thank you," I said, sitting in my chair as usual, hoping he would do the same, but instead he danced over to the sideboard to refill his glass. "Hugo, I hate to say something, but—"

"You're totally right!" he cut me off. "I shouldn't drink alone. How rude of me." He thrust a glass into my hand, and I took small, careful sips where Hugo did giant gulps.

"Where do you get this stuff?" I asked, trying for innocuous conversation. "On the *Stalwart* we had some vile backroom hooch, but your supply is of such high quality."

"This is from the *Islay*, the fleet's whiskey ship. I didn't take you for a connoisseur of fine spirits," Hugo quipped.

"Oh, I'm not. This just doesn't taste like jet fuel, so I assume it's good."

"Tell me more about the *Stalwart*. And the *Empire*. About your life before the *Rochester*."

"What do you want to know? My life story isn't that interesting."

"I don't believe that. Why did you transfer from the *Empire* to the *Stalwart*? There must be a story there."

Oh, was there. Given the topic of the day, I wasn't sure it was the best story to tell, but Hugo prodded me on.

"I left the *Empire* because my family didn't want me anymore." I hadn't ever said it out loud—I was too diplomatic for that, I told myself—but there it was. After that, it all came pouring out of me, like the tears I'd stubbornly refused to shed all those years ago.

"I joined my aunt's household after my parents died, when I was seven. She didn't really want me, but my uncle, who was my mother's brother, insisted. But then he died too." I found myself choking on the words, so I took a serious draw of liquor to fortify myself. There was no point in crying over it now. My poor uncle had been gone for nearly a decade at this point.

Hugo politely remained mute, neither offering platitudes that would make me uncomfortable nor avoiding my gaze. I appreciated it.

"She kept me around as long as was fashionable," I continued. "She didn't want to be seen as kicking out an orphan right away, you know? The other ladies showered her with such praise for taking me in from the poor part of the ship. But when I was eleven, after the Kebbler virus, the fleet enacted the Orphan Transfer Program, and she jumped at her chance. I'm sure she told everyone I volunteered to go. The *Stalwart* needed warm bodies for their farming pipeline and, as it turned out, junior ship-engineering apprentices. So that's where I ended up."

"I was curious about that, actually," Hugo said, hopping up to go to the sideboard again. This time he brought the decanter with him, refilling my glass before I could protest, then topping off his as well. "Why ship engineering? It's not a common field for women, for one, let alone one from the *Empire*."

"And yet *you* have a woman ship engineer. *Two* now. So how uncommon is it?"

"Fair point. But Lieutenant Poole… her gender is incidental. Her father had a daughter instead of a son, and the position of ship engineer has been passed down from generation to generation on the *Rochester*, so, ipso facto, Lieutenant Poole became our engineer."

"I can tell a similar story," I said. "My father taught me everything he knew, up until he died. I'm sure if he'd lived, there would have been enough talent on board the *Empire* that I wouldn't have necessarily taken his place. But who knows?" I shrugged. "Maybe I would have wanted to take his place. On the *Stalwart*, however…"

"You didn't like your job?"

"I didn't like being on a ship that's rumored to be next in line to be decommissioned," I put it bluntly.

"Cheers to that." Hugo raised his glass to mine. Just when I thought perhaps Hugo wasn't so drunk after all—he seemed perfectly composed insofar as he was speaking in complete, cogent sentences—he said, "So tell me how your parents died."

"That's a bit morbid, don't you think?" I scoffed.

"Oh, come on, I'm allowed a bit of latitude for morbidity today. It's my anniversary. I know they told you."

Busted. I didn't bother denying it. So I told him about my dad, how he'd been crushed by a machine part on a Monday in October, his broken body vented into space on Tuesday. And my mother fell into a deep depression—not her first bout of it, but certainly the first that I recognized for what it was, with my father no longer around to mask her symptoms from me. How, despite that, I didn't recognize how bad it had gotten, and that on a Thursday that November, I found her dead in our quarters.

I left it at that, sticking to the facts. Hugo didn't deserve the burden of hearing about my guilt, or my regrets. George's voice echoed in my thoughts: *You were only seven. It's not your fault.*

"Thank you for telling me," Hugo finally said. Then with a deep breath, he began to tell me his own tale of woe. "Five years ago, my mother murdered my father. She threw him out of the airlock."

It was far more brutal than I'd been expecting, but I paid him the same courtesy he'd given me. I didn't say anything, and let him go on in his own time.

"I don't know how to explain it. She just... lost herself. I was fourteen; Jessa was five. I've never told Jessa the details; she just thinks they died."

He didn't have to explain any further. Killing another human being was a capital offense in the fleet, so I could only imagine what happened to his mother. Flushed out an airlock herself, I reckoned. Hugo fell back into his drink, while I went ahead and tried my best to finish mine and give *And Then There Were None* a try. The prose was engaging, if old-fashioned, and I couldn't help but dwell on the fact that this was a murder mystery beloved by an actual murderer. It lent an additional weight to each word and phrase.

I noticed Hugo had finished his drink and was now pacing before the window, his silhouette dark against the glow from the stars outside. I got up to join him, driven by tingly warmth that spread from my toes to the tips of my fingers, the alcohol at work in my blood. I was light as a feather, Hugo like the wind, buffeting me in his wake.

"Hugo, I'm so sorry," I said, touching his shoulder, sighing with relief when he neither jumped at the contact nor shook me off. He turned, honoring me with a crooked, halfway smile.

"Thanks. It's nice to talk to someone who can understand."

My heart felt like it had burst wide open, and my body moved on instinct, encircling him in a hug.

He was stiff. Unsure. But that only made me grasp harder, because if I pulled out now, it would make it too obvious how awkward this was. Hugo relaxed, just the tiniest bit, leaning into me. And then with a rush of clarity, I realized what I was doing—hugging the captain—and immediately was reined in by my better judgment. I pulled back.

"I am absolutely toasted," Hugo said, swaying on his feet. "We should turn in a tick early, I think."

I nodded, tamping down any disappointment I felt and following him with numb feet from the study and to our quarters. Luna, who must have lurked outside our bedrooms waiting for us to return, circled my ankles with a purr, following me to my door, clearly choosing me as his companion for the evening.

"Luna, you turncoat," Hugo muttered without much heat.

"Good night, Hugo," I said as I stepped through the door, poking my head back out to catch one more glimpse of him.

"Good night, Stella. Sweet dreams," he returned, bidding me adieu with a small wave.

Once the door shut, I did not allow myself to wallow in my dizzy-headed space. I made haste to the bathroom, where I gulped down three glasses of water. Uncanny how two months ago, such water consumption would have been unfathomable. Life aboard the *Rochester*—a macabre wonderland.

As I turned in to bed, not for the first time I wished that Hugo would bend his rule about not taking books from the study. I wanted to dive back into Agatha Christie but instead settled for an oldie but a goodie, relying on Harry Potter and the whirlwind of the Triwizard Tournament to engage and tire me. Harry had just taken a bath with the golden egg, and my eyes started to flutter as Snape confronted him on the stairs.

Then… a laugh.

I heard it—I definitely heard it. A human laugh. Not a cat.

I looked to the cat I had with me, who arched his back, hissing at the door. Luna agreed. There was something out there.

Putting down my reader, I catapulted out of bed to the door, pressing my ear against it. I waited—ten seconds. Then twenty. Then, screw it, I hit the OPEN button, holding my breath as the door slid open.

The hallway was dark. It was likely close to midnight. I stepped out into the blue haze, the black finish of the ship's interior reducing visibility to nil. I counted the space between breaths, staring into the black, willing something to announce itself. But nothing did.

I retreated into my chambers, half convinced I was going mad. After forcing myself to calm, I fell back against my pillow, determined to find sleep.

An alarm blared in my ear, too loud, too close, setting my heart into a gallop. My eyes clicked open, the room spinning, the bed seeming to vibrate beneath me. "Rori, what is it?" I sat bolt upright, looking for an explanation.

"Stella, I am sorry," Rori said, calm and contrite as always. "I cannot rouse the captain. There is a fire in his chambers. Emergency fire protocols will go into effect in one hundred and twenty seconds."

Emergency fire protocols? On the *Stalwart*, that meant whatever room was affected by fire would vent its contents into space, in order to seal the wound and save the rest of the ship. Which meant I had...

"Emergency fire protocols will go into effect in one hundred and ten seconds," Rori updated me.

Less than two minutes to save Hugo's life.

twelve

I bolted up from bed and to my door, slamming my hand against the OPEN button and rushing into the hall. The blue emergency lights glowed eerily as always, with not a hint of the true emergency going on just a few feet away. They should be screaming red. I sprinted to Hugo's door, but of course it was closed.

"Rori, the door!" I cried, and thankfully she overrode the bioscan protocols, letting me in.

I was hit in the face with heat so strong that I threw both hands up, squinting against it. Against my better instincts, I pushed myself forward, toward the fire, which lit up the sheets at the foot of Hugo's bed like a bonfire. I dropped to the floor, crawling toward Hugo's prone figure.

"Please don't be dead," I pleaded to no one but the fire, until finally I reached the head of the bed. The fire hadn't spread this far, and I found Hugo in a fetal position, knees tucked against his chest, the only thing keeping his toes from being roasted. I shook him, but he did not wake. A whiff of stale liquor hit my nose—he was passed out drunk. Of course.

"Emergency fire protocols will go into effect in sixty seconds," Rori provided an update, and I couldn't believe I'd burned through half my time already.

"Hugo!" I shouted, shaking him again. This time he stirred, only just, mumbling and batting at my hands, trying to push me away.

"Emergency fire protocols will go into effect in forty-five seconds."

Screw this. I grabbed Hugo by the arm and hauled him with all my might, out of bed and onto the floor. Then I dragged him along the floor, even as he came properly awake. He didn't fight me; indeed, he began to cough, deep, bone-rattling hacks that continued as we made our way through the hatch door and he collapsed in the corridor.

"My book," he coughed. "I need—" He tried to heave himself up and go back inside, but I stopped him cold. He was in no shape to run back into a burning room that was twenty seconds from venting. I popped my head back inside, crouching low, and saw a single hardcover volume on Hugo's bedside table. Without thinking, I sprinted back inside, precious seconds ticking away, Rori's voice overhead.

Fifteen seconds.

Ten.

I grabbed the book, flying back toward the door, ferocious

heat from the fire that now consumed the bed singeing my lashes as I literally hurled my body over the threshold and into the hallway, landing practically on top of Hugo.

"Emergency fire protocols active," Rori intoned as the door shuttled closed behind me, followed by the hollow thump of the window blowing out and all the fire, oxygen, and unbolted contents within being sucked out into space.

We stared in disbelief at Hugo's door from the wall opposite, chests heaving shaky breaths while the *Rochester* hummed along quietly. As if we hadn't battled a raging fire moments before. Exhausted and numb with shock, I rested my head against Hugo's chest, suddenly realizing it was bare. My gaze traveled down, and I found him naked but for a thin pair of undershorts. My breath stopped short, but I didn't pull away. No, I let myself enjoy it for just a moment, Hugo clinging to me, his heartbeat sounding in my ear. It was unlikely to happen again.

"You saved my life," he rasped. "Again."

I raised my eyes to meet his and found more fire than I could bear. His gaze burned with bewilderment, gratitude, and something else I was afraid to place. Forcing a cough, I pulled myself up to sitting, pulled myself away.

"I hope this was worth risking my life for," I panted, turning over the book in my hands. It had been well kept, the golden lettering of its cover still visible. *The Jungle Book* by Rudyard Kipling. I didn't know it, but it clearly was of great value to Hugo. He would have died going back for it.

"It was my father's." Hugo coughed, now leaning against

a bulkhead to gather his bearings. "And his mother's before him. And so on. I would imagine a book lover such as yourself would understand."

I nodded for the sake of avoiding argument. I loved books as much as the next person, but I loved living even more.

"Now, what the hell just happened?" Hugo demanded between coughs.

"I don't exactly know," I said. "I woke to Rori sounding the alarm, and there was a fire in your room. Someone set the bed alight."

"Someone? How do you know it was someone?"

"How else could it have happened? You certainly didn't do it yourself. And I heard—" No. I stopped myself. It was stupid.

"What did you hear?" Hugo grabbed my wrist, his grip weaker than it could be but still strong enough that the pressure was uncomfortable. "Tell me."

"I heard someone outside my door. Laughing. In the corridor. I don't know how long before it happened. I drifted off. But Luna heard it too. He hissed at the door."

Hugo nodded, like he wasn't surprised to hear it. "Stella, I need you to go into your room and lock the door behind you. Stay there until I come back."

"Where are you going? You need to see Officer Hanada about smoke inhalation, and it may not be safe—"

"I'm fine," Hugo insisted, pulling himself to standing by grabbing firm hold of the bulkhead. Chivalrous to a fault, he offered me a hand, but I wasn't dumb enough to take it. My weight would pull him back down, and while I was winded from my sprint and numb from adrenaline, I was otherwise healthy. I got to my feet without aid, ignoring Hugo's pointed frown.

He grabbed ahold of my arm and started walking me toward my door, not fooling me one bit—he needed my support to stand. And he thought it was wise to leave me in my room while he went off to do who knew what?

"I should go with you," I said, even as we stopped before my door and I pressed my fingers against the bio-lock.

"Absolutely not." He led me inside and deposited me by the bed. Luna leaped up from my pillow, rubbing himself against my side, poking his nose against Hugo's hand. Hugo ruffled the fur between Luna's ears and with clear effort righted himself to standing, no longer able to depend on anything for support. He managed it, though not without a few more dry hacks. "Stay in here until I come back. Don't leave this room under any circumstances."

"Why?" I pushed back. All this cloak-and-dagger was ridiculous. "Is there someone dangerous on board? Do you know who tried to kill you?"

"No one tried to kill me," Hugo said, I suspected mostly for his own benefit. Like he was trying to convince himself. "I'll be back soon. Don't open the door." Then he swept out without answering my question, leaving me in darkness.

"Lights on," I said, annoyed to find my voice wobbling. Rori obliged, taking it upon herself to only half raise them, leaving the room moody but not too dim. Luna let out a pathetic mewl, talking to me as he liked to do, asking me what was going on.

"I know, Lun," I said, stroking his back, finding the soft fur beneath my fingers and the way he broke out into a purr unduly comforting. I understood why Hugo's ancestors had brought cats on board in the first place. They provided a welcome distraction from loneliness. My gaze flicked to the window, which I'd taken to leaving open most of the time. There was debris floating by, anything that wasn't bolted down in Hugo's room now a permanent part of the moon's orbit, unless someone went out to collect it. I thought back to the claustrophobic spacesuit with my name on it in the transport bay and hoped I wouldn't end up being the one to do it.

Minutes ticked by into hours, alertness giving way to restless sleep. I woke several times, looking to the door, listening for Hugo's voice, believing more than once he was there, sitting beside me, only to realize I was dreaming.

"Rori, what time is it?"

"Five a.m.," she told me. Only four hours since Hugo left me, yet somehow it felt much longer. No longer feeling the pull of sleep, I padded over to the bathroom, glimpsing myself in the mirror for the first time. Dark smudges dashed across my forehead, down my cheek. I leaned close, smoothing fingers over my eyebrows. Still there, but more than a few hairs came away under pressure. That blast of heat to the face had done some damage.

I took a shower, happy to let Rori notch up the heat, creating a fine steam, which I let seep into my strained muscles. Still, I couldn't dawdle, in case Hugo came back. I was dried off and dressed by half past five. Then I waited, too keyed up to read or sleep, but simultaneously weary. Something awful had happened last night—or was it this morning?—and I needed to get to the bottom of it. Sergei had said this place was haunted, but I didn't believe in ghosts.

Six a.m. The lights in the corridor would be going on about now, signaling the start of a new day. Somewhere on board, Officer Xiao was seeing to her duties on the bridge. But I'd promised Hugo I wouldn't leave, so I stayed put. Yet I itched to speak to someone. I pulled up to my desk tab and checked my messages. Another day with no message from George. He'd dropped off from daily missives to just a few a week.

I ignored the pang I felt at the thought of George moving on, and clicked on a message from Karlson. His messages were positively persistent, but I almost didn't mind. George found my book-talk boring, but Karlson was kind of into it.

Hey, Stella—

I can't believe you had eggplant! Can you ask the cook where he got that? We've never grown that on the Stalwart *and I can't imagine where it came from. Interesting that you had zucchini, too. We haven't grown that since last season's blight.*

My uncle got me a reader tab like I asked, so now I can try to read some of those books you've been telling me about. We didn't have that mountain book you mentioned, but I did find some Le Carré in the Stalwart archive. I'll let you know what I think.

Hope you're OK. I asked my uncle about your ship and he said that it has a "reputation." He didn't know anything about your current captain, but said there was some sort of incident with the last one. He didn't go into details but made his serious captain face, and then yelled at me for wasting his time with gossip. Never mind that he's the one who started talking in the first place. Anyway, let me know how things are. You know if you need to come back, all I have to do is talk to my uncle.

Jon

The message was eerily well-timed, and everything came pouring out of me like a current. I even used his first name.

Dear Jon,

Actually, I am seriously freaked out right now. I just had to rescue Hugo from his room on fire—literally had to pull him out of bed before he was vented into space. I told him I'd heard someone in the corridor before it happened, and it didn't even faze him! Something is definitely going on.

I'm afraid of saying something, because I don't want to leave. I know you'll help me get back to the Stalwart, and I really appreciate it, but I really do like it here. When airlocks aren't failing and people aren't setting things on fire.

Typing that out, I sound crazy. I don't know—

I was interrupted by a knock at the door. "Stella, it's me."

Hugo! I flew to the RELEASE button, and the door slid open to reveal a Hugo none the worse for wear. He'd changed into clean clothes, though who knew where he'd gotten them, and he appeared flushed, a bit sweaty, but otherwise calm.

"Everything is fine," he said, firmly maintaining his ground on the other side of the door, even though I invited him in. "I forgot I had candles burning in my quarters last night, but I've seen Mari and she says I'm fine." He offered me a hand, which I shook. "Thank you for saving me, and I apologize for putting you in that position."

My body ran cold. Why was Hugo being so formal?

"Please report for breakfast as usual, and I'll see you when I return."

"Return?" I tried to stem the panic in my voice, even as it spiraled out from the pit of ice forming in my stomach. "Where are you going?"

"I have to run an errand off-ship. It should take only a few weeks."

A few weeks? He'd only been home about as long.

"Jessa will be devastated," I said, blatantly using Jessa as a proxy for my own feelings.

"Just reassure her that I'll be back soon, hopefully with good news and some exciting company," he said, forcing a smile.

I had a million questions—What good news? What did he mean by "company"? But before I could ask, Hugo bid me farewell with a curt nod and walked away, heading toward the transport bay. I returned to my desk tab in a daze, reading over what I'd written to Jon. No longer was I alight with apprehension, curiosity. Instead, I felt bogged down by new emotions, which stuck to my skin, my bones, as if someone had poured concrete over me: disappointment and confusion. I saved the message and resolved to finish it later. There was nothing more I could possibly say. Not to Jon. I could barely admit it to myself.

The captain was free to come and go as he pleased, I reasoned. I was just his employee, so there was no use getting upset. Even though I was stone-cold sober, I blamed the alcohol I'd had last night for muddling my mind and senses. Any connection I'd felt between us was only in my head.

I threw myself into the day's tasks, starting with breakfast, which still featured meat, reinforcing my suspicion that the captain's departure was unexpected. Neither Xiao nor Lieutenant Poole appeared, and Orion seemed none the wiser as to what happened last night—he asked me no questions and seemed perfectly surprised when I told them the captain had left. Jessa was, indeed, upset, but years of Hugo's sporadic presence had inoculated her to the initial shock. When I told her, she sighed, long and deep, but then schooled her features and asked if we could swap math for literature today. I said I'd be glad to, but before we could head down to our classroom, a *ping* came in over the comms. Officer Hanada was calling.

"Hello?" I answered.

"Hello, Stella," Hanada singsonged in my ear. "I hear

you ran into a burning room this morning and might have suffered a little smoke inhalation. Please report to the medical bay ASAP."

"I have class, so—"

"Have Orion watch her. I have a busy day ahead, and Hugo insisted I see you, make sure you're not dying."

"I feel fine."

"Even so."

She was a force to be reckoned with, and so I instructed Jessa to do independent reading until I could join her.

"Where is the medical bay, exactly?" I asked, comms still on.

"You know where you found the dead rat? There's a corridor about five feet from there on the right. Go all the way down it, and you can't miss me."

I followed her instructions, though thankfully there were no more mangled cat treats marking the spot this time. The corridor to the med bay was dark, no emergency lights lining the walls here, but Hanada hadn't been wrong. The light spilling out from a glass window in the med bay door made it easy, a beacon in the expanse of black.

The med bay was nothing special, the only notable detail being that it was eight times nicer than the one on board the *Stalwart* had been. Everything was made of shiny silver and frosted glass, all kept pristine from either diligent upkeep or lack of use. Given the size of the crew, I assumed the latter.

Hanada ordered me to hop up onto a gurney so she could check my breathing. Her stethoscope pressed cold against my chest as she leaned in close. The tips of her hair were purple now.

"Do you do that yourself?" I asked, pointing.

"Hmm. I'm the only scientist on board."

"Wait, you're not a doctor?"

She looked at me like I was stupid, then switched to checking my eyes with a bright light.

"I'm a virologist. I just moonlight as a doctor when people run into burning rooms or little girls decide to take a flying leap off a table."

"What does the *Rochester* need a scientist for?" I took a closer look around. The med bay didn't see much use, but there was a door to my right. *Must be a lab.*

"The Fairfaxes were all scientists. Until this generation, at least." She rolled her eyes, and I would have asked for the story if I hadn't been afraid she'd bite my head off. "The ship houses an archive of old Earth drugs, cures, and the like. I keep everything in good condition for when we eventually deorbit."

"There's a lot about this ship I don't know," I said, half to myself. Hanada moved to check my reflexes, hitting a metal prong against my knees.

"Hang in there. Remember, I need you to last at least a year. For the betting pool."

"Hugo says that isn't real."

"Hugo likes to tell people what they want to hear," she volleyed back. "Have you been experiencing any nausea or vomiting, confusion or sleepiness?"

I shook my head. "So what do you do when you're not in the lab, then? Don't you get bored? We never see you on the main deck."

She eyed me, clearly skeptical of my attempt at small talk. But she answered. "I read. Poker on Sundays with Hugo and Poole. I write to my parents. Dye my hair. We could do yours, if you want." She took a step back, examining me. "Magenta might look nice. I think I have the colors to mix that."

"No, that's okay." I could already feel my cheeks heating just at the thought of standing out like that. *No, thanks.* "Wait, you have parents?"

"Most people do."

"I just mean, I assumed you were an orphan," I said.

"Almost but not quite. My parents live on the *Nikkei*. They shipped me off to the *Marie Curie* when I was thirteen, so I haven't seen them in a long time. But they like to write."

"Then when did you come to the *Rochester*? How long have you been here?"

"You're oddly inquisitive." She stashed the stethoscope in a drawer. "Also, perfectly healthy. Congrats."

"Just thought I'd get to know you. Since I'll be sticking around. For your betting pool."

Hanada smiled like a cat. "I came to the *Rochester* when I was eighteen. Ten years ago." She took up my left arm, turning it over and running two fingers along it. Weird, since I thought the examination was over. "And where were you ten years ago?"

"The *Empire*."

"That's what I thought," she said, tapping her fingers at the crook of my elbow, then letting go, seeming satisfied. "Did you have the Kebbler virus? Or were you vaccinated?"

"Why do you want to know that?" The tables had turned, Hanada grilling me for information.

"Science. I'm a virologist, remember?"

"Then, yeah, I had the Kebbler virus."

"And you survived?" Her tone was positively gleeful. She went back to the metal drawer and pulled out a tourniquet and syringe.

"Clearly," I said, eyeing the door. "Can I go now?"

"Let's make a deal." She reached for my arm again. "You let me draw some blood—for science—and I'll answer whatever burning question you were quite indelicately trying to butter me up for."

My whole body burned at being caught, but a surge of triumph pushed through the heat. She was willing to talk to me. Now I had to figure out what question I wanted to ask.

"You think about it while I take care of this." She tied the tourniquet just above my elbow and picked up the needle.

I could ask about the other governesses, or about the sounds I'd been hearing, but the former wouldn't get me closer to figuring out who was trying to hurt Hugo, and the latter might make her think I was losing my mind. "Is there anyone on board who would want to hurt Hugo?" I asked finally as Hanada plunged the needle all the way into my vein.

"That's a dangerous question to ask."

"Why?" I focused intently on her purple-tipped hair to

distract myself from the pressure of the needle. I couldn't look.

"Because if there were, I might be the one, and I have a needle in your arm?" She was quick to let me know she was kidding before I could jerk my arm away. "No one is trying to hurt Hugo. I mean, you've met all of us. Who exactly do you think is a secret killer? The fire was an accident."

I bit my tongue, unsure I wanted to tell her about the airlock, or the laughing. Hanada did not exactly inspire trust. When she withdrew the needle from my arm, I let out an involuntary sigh of relief.

"This was nice," she said, signaling question time was over. Then she shooed me to the door, leaving me in the dark and feeling entirely unsatisfied.

The feeling stayed with me all day, like a second skin. Hanada's question rattled around in my head. I had met everyone on board the *Rochester*, so who did I think could be trying to harm Hugo? Hanada was odd, but if their weekly poker game was anything to go by, Hugo and she were friends. Xiao, Orion, and Jessa were out of the question— too motherly, too friendly, and too young, respectively. I didn't know Lieutenant Poole well, but it was a big leap to brand her a killer. And Albert could have simply poisoned Hugo if he wanted.

But then there was that laugh. Someone had been in the corridor last night before the fire. I was sure of it.

Reasonably sure.

Before dinner, I went back to my unfinished message to Jon, rewriting it now that I'd had some time to collect my thoughts.

> *Dear Jon,*
>
> *Something happened last night… It's turning into a blur now, and I'm not sure what to think. Long story short, there was a fire in Hugo's room. I saved his life, and then he left. And everyone says it was an accident, but I'm not sure.*
>
> *I've gone over it in my head, and I can't imagine who on board would do such a thing. But then I guess I've only been here two months and don't really know them. Does your uncle have access to the fleet-census database? Maybe he could do a quick lookup on the crew? It's Iris Xiao, Grace Poole, Mari Hanada, Orion Carmichael, and Albert Hawes. No need to check on the ten-year-old.*
>
> *Don't worry about me, though. I'm still happy here and don't want to come back. I'd just like some peace of mind that no one on staff is a pyromaniac.*
>
> *Stella*

Dinner was fully vegetarian again, pleasing Officer Xiao, the rest of us not even bothering to mention the change. The crew was used to this. Hugo came; Hugo went. I would get used to it too.

After dinner, I headed for the study. Only once I got there, I remembered: no Hugo, no evening reading appointment. I scoured the corridor, looking left, right, and behind me for good measure before I pressed my fingers to the OPEN button.

And nothing happened. I tried again. Same result.

I was locked out.

Hugo was gone and, with him, access to his favorite spaces on board. To the spaces we shared. Something inside me boiled, like anger. It didn't seem fair—I really wanted to read that Agatha Christie—but I couldn't because Hugo had chosen to run away.

I retreated to my quarters and, for the first time since I'd left the *Stalwart,* allowed myself to cry.

thirteen

Hugo unwittingly left one piece of him behind. His precious *Jungle Book* lay forgotten in my quarters until two days after his departure, when I found it inside my bedside storage drawer. At first I ignored it, stowing it at the bottom of my wardrobe, underneath a pair of dress shoes I'd not yet worn. But each morning and evening as I dressed and undressed, it called to me. I had to know what was so beloved by Hugo and his father and grandmother before him that he'd been willing to die for it.

Fortune would have it that I wasn't locked out of the library. I found a copy of Kipling's biography in the archives, transferred it to my reader, and devoured it alongside *The Jungle Book*. I also found Agatha Christie's entire catalog digitized, easing the blow of the study a bit. I dug in to her mysteries just as the mystery of the ship quieted down to nothing. There were no more strange sounds, and two weeks after my plea, Jon responded and put to rest my paranoia.

Hey, Stella—

I'm sorry it took me so long to respond. The water-filtration system broke, so that's forty-eight hours of my life I won't get back again. Then, when I tried asking my uncle to check out your crew, he gave me The Look again, so I had to implement a different tack. You are looking at Captain Karlson's new apprentice! Part-time, of course, on top of my engineering shifts. My uncle is finally happy with me, though I don't plan on telling him that I have no intention of taking over as captain someday. I'll be on Earth before that happens. But in the meantime, I have occasional access to his tab unit, and it only took me three days to figure out his password.

So basically: I didn't find much on your crew. Poole and Xiao appear to have been born & raised on the Rochester, *and there is limited data, since the private ships don't have to release medical records or work progress reports. Carmichael comes from the* Lady Liberty— *school records are standard. He's gay, and yes, you should be as disturbed as I was that that was in his fleet record. I probably don't want to know what they know about me. Hawes also comes from the* Lady Liberty *and graduated top of his class from their culinary program. There's a note that Fairfax must have paid him top digicoin to transfer to the* Rochester, *given the* Lady Liberty *was paying him a fortune to head their entire food program. Hanada comes from the* Nikkei, *transferred to the* Marie Curie *as a teen, where she rose through the ranks until she transferred to the* Rochester. *Her files note, more than once, that she has a genius-level IQ and was at the top of the list for fleet enrichment. Apparently smart, talented people from rich ships get special enrichment! I'm learning so much already in my apprenticeship. Oh, and there's a note of dismay that she chose to transfer to the* Rochester *instead of staying on the* Marie Curie.

I know you didn't ask me to, but... I checked on your captain, too. Out of everyone, there was a ton of information in his file. The fleet has been keeping tabs on him. I couldn't memorize it all, but I did note that he's been sanctioned for drunk & disorderly conduct more than once on the Versailles *(he frequents the Moulin Rouge Deck, apparently). Watch out, Stella.*

Jon

Hugo and the Moulin Rouge Deck? I couldn't help the furious heat that rose to my cheeks reading it. The stories were notorious—any salacious pleasure one could hope to find, the *Versailles*'s Moulin Rouge Deck had. High-stakes poker, drugs, men and women—all available for a price. Perhaps that's where he was right now. I just hoped he didn't gamble away the *Rochester* on his bender. No one came to claim the ship, so I figured we were in the clear.

But soon Xiao enlisted me to prepare several rooms. When

I asked her why, she replied, stonefaced, "Guests are coming."

"Prepare," as it turned out, meant I was to sub in as a chambermaid. Xiao and I went to the lower deck, and I finally got a look inside the old crew quarters. We opened each room, instructing Rori to leave the doors open to get a bit of air circulation going, then fitted freshly laundered bedding onto each mattress. There were four beds—two bunks—and a bank of lockers in each room, like what we had on the *Stalwart* before I'd been promoted to a single.

"Am I allowed to ask who the guests are?"

"It's technically insubordinate, but I'll allow it," Xiao said, clearly joking, while she aggressively tucked in a bed corner. "Captain Fairfax will be bringing back with him visitors from the craft *Ingram*. Needless to say, they are used to a higher level of service than the crew of the *Rochester* can provide, and thus some members of their crew will be joining us ahead of the party. Maids, valets, a personal chef."

"Albert isn't good enough?"

"They're picky," Xiao said. She clearly was not the biggest fan of the impending party.

"How long will they be here?"

"It was a month last time, though that was before…" Xiao grimaced. "Well, it was a long time ago. This time, I'm not sure. Bianca is older, and I suspect, well… that is neither here nor there."

I didn't know who Bianca was or what Xiao suspected, but it was clear she didn't plan on telling me. She fluffed the last pillow, and we headed back upstairs.

"Now, when they arrive, I will guide the more senior members of staff, and I'll expect you to see to the more junior." She dismissed me, and I hastened to get to my lessons with Jessa. We barely made it through an hour of math and two of history when my comms buzzed. It was Orion.

"Incoming birdie, Stella," his voice rang in my ear. "They'll be docking in the transport bay in ten."

"Roger wilco," I replied, drawing a satisfied smirk from Jessa. I'd finally learned the jargon.

I left Jessa watching a movie and hurried upstairs to change into a more formal dress. As I arrived, breathless, at the outer transport-bay door, I quickly smoothed back my hair into my bun before the outer airlock door opened to admit a small shuttle. Once it had docked, with the airlock closing and the red light above the door switching to green, I opened the door to greet them.

The first thing I was struck by was the uniforms. On the *Rochester,* we wore a lot of black, dark blues, and stiff, structured styles I had quickly become accustomed to. But our clothing wasn't identical; we didn't wear uniforms. The *Ingram* staff emerged from the craft like a mini army, the men in navy waistcoats with brown insets over navy slacks, the women in navy-and-brown dress coats like mine, but stiffer.

Xiao appeared behind me, pasting on a smile and approaching the figure at the head of the procession. "Lieutenant Peters, welcome." She shook the hand of a man who looked to be in his forties, continuing the trend of private ships having a considerably older personnel roster.

"Good to see you again, Iris," Peters said. "May I introduce my staff? Much the same as last time, though with a few additions." They lined up in front of their craft in a coed formation that made it clear they delineated themselves by rank. The senior staff members wore insignia on their left shoulders—all lieutenants. There were three junior staff among them—two maids and a valet, with titles familiar to me from the *Empire*. The maids were to serve the ladies of the party; the valet, a high-ranking male. It gave me a good idea of the gender balance to expect.

Xiao busied herself with the eight senior crew members, leading them off into the ship sans any bags. Instead, the junior members began to haul bags and trunks from the ship—one of each for each member of staff.

"Hello. I'm Stella Ainsley, the *Rochester*'s governess and auxiliary engineer." I shook each of their hands, though both ladies stared at my outstretched hand like I'd sprouted tentacles before reluctantly offering me their weak grips. Guess the *Ingram* wasn't into that form of greeting. They rattled off their names for me in short order—Griegs was the valet, and the maids were Elizabeth Greene, Lizzy for short, and Preity Khan. I hailed Orion on comms to come help us with the cargo.

"Who did you just ask to help us?" Lizzy asked, mouth agog.

"Orion, the communications officer. Why?"

"You can just ask senior officers to assist with manual labor?" Preity chimed in. I didn't think of Orion as my senior, and said as much. All three looked uncomfortable.

"I'm guessing none of you have been aboard before?"

I asked, though their relative ages told that story obviously enough. Griegs and Lizzy were probably in their early twenties, and Preity looked closer to my age. "Well, welcome to the *Rochester*. We're pretty casual around here."

Orion arrived, and the boys exchanged brief greetings, not even hesitating before shouldering a bag and a trunk each. The trunks, thankfully, were on wheels, but the addition of a bulky bag had me spitting curses under my breath.

"There are six rooms, twenty-four bunks," I said as we reached our destination. "So you can spread out if you want."

Griegs shook his head. "There are more coming with the *Ingram*, so we'll need the space."

Accordingly, we deposited the senior officers' belongings into two rooms, and the junior staff's into a third. We would leave them to sort out their gender splits on their own. From the way Griegs eyed Lizzy, cohabiting didn't seem like the best idea. I showed them the basics, how most of the doors they'd have to worry about operated on simple button switches, and how most other things were voice-activated through Rori. Upstairs in the dining quarters, Griegs made inquiries as to which member of the *Rochester* staff was responsible for serving meals, and when I told him none, he nearly lost his balance.

The arrival of the *Ingram*'s staff was a harbinger of Hugo's return, something I both craved and dreaded. Would he be stiff and formal with me, like our last encounter? Or could we reclaim the easiness we'd had between us, get back to reading and talking like we were friends? The *Ingram* represented the unknown variable.

The junior crew provided little elucidation over the next day, choosing to spend most of their time separate from the *Rochester* staff, alternately sleeping, playing games, and eating. It seemed to me they were taking the opportunity to rest as much as possible until their charges arrived. When I asked how long they thought they might be staying, all I got in return were shrugs and, from Preity, a cryptic "Well, that depends," followed by a pointed look shared among them.

They, on the other hand, prodded me for information on Hugo.

"So, what's the captain like?" Lizzy asked over dinner on the second night post-arrival. Preity and Griegs—who was called Thomas by the girls but never invited me to do the same—leaned in with interest. They'd waited until Xiao left with Jessa, and Orion had also excused himself, before jumping on me. They clearly saw me as nonthreatening, but I wasn't delusional enough to assume they considered me a friend.

"We heard he was a bit of a character," Preity added. "I mean, when he brought the *Rochester* out to orbit the moon, everyone assumed he was either stupid or crazy."

"You mean it didn't always orbit the moon?" I asked with little hesitation, belatedly kicking myself for participating in idle gossip about my ship.

"You didn't know?" Griegs said, not without a seriously judgmental tone.

"I've been here only a few months," I admitted.

"Where were you before?" Lizzy this time, same tone.

"I was on the *Stalwart*."

All four hissed air through their teeth.

"No wonder you're clueless."

"Do they even have fleet comms on that bucket?"

I ignored the first—Lizzy was tactless but sweet—but responded to Griegs with my head held high. "Of course we had fleet comms. But we didn't busy ourselves with the affairs of all the private ships. We had more important things to attend to. Like growing most of your food supply." They appeared rightly cowed by that. "It seems you know more about this ship than I do."

"No one from the *Ingram* has seen him in years," Lizzy said. "We used to be neighbors, part of the same orbit cluster around Earth. For almost two hundred years. But then there was the... incident with the Fairfaxes, and Hugo became captain and hightailed it out here... We've heard rumors, that's all."

Moving out to the moon was an extreme, if odd, reaction to his parents dying, but it didn't make Hugo crazy. I didn't like them using *crazy* as a pejorative and I told them as much. "The captain is exactly what you'd expect for someone who had to take over when he was fourteen, in not exactly ideal circumstances," I said. "He's mature beyond his years, responsible; he can be kind of quiet. But he's kind to all of us. We're not expected to put on airs and graces, as you may have noticed."

"Just wait until Bianca gets here," Preity said below her breath. "That'll change."

It wasn't the first time I'd heard lightly disparaging comments about Bianca Ingram, about whom no one had yet adequately provided me information. I'd asked several times, but the junior crew was as mum on the subject as Xiao. I didn't bother to pry again, instead castigating myself for saying anything about Hugo. Hopefully nothing I'd said could be misconstrued as overly affectionate.

The senior *Ingram* staff arrived for dinner, summarily kicking us out. I didn't like the segregation by rank they engaged in, nor did I appreciate it when Lieutenant Peters asked me to stay behind to serve them. I politely but firmly declined, most likely earning myself an enemy in the process. But I didn't care. I was not beholden to them, not because I had lower rank, nor because I was a woman. I was an equal for the first time aboard the *Rochester,* and I would not yield that for anyone.

"You are stupidly bold, Stella Ainsley," Preity said to me as we left Griegs behind to bear the job of food service. Lizzy ran off to do whatever it was she did after dinner, but Preity hung back with me. We made our way slowly toward my quarters. "I would say you were a role model, but the Ingrams would vent me into space if I conducted myself as you do."

"They sound awful," I said, but Preity only shrugged.

"It's a nice ship and a good life. They're strict about protocols but otherwise undemanding. We have plenty to eat; we're allowed to do as we please on our own free time. Of all the transfers I could have gotten, I'm happy with it."

"You were a transfer? From where?"

"The *Empire*. I transferred out as part of the orphan program six years ago."

"Oh. Me too." I couldn't believe it. The fleet wasn't huge, but who would have thought it could be this small? "How did we not know each other from the *Empire*? Wait, did you know George Davies?"

The light of recognition lit behind her eyes. "Ginger bloke?"

"Yes! He ended up with me on the *Stalwart*."

"Wow. How is he?"

I said the first thing that came to my mind. "Hot. But, you know, in an annoying kind of way."

Preity simply laughed. "Yeah, he was annoying on his best days when we were kids. But I could see him going the way of seriously attractive. What part of the ship were you in? Maybe that's why we never crossed paths."

"Engineering," I said.

"My family was in textiles, like George's. That explains it, then."

"This is me." I indicated my door.

"Oooh, can I see?"

I gave Preity a tour of my humble abode, watching her eyes become saucers as she took a turn of the room. "No wonder you like it here. This is orbital." A reply was halfway out of my mouth when Preity went still and began talking to herself. Then I realized she was receiving a message on comms.

"Roger that; I will be there in five," she said. Then she turned to me with a grim look. "The *Ingram* has arrived."

fourteen

I did the sensible, mature thing and hid in my room for the rest of the night. No one hailed me to go help with bags, and I was hardly going to volunteer. I was in no mood or shape to play purser. I needed a full night's sleep and a long, hot shower before I discovered what kind of captain had returned to the ship.

Regardless, I spent the better part of forty minutes with an ear pressed against the door as our new passengers moved into their quarters. I heard a laugh, which sped up my heartbeat threefold, but this was a light, tinkling laugh. The laugh of a woman who was trying to impress a man. Was it for Hugo? Or a man of her own party? I pushed my body harder against the door, but the laughter and the chatter only seemed to drift farther away.

Eventually I gave up, treating myself to a steamy shower,

then distracted myself with a vampire book until I was groggy enough for sleep.

Morning came too soon, dread weighing down my limbs as I pulled myself through my a.m. rituals. I chose a simple black overdress and made my bun particularly neat, carrying them out with me into the greater ship like armor. Immediately, I sensed a shift; the atmosphere of the ship was different. Busy. Full. Chatter echoed from an adjacent corridor, the hum of humans replacing that of circulating air, buzzing machinery. I ran into Lizzy and Preity on my way to the dining quarters, where we were met by Xiao.

"Good; you're all prompt. A great start to our new schedule. Junior staff eats breakfast at seven, senior staff at eight, and then civilians and the captain at nine. *Ingram* staff, I take it you're aware of your duties beyond breakfast?"

The girls nodded and went into the dining room, but Xiao grabbed my arm, holding me back. "Stella, I may be out of pocket while the Ingrams are here, but if you need me, I'm here for you." She then lowered her voice just above a whisper. "And, well. I hate to say this, but the Ingrams are accustomed to a very different ship and crew dynamic, so it would be best if you were… seen and not heard while they are here."

I had figured out as much from interacting with their crew, and had already resolved to be seen as little as possible myself, let alone heard. Xiao apparently wasn't done, though she seemed to be trying to find her words. She pursed her lips and furrowed her brow.

"You also may find that the captain is… different with the Ingrams on board. Just don't take it too much to heart, and take care of yourself." She patted me on the arm and went off in the direction of the bridge.

Xiao's words did little to quell my mounting anxiety. As the day progressed, I started to suspect the new schedule was designed to keep me and Hugo apart. I was officially "junior staff" now, and my duty was to mind Jessa, who was even more cut off than I was.

"He's been back a whole day and hasn't come to see me." Jessa pushed away her plate with a huff. I would now join her for dinner in her quarters, as the Ingram party was to monopolize the dining room each evening from now on.

"I'm sure he's just sleeping off some jet lag," I said, picking at my chicken with a fork. Not even the return of meat to the menu could buoy my spirits. I was distracted by nerves.

"Sure," Jessa grumbled. "Or he's spending all his time with Bianca, like he used to."

My comms pinged in my ear. Incoming message from Officer Xiao. "Stella, the captain requests that you dress Jessa in something appropriate for company and bring her to the drawing room."

"Roger that," I said with a sigh. I'd barely managed twenty-four hours avoiding him. But at least I had Jessa to hide behind. Dinner had involved a red sauce, which she'd somehow managed to get in her hair. I ordered her into the shower while I picked out one of her nicer overdresses, which, unlike mine, came in a variety of vibrant colors—saffron, lilac, azure. I chose the lilac, to which Jessa wrinkled her nose.

"I want to wear pants. And a black top. Like you do."

I ordered her to lift her arms so I could pull the pinafore wrap over her underlayer. "Nice try, but I wear dresses every day."

"Why is that? Pants are more comfortable."

"And dresses are more comfortable to me," I said. "You should be able to wear what you like, I agree." Jessa opened her mouth to reinvigorate her argument, but I stopped her in her tracks. "But. Some people have certain ideas about what girls should wear, so that means a dress in a pretty color."

"My brother doesn't care what I wear."

"But the Ingrams do, and your brother cares about them."

I'd been through this pageantry aboard the *Empire,* where girls were expected to adorn themselves as best they could like beautiful flowers. Impractical accoutrements such as lace, gauzy overlayers, and even silk abounded in the fashions of the finer ships in the fleet. I preferred dark colors and the more practical fabrics, even as a child. My aunt had been more than happy to oblige me, as vibrant colors were the domain of only those with money and resources, and she didn't wish to waste any on me.

Jessa pouted but allowed me to dress her: the price she had to pay to see Hugo. I checked myself in the mirror. Same old—plain face and hair that threatened to escape my bun, which I smoothed back. The stiff bodice of my overdress caused strain in my back but gave me the clean lines and unassuming airs I desired. To blend into the background of the party was my aim. To hide.

We found the drawing room easily enough by following the tinkling of glasses, the raucous laughter of a large party, which you could hear from the bridge. We followed the noise to the third bulkhead down from the dining quarters to find several people spilling into the corridor, some precariously holding glasses whose contents sloshed over the sides as they moved. They must have started drinking with dinner.

The drawing room boasted a collection of fine couches, chairs, and tables, plus Hugo's promised pianoforte. You couldn't miss Hugo, who was the center of attention as he sat in an armchair surrounded by a trifecta of couches filled to the brim with ladies. I found myself pulled along behind Jessa, who eagerly charged inside and headed straight for him. As usual, she launched herself at her brother, shouting his name, and while he hugged her, he did so more stiffly than I had ever seen him do. A sea of judgmental eyes turned on the reuniting siblings; I watched them as they watched, passing my own sort of judgment in kind.

The overwhelming theme of the party was blond and haughty. Everyone was painfully overdressed in evening gowns of taffeta and silk and horribly impractical high-heeled shoes, which poked out from underneath their gowns. I skimmed them, identifying the likely culprit of the captain's wife—in her forties, straw-colored hair piled high on her head, culminating in a tiara. Only a captain's wife would be so stupidly audacious. And to her right and left were two young facsimiles, their golden hair tumbling down their backs freely over elegantly boned bodices of magenta and royal blue. No one had to tell me that the more beautiful of the two—her features more delicate, her hair that much glossier—was Bianca. I could tell from her primary position closest to Hugo, and the way she leaned toward him with purpose. She lit up the room like a star.

"My, she's only grown more precious with time, hasn't she?" Bianca said of Jessa, her lips set in a smile that didn't quite reach her eyes. I could see Jessa in profile, and her expression echoed my thoughts exactly: what kind of pandering orbit junk was this?

"Do you remember me?" Jessa shook her head no. "Well, you were only four last time I saw you, so I'm not surprised." Bianca sat back on the lounge, her direct attention for Jessa having ebbed; now she regaled her audience like the headliner that she was. "You know, we used to think she might be a bit slow! She didn't talk until she was nearly four, and even then could barely string sentences together."

I saw Jessa flinch, caught the tightening of Hugo's jaw— the first time I'd allowed myself to look at him since entering the room—and was spurred into action before I could think.

"Jessa is quite bright, actually." I stepped forward into the light and saw the way the party peered at me with genuine surprise. They'd not seen me until now, though I'd been standing not even five feet behind Jessa the whole time. "She excels in all her subjects, including but certainly not limited to extemporaneous speech and debate." Or, at least, she would as soon as I started teaching her in those subjects, which I resolved to do starting the next day, just to show Bianca Ingram.

"Now, who is this bold creature?" Bianca said, that forced smile back on her face, her outrage leaking through in the way she spat the word "bold" like it was a curse.

"This is Stella Ainsley, our new governess," Hugo said, his voice like an electric current running through me. He acknowledged me, our eyes met, there was the briefest spark—of happiness to see me, of pride—but in a second it was gone, and everything that followed served to convince me I'd imagined the moment, a trick of the light and shadows. "She comes to us from the *Stalwart*."

"Ugh, a governess." Bianca moaned with exaggerated force. "I think we can all agree that governesses are the absolute worst. Lucy and I used to play the most delightful tricks on ours. She'd squawk bloody murder at us, and we'd just laugh ourselves silly."

Lucy, the blond doily in magenta, tittered in agreement. "But this one is so much younger than ours were. How old are you?"

"Seventeen," I responded.

"Just seventeen and from the *Stalwart* to boot," Bianca scoffed. "She can hardly be qualified to teach, Hugo. I heard they teach only farming aboard that old bucket."

"I was raised and educated aboard the *Empire*," I defended myself, feeling my whole body go hot from both adrenaline and embarrassment. All eyes were on me, including Hugo's, whose expression was unreadable. "And I'm well qualified to teach Jessa in a variety of subjects, including literature, history, mathematics, science, and art."

"No foreign language?" That was Bianca's mother, voice dripping with condescension. "It would be such a shame for Jessa to miss out on a good, classical education. French, German, music. We can recommend someone if you like." She addressed Hugo like I wasn't even there. I realized they were all doing it—speaking about me, and Jessa for that matter, in the third person. We were conversation pieces, not people.

"That won't be necessary," Hugo said. "Xiao has been teaching her Mandarin, and I can relay passable French and music instruction."

"Oh, yes, I had nearly forgotten!" Bianca leaned forward, running her fingers over Hugo's arm. "You were always my piano man. Shall we again, for old times' sake?"

Jessa and I were promptly forgotten as Hugo and Bianca got up to put on a show, so I found an empty love seat by the door for us.

"I don't like him with these people," Jessa muttered to me as the chords of an old fleet anthem rose above the din.

I had to agree, but for Jessa's sake, I made excuses. "I'm sure he'll be back to himself in a day or so. I could tell he was really excited to see you." Jessa tossed me a skeptical look but didn't argue. We both turned to watch the performance. Hugo's playing was passable but unpracticed, the opposite of Bianca's song. Her talent was annoyingly superior—tone clear as a bell chime, each note strong and unwavering. I'd bet my tablet she practiced every day, likely after years of learning from masters.

"I do remember that Bianca lady," Jessa whispered to me. "I didn't like her. That's why I didn't talk to her."

"You're a smart girl." We shared a conspiratorial smile. Then we sat through two more songs from Bianca, three moderately less enjoyable attempts from Lucy, through which at least Hugo demonstrated some improvement on the keys. I hated that he played for them but had never played for me, like he'd promised. But then I shook the thought away. We'd had our dreaded reunion, and it was basically a big fat nothing. I tapped my comm piece and asked Rori for the time, and she confirmed my suspicions.

"It's past your bedtime," I informed Jessa, who, as if on cue, yawned.

We slipped out as another young woman, a cousin, I guessed, sat down to the piano and I saw Bianca pull Hugo into a dance. It was usually not my role to put Jessa to bed, but I had no desire to disturb Orion or Xiao. I talked her out of watching a movie, got her into her sleep clothes, and made sure she was in bed with the lights out before retreating upstairs to my own quarters. I was nearly there, counting the steps until I could sleep, when my comms buzzed.

"Captain Hugo Fairfax calling," Rori announced in my ear. I nearly tripped over my own feet. Why would he be calling me? Hugo had never used comms to hail me the whole time I'd been here. With a shaky voice, I accepted the connection.

"Hello?"

"Stella, why did you leave?" a brusque voice demanded.

"I had to put Jessa to bed."

"Oh," he said as if the thought never occurred to him. "Well, then, come back if you're done. I want you here."

"I'm quite tired."

"Nonsense," he insisted. "The night is young. I'll see you in five minutes."

The captain had given me a direct order, so back to the drawing room I trudged. I sat myself quietly in my love seat again, observing how the mood of the room had shifted since I'd left. The whole party was at least four or five drinks in, and Hugo was finally getting to play his precious poker. I found him holding court at a round table, half his face hidden behind a spread of cards. Bianca and several people I didn't have names for yet were playing along. No Poole or Hanada.

Whisper-soft, Lizzy ducked in through the door and took a seat next to me. "I'm here to collect the missus when the time comes," she informed me, indicating Mrs. Ingram, whose face was now bright red, her tiara half-slid down her head. I pointed her toward the poker table.

"Who is everyone? Other than Bianca. I've already met her."

"She's a peach, right?" Lizzy's grin was wicked. "Next to her is her older brother, Braxton, who likes to put his hands in all sorts of interesting places, so watch yourself. And over there"—she pointed to a sour-faced young woman with an unfortunate snub nose watching the poker game from the sidelines—"is his wife, Justine. She came to us from the *Versailles*, speaks mostly French, and the captain and Mrs. Ingram are quite put out that after nearly two years of marriage, she's not yet produced an heir.

"The mousy brunette is cousin Cecily, who has nothing much to recommend her except that she's always game for a round of poker, and next to her is the captain himself."

I looked him over and found a man who matched his wife in his audacity. Taking the captain title rather literally, he was dressed in Old-World naval attire, complete with gold aiguillette and cap. "Did he think this was a costume party?"

"Good one, Stella!"

Only I hadn't been joking. Lizzy continued to give me the gossip I didn't ask for. "The captain has spoiled his precious children rotten at the expense of his ship, and so here we are, throwing ourselves at the Fairfaxes."

"What do you mean?"

"You didn't know? I thought the *Rochester* crew was all cozy. Guess not. Captain Ingram is here to discuss a merger with Captain Fairfax. Combine ship crews and resources so we can stay in space a bit longer. The *Ingram*'s on its last legs, though they'd never admit it."

"Does Captain Fairfax know?" I asked, watching the poker game with renewed interest, especially noting the way Captain Ingram deferred to Hugo—I was sure he was letting him win—and how Bianca batted her eyelashes just so.

"Of course," Lizzy said. "They've been going back and forth on it for years. But they wanted to wait until Bianca was older, and just between you and me, Captain Ingram has been taking meetings with several other ships in the hopes of finding a less… risky match."

She leaned close, practically whispering in my ear. "Rumors are that he spends most of his time drunk, gambling away favors, and partaking of the company of various men and women on the pleasure cruisers. And then there's what they say about the family curse." Lizzy dangled her gossip like fruit, pausing a moment, clearly expecting me to urge her on. I did not, and she continued, regardless. "His mother wasn't well at the end, and everyone wonders whether it may be genetic. But Bianca's rejected everyone else. Too old, too ugly, the ship wasn't nice enough. So here we are, in the middle of nowhere with Captain Crazy."

"He's not crazy," I mumbled, though my heart wasn't quite in it. I was distracted by a leaden feeling in my stomach and the view of Bianca leaning into Hugo's shoulder, whispering something in his ear that made him laugh.

It was the last of a bitter cocktail I needed to swallow. This wasn't a normal visiting party. It was a courtship ritual. Bianca and Hugo were intended for each other.

fifteen

I fled the drawing room with the same lack of fanfare as when I had arrived, making excuses to Lizzy and slipping silently out into the hall. I sought out the stars, craving their communion in my despair. I went right to the bridge, not only the best spot for a panoramic view of the stars but also one that I knew would be empty at this time of night. Xiao had long since gone to bed, and none of our guests would dare intrude on their hosts' command center. I made my way through it, past the outer ring that housed Orion's comms station, into the darkness, led by the light, until there was just the captain's chair and a bank of tab controls between me and the view beyond. I sat in the chair, in *his* chair, which offered a perfect viewpoint through the expanse of windows. And I said something akin to a prayer. A plea.

"Please don't let it be true."

But I knew in my heart that it was. That soon I would lose the only place I'd ever truly felt happy, welcome, and wanted. I couldn't possibly stay here, not once Hugo and Bianca were married. I said it out loud to make it true. "I will leave when Hugo and Bianca are married." The words turned to ashes in my mouth.

And then I did something I hadn't done in a long while. I talked to my parents.

That's how Hugo found me, prattling away at triple-paned glass like a madwoman. "Stella, is that you?" I nearly jumped out of my skin at the sound of it, cursing under my breath. "Wait, are you in my chair?" I jumped again, this time up and onto my feet. And there he was, Hugo in all his glory—tall, broad shoulders, furrowed brow—shadows and lines that made me want to draw him. An expression that made me melt.

"I looked up and you were gone. I wanted to talk to you. Say a proper hello."

The evening's earlier humiliation came rushing back. He ignored me in front of company and was talking to me only now, when no one could see. "Why would you want to talk to the lowly governess?" I replied with more petulance than I intended. Hugo laughed.

"Oh, Bianca is an idiot. Don't mind her."

"Is that what you wanted to talk to me about? Bianca?"

"No, of course not." He frowned. "I wanted to see how you were doing."

"I'm fine," I attempted breezily, but it came out tight. "I have your book, by the way. I would have returned it to the study, but unfortunately I found once you'd left that it was locked."

Hugo's eyes searched my face, which I kept steady in challenge. "Of course. I'll collect it from you promptly." All softness and humor had left him.

"Thank you. I should be going to bed. It's far past my bedtime." I swept past him and immediately regretted my coldness, but as I turned back to apologize, I stumbled right into Bianca Ingram. She jumped back from me like I was a demon, shrieking that I should watch where I was going. Then she turned to sweetness and light as Hugo came up behind me. He ignored me and beamed at her, piercing my heart in two.

"Hugo, darling, you must walk me to my quarters. A girl could get lost in this place," Bianca trilled. He obliged, offering her an arm so that they might stroll to their destination linked. We walked in near unison, me five steps ahead of the couple until they tapered off at what I assumed was Bianca's door. I was happy to lose them.

I slowed to a stop in front of Hugo's old door, dwelling briefly on that night just a few weeks ago. The fire, the panic, Hugo leaning sweaty against me, half naked. I lingered too long, snapped out of my reverie by a giggle and a voice that was gratingly familiar.

"Come on, Hugo! I want to see where you sleep."

I hurried to my door, making it just in time before Bianca and Hugo came around the bend. They passed me, because of course Hugo's old room was out of commission until they replaced the window and salvaged the room. But then they stopped just one door down, on the other side of me.

"Your room is next to the governess's?" Bianca said. I shared her surprise. I hadn't realized Hugo was still my neighbor. "How gauche."

Finally, I opened my door, stepped inside, and promptly shut it behind me so I wouldn't have to hear their courtship go on. A stampede of emotion bubbled up from inside me with nowhere to go, so I settled for penning a quick message to George before I went to bed.

Dear George,

If I've done the math right, today should be your eighteenth birthday. I can't believe I'm not there with you to celebrate. We had plans! I hope you're off somewhere doing something insanely fun, which is maybe why I haven't heard from you in a while.

I finally saw that nun musical you told me about, and you were right—I really loved it. So did Jessa. You should have told me the captain was so handsome. I would have watched it sooner. Stop making whatever grossed-out face you're making right now.

Things here are… different. I don't know why I thought things would stay the same way forever, but I guess I did. Now we have this group of people here from the private ship Ingram, *and they're pretentious, rich jerks that I have to tiptoe around. It's like the* Empire, *except this time I'm an employee, so I really can't mouth off. George, you would hate all of them. There is one funny thing—do you remember a girl from the* Empire *named Preity Khan? She works for the* Ingram *and says she remembers you. Said you were obnoxious, so I knew it was true. Kidding.*

I wish you were here. Things are changing quickly, and I have no one to talk to.

Love,
Stella

My pupil yawned through most of her lessons the following day, her mood as sour as mine.

"He didn't even bring me a present," Jessa complained, abandoning a difficult math set. "Hugo always brings me something, but he was too distracted by those stupid ladies."

"I'm sure he has something for you," I reassured her, despite my doubts. Hugo had returned to this ship with the singular purpose of marrying Bianca, so I didn't trust him to remember gifts. "We'll see what happens tonight in the drawing room." We both made faces. I'd received the order shortly after breakfast that we were to return for another evening of humiliation and boredom.

My comms pinged with an incoming hail from Officer Xiao. "Stella, I'm sorry to bother you during lessons, but please find a sensible stopping point and come see me on the bridge." Her tone lacked her usual underpinnings of warmth. I must have been in trouble for mouthing off to Hugo. I found a grim-faced Xiao waiting for me, but what set my heart pumping and anxiety creeping up my spine was another look I knew well: pity.

"Stella, I'll need you to go to your quarters and pack up your things."

My breakfast threatened to return up my throat, but I pushed it down, maintaining a stoic expression as best I could.

"You'll be moving down into the crew quarters with the *Ingram* staff temporarily." Xiao flashed me an uncomfortable smile. "For the duration of their stay, that is." Did she know the "duration of their stay" was likely to be forever? I couldn't read her.

"May I ask why?" I needed to know if I was being punished for my insolence with Hugo.

Xiao hesitated. "Two of the Ingram cousins were doubling up, and when it came to Miss Bianca Ingram's attention that you had a room right next to the captain's… she suggested she move into your room so that her cousins might be made more comfortable."

Bianca. Of course.

"I'll meet you at your quarters in twenty minutes to help you move," Xiao said, dismissing me. I didn't understand what she would possibly need to help me with until I took inventory of my belongings. When I'd come to the *Rochester,* I'd been able to fit all my worldly possessions into a single bag. Now as I extracted the contents of my storage unit and my clothing drawer and surveyed them on my bed, I realized I owned far more than I could carry.

Xiao was prompt, and without a word folded several dresses over one arm and took up two pairs of shoes with her free hands. I grabbed the remaining clothes, Hugo's *Jungle Book,* and my drawing tab. I cast a longing look at my desk tab, which was fixed and could not be moved.

"Don't worry. We'll have Rori add a profile lock to it so the next occupant can't root around in your files. I'll set it up so you can check for messages on the bridge in the meantime."

We moved down to the crew quarters on the lower deck without talking, Xiao respecting my need for the head space to process it all. For my part, I was concerned if I tried to talk, I might cry. I felt stupid, vain at the thought of it— crying over having to share a room again—but it was more the *why* than the *what* that affected me. Someone with everything had gone out of her way to take the one space that was mine. Bianca was putting me in my place, and a bitterness swelled up inside me that I was determined would not spill out as tears.

"Stella, what are you doing here?" Preity jumped down from her bunk to greet us. At least I wouldn't be sharing with strangers.

"Miss Ainsley will be sharing space with you until the conclusion of your visit," Xiao informed her, taking it upon herself to locate an unoccupied locker and transferring my clothes into it. After that, she didn't stay, bidding me farewell with a terse nod of her head, her feelings on the situation once again unspoken yet abundantly clear. She did not like this any more than I did.

Once she was gone, Preity pounced. "It was Bianca, wasn't it?"

"How did you know?"

"Lizzy said she was all in a huff over it this morning, how you had such a nice room, and next to the captain's, no less. It doesn't surprise me one bit she schemed to get you out of there. Anyway, I'm sorry you have to slum it down here with us."

"This is hardly slumming it," I said, determined to remain good-natured and not to put myself on wrong footing with my new roommate by acting like I was above this, or her. "They're the nicest bunk quarters I've ever seen."

"You and me both," Preity said. "You can go on the other top bunk." She pointed to the one opposite hers, which seemed to be operating as a second closet, clothes strewn all over it. "Just move that stuff. Lizzy's been using it as storage." Knowing it wouldn't earn me a friend later, I did so, transferring Lizzy's things to her bed below, tucking my drawing tab under the pillow.

I excused myself to get back to lessons with Jessa, though not before Preity invited me to hang out with the *Ingram* crew later that evening. It seemed now that I had been demoted in my quarters, I might be accepted by the group. A silver lining. I warned her I might not make it that evening on account of being ordered to the drawing room again, which drew me a look of pity and words of luck from her. I would need it.

Jessa was even more reluctant to wear a dress that evening, though eventually I cajoled her into a blue frock, to which she agreed only on the condition that she could wear pants underneath it. I chose my battles and managed to bring a presentable ten-year-old along with me to the drawing room earlier than the night before. The mood was more subdued, either because of the earlier hour or because several people were still hungover from the night before.

Hugo's happiness at seeing his sister seemed genuine this time, which indicated he was likely sober. And he almost fully redeemed himself by pulling a wrapped package from the recesses of his chair, presenting it to Jessa with a flourish.

"Consider this both a sorry-I-left present and a gift for your impending eleventh birthday," he said as Jessa ripped into the brown packing paper to reveal a slick new tab unit and stylus. Jessa cottoned onto it as soon as I did.

"Is this a drawing tab?" she asked breathlessly, looking back to me with a grin. "Just like Stella's!"

"Yes," Hugo replied. "I stopped by the *Nikkei* and got you one. And after you get the hang of things, send me your favorites, and I know a printer who will put them on canvas."

I allowed myself to observe the rest of the company besides Hugo. I found Bianca with a smile plastered upon her face, but it was obvious she thought the display something of a bore. Indeed, she wrested focus back onto herself by asking Hugo a question about some story for which I had zero context, and I took this as my cue to move with Jessa to the back of the room.

ALEXA DONNE

We powered on her new drawing tab, and I showed her the basics, from all the different drawing tools she could employ to how to pull up the tablet's built-in photo-reference aid. This model was much newer than mine, so I found more bells and whistles that I was eager to explore, but I resolved not to snatch it away like a toy from a child. Like a grownup.

Xiao came to collect Jessa not even an hour later, much to my surprise and consternation. "Oh, I can put her to bed," I assured her, but she waved me off.

"Captain's orders. He wants you here." Xiao took Jessa by the hand and left me to fume. Jessa's bedtime had been my out, but instead Hugo was tethering me to the drawing room for some reason. Ritualistic torture, I was sure.

The party moved around the table tab to play a game, while I sat in the shadows, plotting how I might escape. I needed a sound excuse, or else Hugo would just hail me on comms again, ordering me back. So preoccupied was I in my scheming that I lost sight of Hugo, allowing him to take me completely by surprise.

"I have a present for you, too," he said, sitting next to me, leaning close, his voice low and conspiratorial. I sat straight-backed and stiff, just inclining my head to acknowledge him. He handed over a rectangular wrapped package. I tried tucking it away to open later, but Hugo would have none of it. At his urging, I peeled back the paper to reveal a new drawing tab, identical to the one he'd given Jessa. It stole the breath from my lungs.

"This is too much," I said, forgetting myself and turning

188

full on to face him. He looked to me eagerly, biting his lower lip. "How much did this cost you?" I asked, turning the tab over in my hands, my heart swelling two sizes.

"Don't worry about it. I saw it and knew I had to get you one. Now you and Jessa can draw together."

It was like he'd taken a pin to me, deflating me back down to size. Matching gifts for me and his sister. I was like a sister to him. It was all clear now. I smiled, thanking him genuinely, if a bit sadly.

"You should draw our guests," he suggested, pointing to Captain Ingram, again in his ridiculous naval attire, then to Lucy and Bianca. "Put your time in here to good use."

"Why do you want me in here? I'm not contributing anything. No one speaks to me."

"Frex them. You're here for me. I missed our evenings together."

"I would be more comfortable elsewhere," I insisted. "With Jessa, or the other junior crew. I don't belong here."

"I happen to disagree." Hugo remained stubborn. "I want you here every evening, for at least two hours. There's an hour left tonight."

"Fine," I said, acquiescing, pretending it wasn't an order, "but only if you agree to actually talk to me for at least a half-hour every night. And speaking at or about me doesn't count." It was my small piece, my line in the sand.

"Agreed." His gaze flicked away, over to the table tab, where the Ingram family was playing a game, catching on Bianca, who beckoned him back over with a measure of haughty aggression. But Hugo waved her off and turned back to me. "Then I should start with an apology about your room demotion."

My heart sped up. "It's okay. Not a big deal," I said.

"No, it is a big deal," Hugo insisted. "I want you to know that I had no idea. I was still asleep when Bianca and her father strong-armed Officer Xiao." Translation: he'd been hungover. "If I'd been awake, I might have stopped it. I still could. Say the word, and I'll change it back."

Why did he have to put this on me? There was no scenario in which I could assert myself and come out the winner. "No, really, it's fine. I hadn't realized two of the cousins were doubling up, and that room is bigger than I could ever need. Please don't make a fuss over me."

Hugo locked gazes with me, his searching, skeptical, while I kept mine neutral, resolute. I would not have him upsetting the social balance in my name, painting an even worse target on my back.

"As you wish, then," Hugo finally said. "Listen, about Bianca…"

We both looked over to her as he trailed off. Engrossed in the game, she looked unusually harmless and especially beautiful. When she wasn't snapping her fingers at Hugo or sneering at me, she was lovely. I looked at him looking at her, wincing when he smiled to himself.

"We go way back," Hugo continued. "The Ingrams are my family's oldest friends, and the only ones who kept in touch after... well. I know they're a bit much, and far more hierarchical than the *Rochester* is. But Bianca's not half bad, when you get to know her."

"Oh, I'm sure," I offered weakly, unsure what Hugo wanted me to say. I wasn't about to become friends with her. I felt stupid that I'd entertained feelings for him, even though he'd been flirting with me, when he so clearly wanted someone like her.

Hugo sensed the topic's end. "We have twenty-five minutes left," he said. "What else do you wish to talk about?"

"Tell me about the *Nikkei*," I said, desperate to dwell on subjects that didn't make my cheeks burn and tears threaten to come. "I've heard it spoken about, but never in great detail. I had to leave the *Stalwart* before my supervisor returned from his trip, or I would have grilled him."

Hugo spent the next half-hour regaling me with stories of the ship reputed to be the most technologically advanced in the fleet. Meanwhile, I watched as Bianca became more and more incensed from afar. She toddled over in her impractical heels and whined at Hugo to join them in their next game, claiming she was losing hopelessly without him. He tried to beg off on my account, but I deferred to Bianca, insisting he go. She'd demonstrated the power she wielded when it came to Hugo. I wasn't going to intentionally cross her.

I used the opportunity to slip out and head for the bridge, where Xiao said I could check my messages in the evenings. I had one from George.

Hey, Stel—

I know I am the worst friend for not writing sooner. You were right—it was my birthday—and they moved me up to field duty a few days early. It's been a whirlwind. They made me a supervising officer, right out of the gate. Jon might have pulled a few strings. He's in his uncle's good graces now that he's apprenticing with him. If I play my cards right, I'll get a promotion to lieutenant in the next few years, maybe get involved with the decision making when it comes to the supply chain. Jon has all these ideas about staging a mini-coup, keeping more of the food we grow on board. Of course, Jon also thinks there's a conspiracy to move food production off the Stalwart altogether, but that's a whole other thing.

We watched another movie I think you would like. It had all sorts of weirdness and layers and stuff, about dreams within dreams or something—right up your alley. Not so much mine, but at least I had Joy to keep me company. I took your advice and asked her out, and before I knew it, we were an item. For some reason, Destiny has stopped speaking to us, but everyone else seems supportive. I know you were rooting for Joy, so thanks for your advice.

Until next time,
George

George and Joy. Of course. I seemed to have a talent for willing other people's relationships into existence. I typed up a quick response, conveying my congratulations on his relationship, and then headed for bed. I was halfway to my old quarters when I realized my error, redirecting myself downstairs to the crew wing with slightly heavier steps.

"You must be lost."

It was Hanada, just a few steps behind me. It was strange seeing her down here with full-on lighting. She almost looked normal. It seemed rude to run away from her, so I let her catch up and we continued on together.

"I moved down here. With the *Ingram* crew," I said, like it was perfectly normal. Like I'd had some choice in the matter.

"First he cancels our weekly poker game, and now he makes you move? That frexing—"

"Hugo didn't do this," I cut her off.

"Then I can guess who did. You know, he used to follow her around like a puppy, and now it's her family who's desperate for our affection."

"You know about the whole merger thing, then?"

Hanada stopped us just short of where the corridor widened and the crew quarters began. A wild shriek of laughter from the mess hall signaled the *Ingram* crew's party was in full swing.

"The Ingrams have been gunning for a merger since before Phillip died."

"Phillip?"

"Fairfax. Hugo's father. He couldn't stand the Ingrams, but they were old family friends of Cassandra's—Hugo's mother— and so he indulged it."

"And Hugo had a thing for Bianca?"

"He was thirteen. I think he had a thing for everyone."

I laughed, because I was sure I was supposed to. "Then some things don't change," I said. "He's smitten with her."

Hanada narrowed her eyes. "I wouldn't be too sure. In my experience, Fairfax men are never quite what they seem. They're stubborn."

"What does that mean?"

"We can engage in idle girl talk some other time," she said, entirely unhelpfully. "Just keep your wits about you. Good night, Stella." Hanada slunk off to her quarters, and I continued to the mess hall.

The junior crew and two lieutenants were deep into a game of poker, though their cards were cruder than those I'd seen the Ingram party and Hugo using. I drifted to the edge of the room, where Preity was sitting, cheering on Lizzy as she stared down Griegs. Hanada should have stayed. This was right up her alley.

"Did the crew-member princess decide to slum it down here with us?" Griegs sneered over his hand. Lizzy promptly smacked him on the shoulder.

"She's bunking down with us now, so be nice. Her Grand Highness Bianca saw to it." Everyone tossed me a bit of sympathy.

"Yeah, and it's not my choice to spend hours up there in that awful drawing room," I said, deciding to use the truth to my advantage. "It's dreadfully dull when I'm sitting in the corner being ignored, and the epitome of humiliating when they pay me any mind. I'd rather not go, but Captain Fairfax is requiring it."

"That's weird," Lizzy said, trading a look with the others.

Was it? I supposed I was used to Hugo demanding my company on a nightly basis. I both hated the humiliation of the drawing room and craved his company, like a masochist.

We stayed in the rec room until Lizzy took the kitty with a royal flush, causing a red-faced Griegs to stomp out of the room. Then I got my first taste of communal life in years, dancing around with the rest of the girls in the bathroom, hoping no one could see me blush when I bumped into a male lieutenant named Ritter. I strapped myself into my top bunk as Lizzy voice-commanded the lights off, realizing as I turned my face against the pillow, eyes meeting pitch-black, what I would miss most about my private quarters. This room had no window, and thus I was cut off from the stars.

sixteen

Over the next week, I tried to adjust to the rhythms of my new life. I rose at six thirty to beat Griegs to the showers, as I found he notoriously liked to sleep in until the last possible minute. My new roommates embraced me, becoming friendlier each day, while I felt more and more distant from my friends among the *Rochester* crew. They were all considered senior staff and thus ate with the senior *Ingram* crew. Only Jessa remained constant; I spent my days with her, and my nights in the drawing room for my allotted two hours. Hugo hadn't asked Jessa back since the night he'd given her the gift. She wasn't taking it well.

I made excuses, because I didn't want to tell her the truth. The new Hugo I'd met on the day of his morbid anniversary was a permanent fixture now. Frequently drunk, intermittently hot and cold, not at all thoughtful or sensitive to others. He'd turned into every stupid boy I'd ever known on the *Stalwart* but worse, for every once in a while, there was a glimmer of the old Hugo. He'd make an inside joke about a book we'd read, or ask me with genuine concern about my day. But then he'd pour himself another drink, and Bianca would pull him away. She became his new favorite person. Or an old favorite, as Hanada had pointed out.

I took Hugo's advice and used my time in the drawing room to get to know my new drawing tab. I rendered Captain Ingram in his gold-ribboned shoulders in ink and acrylic blue and gold, and Mrs. Ingram in her successive parade of ridiculous hairdos in pastel oil crayons. I did a watercolor of the trio of cousins whose names I couldn't remember bending their heads together in gossip. A simple, sad pencil sketch of the sullen Justine, who watched her husband flirt with the maids serving drinks.

And Bianca. I drew her most of all, in multiple mediums, over successive nights. I was determined to capture her beauty, as a reminder to myself why Hugo spent each evening accepting her shameless flirtations. Why he always flirted back.

"You capture her well," Hugo said one night in a low voice, startling me so much that my stylus slipped, creating a smudge across Bianca's right cheek. I quickly undid my last move. "You really captured the… spark in her eyes."

I thought the word he was grasping for was "meanness," but I merely smiled and accepted the compliment.

"Do you ever draw me?" he asked, a wicked glint to his

eyes. I did draw Hugo, but always in private, so no one could see the attention and time I spent on him. "I can tell the answer is yes, so you might as well show me."

I found my most recent attempt at him and handed the tab over for his assessment. He frowned. "I look so serious."

"Well, you're a serious person," I said.

"Not around you. You're the one person I feel I can relax around."

I willed myself not to say something that would get me fired.

"Even when you're relaxed, then," I hedged, "you have a baseline of seriousness. It's not a bad thing. I also consider myself a rather serious person."

"That you are," Hugo said. "And do you ever draw yourself? Do you have a self-portrait?"

"There are far more interesting things to draw. Real and imaginary."

"Oh, I don't agree. Would you draw one for me?"

I hesitated.

"Please? If you do, I won't make you come to the drawing room." I perked up at that, but too soon. "For an evening or two," Hugo finished, his smile sly.

"Fine, but only because it's somewhat of a thing artists do. All of the greats created self-portraits, and I am by no means great, but I shall try."

"Good," he said. "But there will be no more drawing tonight."

"What do you mean?"

He clapped his hands together, standing, then announced

to the whole room. "Everyone, stop what you're doing. I propose we play a game."

"Ooh, yes!" Bianca trilled, grabbing Hugo by the arm and pointedly tugging him away from me. "What do you have in mind?"

"Hide-and-go-seek," he answered.

"But that's a children's game." Bianca pouted.

"Only if children are playing it. And you're not a child anymore, are you?" Hugo teased, prompting Bianca to giggle, smacking him playfully in the shoulder. My dinner threatened to rise into my throat.

"Now, everyone must play," Hugo continued. "And the only rule is you must hide in a publicly accessible space. No going into any private rooms. You have the whole ship, both levels, at your disposal. And we're going to make it fun." He strode over to a side table, grabbing a bottle of liquor and pouring a little bit into a dozen small glasses. "One for everyone. You must drink before you run off." A line quickly formed, while I edged toward the door, waiting for the best moment to sneak out.

"Stella, where are you going?" Hugo boomed. "You must play."

Everyone turned to stare, and I stammered out an excuse about being tired, but Hugo was relentless.

"She can be the seeker," Bianca suggested, but Hugo shook his head.

"No, she knows the ship too well. The game won't be any fun. I want you to be the first seeker, Bianca."

"But I wanted to hide with you," she huffed, swallowing down her shot and then snatching up another.

Hugo shook his head. "Hiding with another person is against the rules. If your spot is taken, you must find another one. And anyway... I want you to find me, B." He winked at her and she blushed. I marched over to the sideboard and drank two shots for good measure. When I came up for air, I found Hugo appraising me, seemingly impressed. I just wanted to get this over with.

"One last thing," Hugo said, stopping everyone before they spilled out into the hall. "Rori? Turn off all the lights in public areas. No emergency lights, please."

Several people gasped.

"Now, this is going to be fun!" Hugo said before running off into the black.

All the hiding spots I could think of were taken. I'd tried the bridge, the kitchens, various shadowy alcoves. Basically, everything at front and midship. I was running out of time.

"Rori, how much more time until Bianca starts searching?" I whispered.

"Sixty seconds," she chimed in my ear.

I sighed. Maybe I should just give up and let Bianca find me easily? But no, then she'd tease me endlessly for failing at a child's game. I headed aft, squinting in the darkness as I approached the landing bay. It was technically public, but only accessible via two bio-locked door codes, which defeated the purpose. I could hide there, but Bianca wouldn't be able to get in. The supply room, however...

I crept inside, careful not to trip over Lieutenant Poole's toolkit, or the bench in front of the lockers. I aimed for a pitch-black corner, where the row of lockers ended and a heavy metal cabinet created a shadowy nook at the best of times, when the lights were on. Sixty seconds had to be up by now. I slipped into the darkness, my back to the wall, peering out, around the corner to the door. Worried she'd be able to see me from this angle, I took a step back.

And hit something solid and warm. Not a wall. A person.

I shrieked, but the sound was muffled by the hand that clapped itself over my mouth. Hugo's voice in my ear stopped a full-scale panic.

"Sorry to startle you," he said.

I pulled away, body tingling from the shock. Or maybe from his touch.

"I'm sorry. I'll go find somewhere else." I started to back away, but he grabbed my hand and pulled me back into the shadows.

"No, stay. It's too late to find somewhere else."

"But the rules..."

"Frex the rules. They're my rules, anyway. Stay."

Hugo pulled me in so close my breath warmed the skin of his neck, and he secured his arm around the small of my back, hand resting on my hip. This was as physically close as we'd been since the night of the fire, only this time he was fully clothed. My thoughts flew in a million directions, most of them shouting about why and how and that he smelled like liquor and sweat, but why didn't I mind? I tilted my head up to search his eyes, features rendered in shades of gray by the dark, like one of my charcoal drawings. I couldn't read him or his intent. Was it necessary to be so close?

I exhaled a shaky breath, the sound of it jarringly loud, so much so that Hugo pressed a finger to my lips, shushing me. I kept further attempts to breathe quiet, but he didn't move his finger, the graze of his skin against my lips maddening, only serving to draw my breaths quicker. At this rate, I'd overheat. Or faint. But no, there'd be no falling with Hugo as an anchor. His hand on my hip burned a hole through my clothes.

A high-pitched squeal from the corridor broke the spell. Bianca must have found someone nearby. I startled out of Hugo's grasp, backing against the wall, both savoring and dreading the space. He didn't reach for me again. Minutes passed, and my heart slowed, my mind catching up with me. What was I thinking, hiding in the dark with my boss? When Bianca found us, she'd tell everyone, and all would assume we were doing something untoward. My cheeks burned with new purpose, a preview of the mortification to come. I couldn't let that happen.

"I have to go," I said, stealing away before Hugo could stop me. I flew back to the drawing room, slipping quietly inside and finding it empty, as I'd hoped. The windows offered a meager light and stars by which to distract and calm myself. The party returned some twenty minutes later, everyone laughing and chattering, accusing others of cheating. Not that it mattered, as there was nothing to win. Another round was suggested, but Hugo firmly said no. I returned to my seat by the door, only to find myself the object of his maddening attention. He stared at me, gaze accusing.

So again I fled, out into the hallway, still shrouded in darkness. Except there seemed to be a light flashing off to the right. It illuminated the corridor at regular intervals, every five seconds. I followed the flashes to the bridge, where I found a multitude of screens all blinking the same message: SHIP INCOMING.

I hailed Officer Xiao, her voice thick with sleep, but she came alert as soon as I told her what was happening.

"I'll be on the bridge in three minutes. Get the captain up there immediately."

I touched a finger to my ear, clearing my throat to keep it from shaking. "Comms on. Paging Captain Fairfax."

"Not authorized," Rori intoned. I'd forgotten. Only Xiao and Poole could directly hail the captain. There was no time to get Xiao back on the line.

"Rori, please make an exception. At least tell the captain I'm calling; see if he'll answer."

I waited, silence in my ear until he answered a moment later, voice playful.

"Stella, are you coming back? You know I don't like it when you leave."

"Sir, I need you to report immediately to the bridge. We've got a ship incoming."

For a moment, he didn't speak. I was afraid he hadn't

heard me, so I began to repeat myself, but he cut me off. "Roger wilco," he said, suddenly serious. "I will be there in a minute." He arrived a minute before Xiao, scanning the screens, ignoring me. Then he touched two fingers to his comms piece.

"Incoming ship, please identify and state your purpose." He waited for a response, mouth tight, staring intently at the windows. When his jaw started clicking, I assumed he was hearing a response, one he didn't like. "I will allow you on board my ship to refuel and rest, but I want you gone in twelve hours." Though I saw Hugo sway on his feet, close his eyes, and breathe heavily through his nose to steady himself, his voice remained strong and clear. I'd never seen him so in command. It was a good look on him. "Well, that is your opinion," he continued his conversation as Xiao arrived. He signaled her, then ended his call. "I will meet you in the transport bay in twenty minutes with my First Officer. Do not move from there until we come to collect you."

Then Hugo turned to me, all business, the last hour erased as if it had never been. I wondered if I'd dreamed it.

"Stella, please go to the drawing room and inform everyone that I won't be returning this evening. Encourage them to turn in early, and let them know I will see them tomorrow. Then go to bed."

I opened my mouth to protest, to question him, but a look from Xiao silenced me. I nodded and wordlessly slipped from the bridge, making my way to the drawing room to fulfill my duty. It wasn't easy. I stood in the doorway, clearing my throat and calling for attention two, three times before anyone but the *Ingram* wait staff paid me any mind, and even then, they remained skeptical.

"Are you sure Hugo's not coming back tonight?" Bianca asked, like she was certain I was trying to trick her. "And even so, why should we go to bed just because Captain Fairfax is abandoning us?"

"Because he requested it," I said. "I'm going below decks and will tell your crew to come fetch you. Have a good evening." I didn't give them time to protest.

While my bunkmates went to fetch their ladies, I got ready for bed, playing the events of the evening over in my mind as I brushed my teeth, unzipped my dress. The whole thing felt far away, already unreal to me, the memory fuzzy at the edges, fleeting like smoke. I hardly trusted my recollection of it. I pushed the fabric off my hips, thinking of Hugo's hand in the same place an hour before. I touched tentative fingers to my lips. Had I imagined that part of it? His hand on my hip, of that I was sure, but this... I kissed the tips of my fingers as I'd dared not kiss his. It had to be a mistake. Hugo had no reason to be so intimate with me. He must have been too drunk to know himself.

Yes, that must be it, I decided, settling into bed with my reader tab. I'd fallen horridly behind in my books over the last few weeks. I fell asleep before the *Ingram* staff could return, lights blazing still, with lines from Dickens echoing in my head. They reverberated, poetry-like prose spiraling into vivid images in my mind, until they screamed.

But no. I realized it wasn't literature in my dreams, but real screams I heard. I jolted awake, strap holding me down, surely bruising my ribs as I tried to sit up too suddenly. It was silent now, but I knew it had been real. My eyes darted around the room, and despite the dark, I could make out the outline of the other bunk, my roommates dozing. I undid the strap, climbing down and out of bed, making my way in bare feet to the door. The hallway was quiet, dim. The scream had sounded close, and instinct carried me to the medical bay. The light from the hatch window in the door lit the way, and I tiptoed down the hall until I was flush up against the medical-bay door. I obscured myself in shadows, able to just peek through the glass and into the room.

Inside I found Hanada standing grim-faced over a man who looked vaguely familiar. He was clutching his right hand over his left arm, which bore a bloody bandage. His middle was wrapped up too, like he'd been sideswiped by something. My eyes swept the rest of the room, as much as I could see of it, catching only empty gurneys and glass cabinets lit sickly yellow and full of medical supplies. Then suddenly a lumbering, dark figure appeared in the hatch window, and next thing I knew, the door was sliding open and I found myself pulled inside.

seventeen

I yelped, wholly undignified, and stumbled over the threshold. But a pair of strong arms caught me against a warm chest. I angled my head up to find familiar eyes glaring down. Hugo.

"Miss Ainsley, you should not be out at this time of night," he said, confusing me with my proper name. He gently but firmly pushed me away.

"I'm sorry, but I thought I heard a scream."

The patient opened his mouth to speak, but Hugo cut him off. "Don't you dare speak to her." He turned back to me, his voice lower, softer, but it was still obvious to me that he was wound tight like a spring. "Stella, you should go back to bed."

Hanada cleared her throat. "Actually, it might be a good thing that she's here. She can watch him while we…"

The patient snorted, then groaned as if in pain. Both Hugo

and Hanada told him to shut up, in unison, before he could make a retort.

Hugo nodded, first to Hanada, then to me. "Stella, I need you to stay here while Mari and I go take care of something. Don't talk to him, or let him talk to you, and make sure he doesn't go anywhere, or do anything."

It was both specific and vague at the same time, but I nodded my agreement. Mari grabbed a medical bag, and Hugo flashed me a sympathetic smile and our bloody guest a hard-eyed stare, before they both swept out the door. I followed Hugo's directive, sitting in a swivel chair so I could watch my charge, but I did not talk. He wasn't so obliging.

"A girl so young as you should not be wrapped up in such sinister dealings. How old are you? Fourteen?"

Once he spoke, it clicked: where I knew him from.

"You're from the *Olympus*. You were at the memorial. Meyer?" I said, breaking the embargo on talking myself.

"Mason," he corrected me. "You've come a long way from the *Stalwart* to this place." His beady little eyes narrowed in on me, practically looked through me, and a shiver ran down my spine.

I crossed my arms over my chest and refused to say anything else, though Mason prattled on.

"Do you know the history of this ship?" He coughed, groaned again, but didn't stop his questions. "And of the people on it? Surely you must be curious?"

I swiveled away, concentrating on the wall, running through upcoming lesson plans to keep myself distracted. I didn't know how much time had passed—twenty minutes?

Thirty?—but my eyes began to droop, my head to loll against my shoulder, when Mason spoke again.

"I know you're an inquisitive sort of person, Miss Ainsley. You asked your friend Jonathan Karlson to look into the *Rochester* crew, but he didn't find much."

"How could you know that?" I took the bait, whipping around to face him. He grinned like a cat.

"I had you flagged soon after arriving on the *Rochester*. I've been reading your messages ever since."

"How could you do that?"

Mason sighed. "No one reads the terms of service. It's well within the government's rights to read messages. For the protection of the fleet."

Arguing with him would be fruitless. I turned back around, ignoring him again.

"I have to thank you for giving me a reason to come and investigate. I couldn't have, without due cause, and you were most helpful."

I heard the click-clack of boots approaching at the same time as Mason did. I jumped up.

Mason's lips tugged into an infuriatingly smug expression. "You should tell your friends to stop worrying so much about vegetables. *Que sera, sera.*"

The door banged open, Hugo looming large over us, eyes flashing accusation at Mason.

"Just talking about the weather," Mason said.

"It's time for you to leave, Mr. Mason," Hugo said, ignoring his cheekiness.

"You said I could stay on board twelve hours. I need to sleep."

"I'm sure your ship is equipped with autopilot. You'll have three days to sleep."

They engaged in their politely passive-aggressive battle until Mason finally gave in, using his good arm to leverage himself off the gurney. Hugo was an immovable object, met by Mason's much weaker force.

Mason hobbled to the door with exaggerated slowness, until Hugo called him on his theatrics. "Quit that." Hugo grabbed Mason's good arm and pulled him into the hall. "Stella, please come with us."

It was a short journey to the transport bay, though our elevator ride felt like it lasted hours. Mason alternately sniffled and smirked, more than once looking like he wanted to say something, only to be shut down by Hugo's glare.

I couldn't stop thinking about the vegetables. Jon asking me about them, and Mason specifically mentioning it. What had he meant by "*Que sera, sera*"?

Hugo went so far as to physically escort Mason onto his shuttle. I stayed outside while he went in, making sure the autopilot was programed to take him away. Mason loomed in the doorway as Hugo made his way down the shuttle steps, returning to my side.

"This isn't over, Mr. Fairfax. Sleep tight."

I shivered while Hugo seethed all the way to the outer bay, where we watched Mason depart. Questions bubbled onto my tongue, but I didn't let them escape. The moment was wrong, with Hugo wound tight and likely to snap. Such a different mood from a few hours ago. We were less than fifty feet from the storage room, where a stolen moment in the dark had made my insides writhe. Now all that coursed through me was apprehension.

"I'll see you to your quarters."

"That's not necessary—"

"I insist."

We didn't speak in the elevator, or in the icy blue lower-deck hallway. I walked slowly, forcing Hugo to keep my pace, working my way up to the right moment. It didn't come. I asked anyway.

"Who attacked Mr. Mason?"

"Nobody attacked him."

"Then what happened?"

"He fell. Down the stairs."

"Which stairs?"

"To the upper deck."

I didn't believe a word of it. His answers were too quick. I felt sick at the fact he was lying to me. Keeping secrets. The hallway widened, bringing us to a stop at the crew corridor.

"And why did he come in the first place?"

Hugo sighed. "A surprise inspection."

That, I could tell, was the truth. I opened my mouth, ready to ask a follow-up or three, but Hugo stopped me.

"I'm exhausted, and I'm sure you are too. It's nearly three. Good night."

"Night," I said a moment later, into the dark space where Hugo used to be.

I awoke confused.

Thankfully it was the weekend, so I had no class with Jessa, leaving me to do some sleuthing. I waited until long after breakfast, until Lizzy and Preity headed for the drawing room to tend to their ladies, finally up and past their hangovers, so that their fun could start all over again. The sweet spot was the hours before dinner, while everyone was busy drinking and gossiping. No one would see me exploring the upper deck.

I'd passed it dozens upon dozens of times. The elevator and the staircase were just to the right of the bridge, but I'd never ventured there. I was a rule follower, and no one had given me permission to go above decks. I'd heard it called cold storage, though that's what they called the library, too, so who knew what secrets were up there? And if Mason fell down the stairs, the place where he'd fallen had to have been here. I'd checked the only other stairs on board—aft, leading down to Deck Three; and forward, leading into Jessa's quarters. Neither held evidence of a fall or injury.

The foot of the stairs to the upper deck was clear too. Still, I ventured up, willing some bloodstain to appear. I wanted what Hugo had said to be true. I climbed up the winding stairs until I came to the top of what should have been the landing. In front of me was a haphazardly erected barrier, old ship parts piled on top of one another and fused into a makeshift barrier. It was bizarre. Why would someone block up the stairs like this?

A high-pitched giggle floated up to my ears. *Bianca.* I crept back down to the bend in the stairs, keeping just out of sight.

"While I'm perfectly happy to have you as my neighbor, I don't get why you don't sleep in the captain's quarters," Bianca said.

"I prefer my old room is all."

She was talking to Hugo. Of course.

"You were always too modest." A pause. "Come on. Take me up there, for old times' sake."

"There's nothing to see up there. I don't see the point."

"The point is that I'm asking."

Silence. Then Hugo spoke. "Rori, unlock the elevator." The doors dinged open a moment later.

I rushed back up the stairs to the barrier, pressing my ear against a metal fixture that likely used to be the hatch of a shuttle. A moment later, I heard the muffled rush of the elevator opening, Bianca and Hugo stepping out. I pictured a corridor, gunmetal gray with a pop of pastel from Bianca's dress and heels.

"I want to go in—"

"No."

I imagined Hugo's face as stony as his tone, Bianca pouting. "Why not?"

"I always keep it locked. No one goes inside."

"Hugo, you have to get over this. You'll have to go in there eventually. When…"

She drifted off. I pressed harder into the barrier, ear stinging cold from the metal. Did she touch him? Kiss him? I couldn't hear anything. Then, a scoff.

"What? When you marry me? Cool your heels, B; it's not your ship yet. Rori, elevator open."

Thankfully the ding covered the happy laugh that slipped from my lips. Hugo putting Bianca in her place was the best entertainment I'd had in weeks. I supplemented the lack of visuals with a scene in my mind of Bianca's face colored bright red, shooting daggers with her eyes.

I waited for the elevator to deliver them downstairs, and for them to wander in the direction of the dining room, where drinks started pouring at seventeen hundred hours. I crept down the stairs, rounding on the elevator and trying my luck.

"Rori, can you open the elevator doors?"

"You are not authorized to access this elevator," she said, monotone as ever, yet I swore I detected an undercurrent of judgment. "I'm sorry, Stella." I was imagining sympathy now too.

"No problem," I said.

"You have a message. It just arrived."

I thanked Rori and hurried to the bridge. Maybe it was from Jon. I had to warn him—and George—that Mason was reading our messages. But how could I do that without Mason seeing the warning, too? It would put them both in a dangerous position.

I pulled up the message, but it wasn't from Jon, or George. It was from a ghost from my past.

Dear Stella,
    I hope this message finds you well. I was surprised

to find, when I inquired with the Stalwart to pass on my message to you in person, that you'd transferred to another ship. I'm afraid you'll have to read my sad news.

My mother is very ill, and the doctors believe she will be gone within a fortnight. She has been asking for you more and more as she slips further into delirium. I cannot take her shouting, so I thought it best to summon you to the Empire to see her, as is her wish.

If you choose to come, please hurry.

Your cousin,

Charlotte

eighteen

I went from creeping on the stairs to stalking outside Hugo's study. Pressing my ear to yet another door, I heard a clink of ice against glass. He was inside, but was he alone?

"I need to leave," I whispered, practicing the phrase. I dreaded saying it, though I knew I had to. Leaving would be practice, too.

I knocked lightly, until a muffled grunt granted me entry. The door slid open, and I propelled myself forward with a great big breath, for courage.

"Hello, Stella," Hugo said, low and cautious. He probably thought I'd come to ask more questions about Mason's visit. Luckily for him, my new circumstances had put my curiosity on hold.

My feet carried me to my old chair without a second thought. He had been standing, but Hugo followed my lead, sitting in the chair opposite. I took another deep breath, stretching my lungs until they almost hurt. "I need to leave." I pushed it out before I could second-guess myself.

He stared, dumbfounded. "Where are you going?"

"To the *Empire*," I said. "My aunt is dying, and she asked for me."

"You have to go?"

"I would regret it if I didn't."

A loaded pause, and then: "Fine. Then when do you leave?" He refused to look at me, instead focusing on the rug on the floor, exquisite and impractical as it was. I willed him to look at me, to say what he was feeling. Sometimes I could swear he knew what I was thinking, but just as quickly, he could turn so cold. Distant. Hugo was a planet far from reach, a brightly burning star too distant to fathom.

"Tomorrow night. Xiao already called the shuttle," I said, tamping down my own feelings in favor of facts.

Hugo kept his resolute stare leveled at the floor and began to tap his fingers aggressively against the arm of his chair. "And when will you return?"

"I don't know," I answered honestly.

Finally, he looked at me straight on, eyes locking to mine. "But you will come back?"

"Yes." My reply came fast and fierce, my heart declaring itself before my head could catch up. "Unless you don't need me here anymore." I thought of Hugo and his impending marriage to Bianca.

"Of course we'll need you here," Hugo said, but it

did nothing to reassure me. He might believe that, but I remembered my promise to myself. I would leave when Bianca and Hugo were married. And shortly, I would leave to go make amends with a woman who hated me.

"I need an advance on my salary. I'll be fine to get to the *Empire*, but I need a bit more than I've earned for the return."

"You can charge anything you need back to the *Rochester*." Hugo waved me off.

"I appreciate the gesture, but I'd rather take care of this myself."

Hugo kept tapping those fingers, though this time it was clearly in calculated thought. Finally he ceased his maddening motion, jumping up to retrieve his personal tab. He spent a moment jabbing and swiping at it, then turned it so I could see. "You've been here nearly three months, which means I owe you six hundred, but you'll need more to hail a shuttle both ways. I've given you a thousand. Just in case."

"That's far too generous, I couldn't possibly take it—" I tried to protest, but he cut me off.

"You asked for an advance. Consider it a promise to come back."

"You needn't bribe me for that."

"It's not a bribe," Hugo insisted, though we both knew that it kind of was. A guarantee of my return.

And maybe I was lying, just a little bit. Everything I'd seen and heard aboard the *Rochester* was starting to wear on me. It would be easier to run away. But I wouldn't. I couldn't leave the people behind. I couldn't leave *him*. Not yet.

He was looking at me now, pulling me into his orbit with those eyes that spoke volumes without saying a word. But they were mystery volumes; I could never tell if Hugo wanted to kiss me or throw me out into space.

"If you're leaving tomorrow, that means I can have you tonight," he said, lips curling into a wicked smile. I choked on nothing more than my own saliva at the shock of it, but then Hugo went on. "A little birdie tells me you've learned to play poker below decks. I insist we play."

"My abilities have been overstated. You don't want me at your table. And I have nothing to wager."

"Don't worry about that. Go grab your dinner, and I expect you at the poker table promptly at eight."

And that was how I ended up spending my last evening on the *Rochester* for who knew how long engaged in a most insidious game of poker.

I was a fish among the sharks. They grinned; their teeth glinted in the light, eyes narrowed to knowing slits. I'd watched Bianca, Braxton, and Captain Ingram play from afar many times before, but sitting under the halo of light that illuminated the table, shadows cast in sharp relief across faces that clearly wished my defeat, it was a wholly other experience. I was flanked on either side by Braxton and Captain Ingram, leaving Hugo and Bianca facing me like an elegant couple with a guest at their table.

But I played the part of a shark as well. Poker was all about keeping one's cool, not letting on how good or bad your hand was, maintaining composure. I was an old hand at that. What I hadn't quite mastered was the art of manipulation, of acting to fool my opponents, which both Bianca and Hugo were skilled at. For one thing, I was certain that Hugo was only pretending to be drunk for once. There was a keenness behind his eyes that I recognized. Hugo was sharp. Hugo was paying attention.

Bianca was playing the part of the coquette and simpleton, giggling at every half-clever thing the men at the table said, calling her sister, Lucy, over to ask for her help in analyzing her cards. I didn't understand her strategy except perhaps to look vulnerable and cute for Hugo, given everyone at the table knew how skilled she was at the game. She didn't need Lucy's help any more than I did.

Captain Ingram was, in fact, not very good at poker at all. He could not control his facial expressions when dealt a hand, and he chewed on his lip when he bluffed, making him rather easy to beat, which I did in the first round. Bianca took the second, not at all graciously. She sent me a gloating smirk across the table as Hugo insisted we play again and that I must participate, try to win back my title. I withered a bit in my chair. Then I slapped away Braxton's hand from its attempt to negotiate my thigh.

I approached the next game like a call to battle. I sat up straight, rolled my shoulders and neck, cracked my knuckles. When I looked at my cards, my face remained impassive. They were decent, but not great. Still, I placed my bet—it was Hugo's money and favors, after all. Another element of the game that made me dangerous to my opponents. I had nothing to lose.

And then Hugo went and ruined everything. "What do you say we up the stakes so this game is a bit more personal?"

Bianca lit up. "What did you have in mind? Strip poker?"

"With your father and brother playing with us?" Hugo laughed. "Not exactly. I was thinking more along the lines of putting personal favors on the line." He examined his cards with a sly smile, then looked at each of us in turn. "For instance, I wager a joyride in my private transport."

Joyride in private transport appeared on the tab table screen under the column of Hugo's wagers, setting it in stone. You had to be very careful with what you said at a poker table—everything was registered, and there was no backing out of bets once uttered.

"Or you could wager just your private transport," Captain Ingram said, but Hugo shook his head vehemently.

"Small stuff only. Things those of us at this table can do for the others." Hugo discarded two of his cards, picking up two from the deck.

"Well, then, I fold," Captain Ingram said in a huff, throwing down his cards. "There's no trifle anyone at this table could wager that I'd have interest in."

Or he had a crappy hand, more like. Down to just the four of us with Hugo's new wager literally on the table, I found it a challenge to maintain my outwardly confident demeanor. I had no clue what so-called personal stake I could wager, but Bianca was quick to come up with something.

"I wager a song. If I lose, the winner can ask me to sing anything, and I'll do it." She swapped out three cards—bad hand?

I noticed Braxton roll his eyes when he thought his sister wasn't looking. Then it was his turn to wager or fold. He shrugged. "I'll wager a back massage." He took just one card, but I could tell from his microscopic flinch it wasn't a good one.

If ever there was a disincentive to win a game, a massage from Braxton was it. But I kept my face passive as I tossed my own wager into the ring—a portrait of the winner. I drew two cards, forcing myself not to react—I wanted to smile, since I was on my way to a straight flush if luck kept going my way.

"Now, for this round, a bit of a twist," Hugo said. "I will choose what each of you must lay on the line to raise."

"That's not fair, Hugo!" Bianca smacked him lightly on the arm. "We're hardly playing poker anymore at that point."

"My ship; my rules." He took a swig from the cup I was sure didn't contain a drop of liquor. "I'll start with you, Bianca, since we're throwing out the conventions of poker, as is. My wager for you is your quarters aboard this ship. If you lose, the winner gets your room."

I couldn't help it; my eyes went wide at that, and Bianca made no effort to maintain her cutesy persona. Fire nearly blew out of her ears.

"That is absurd!"

"Not if you have a good hand. Wager it if you're sure you'll win."

Bianca's fine cheeks burned red with frustration, but she

pressed her mouth into a firm line and swapped out another two cards. She was in. I noticed the tab didn't register the bet, and so did Hugo. So he made Bianca repeat it out loud. It was a beautiful thing to hear her say, "I will give up my room."

"Braxton!" Hugo lowered his voice so just the four of us could hear. "You shall wager a public confession about how you've spent all night trying to run your hand up Stella's skirt."

I nearly fell out of my chair. Braxton narrowed his eyes to slits, staring down Hugo, then pushed back from the table noisily, throwing his cards down. "Frex you, Hugo Fairfax, and your frexing games."

Hugo was unmoved. "Stella, you shall wager both your tabs. Reading and drawing." He knew how much they meant to me—they were my sole and primary hobbies, and if Bianca won, I'd never see them again. But from the way Hugo was looking at me intently, the gentleness when he suggested it, I knew he thought I could win. He'd surely given me incentive— save my beloved possessions, get my room back from Bianca.

I accepted his proposal, repeating the wager and drawing just one card. I hid my disappointment that my luck had not held. Maybe I could still go for a flush.

"And finally," he said with a flourish, "for me: I wager my bachelorhood and, in turn, my ship. Whoever wins will get to decide whether or not I will marry Bianca."

Frexing hell.

Bianca made a choking sound, which blossomed into something of a growl. "Hugo, what are you playing at?" Each word was tight, almost violent.

"I'm just putting something on the table that's very valuable to me," he said. I didn't miss the way he looked to me as he said it. He was challenging me to fight for my place aboard this ship. Electricity traveled down my spine.

"Me or the ship?" Bianca asked through clenched teeth.

"Both," Hugo replied, glib.

Bianca was not yet satisfied. "And what if you win?"

"Then nothing will have changed. I'll honor my commitment."

"And if she wins?" She spat her pronoun like a curse, jerking her chin in my direction. I froze under their collective stares. Did I really have to answer that? Hugo saved me the burden.

"I would hope that Stella would follow her heart."

If looks could kill, Bianca's would have stopped said heart dead in my chest. Then her eyes flitted back down to her cards, and her hard look morphed into one of vicious delight. "Then I call. We go one more round to draw, should we need to; then we show our cards," she said, clearly convinced her hand was a winner, or at least that the odds were in her favor. Two out of three that she'd get her way. She pointedly did not take any new cards.

I examined my cards again, sure to keep my features impassive. I had a flush, which would be enough to win if Bianca and Hugo had mediocre hands. Should I swap out the card keeping me from a straight flush, taking the chance? Or stick with my cards, assuming Bianca was bluffing with her cat's grin? The tiniest ball of panic sprang up in my belly, ballooning into a pressure that pulsated with my heartbeat. Looking at Hugo made it worse. I could live without my tabs if I needed to, and getting my room back would be poetic justice, but it wasn't a real need.

But the chance to stop Hugo from marrying Bianca, to keep the *Rochester* from the Ingram family's greedy grasp... I wanted it desperately. Even if I was a fool to nurse feelings for Hugo, I wanted to save him from her. Everything depended on the cards in my hands.

I blinked slowly, breathing steadily like there wasn't a full-scale panic happening inside. "I'm good," I said, forgoing the deck. I just had to hope my flush would be good enough to make a stand.

Hugo looked at Bianca and me in turn, then put his cards on the table. "I fold," he said, to Bianca's frustrated groan. Her odds just went down. But mine went up. And it was time to show our cards. Bianca stared me down, willing me to go first. I refused. Fine ladies of the fleet before governesses and all that.

Bianca read my impassive expression and lack of action as the challenge it was, and finally turned over her cards, laying them out on the table with a flourish. The wicked glint in her eyes told me she was confident her straight was a winner. I let my face fall, increasing her triumph for just a second. Then I laid my cards out for all to see.

"Flush," I said. "I win."

Bianca was struck speechless, choking on disbelief and rage. I refused her the satisfaction of gloating, though

I couldn't help a small smile as the tab table registered the win, transferring all the bets that had been laid down into a column with my name on it.

"Good game," Hugo said, turning to his apoplectic would-be fiancée and attempting to offer some comfort. "I'm sure your cousins won't mind doubling up again." Bianca glared at him hard, and I stifled a laugh. He had to know that wasn't the part of the wager she was upset over losing. The full realization washed over me. I held both their futures in my hands. No, not just theirs, everyone's on this ship. Captain Ingram and his wife, Braxton, Justine, the nameless cousins, Lizzy, Preity, even Griegs. Their ship was dying, and we were their only hope.

Guilt replaced any sense of triumph. There was far more on the line with this marriage than Hugo's—or my—happiness.

The rest of the Ingram party finally noticed that a showdown of epic proportions had gone down, swarming the table and Bianca, gasping at the contents of the winning tally, bombarding both Hugo and Bianca with questions. I slipped away quietly before they could turn their attention to me. But I wasn't fast or far enough when Bianca caught up to me in a dim corridor halfway to my quarters.

"I know you're probably pretty happy right now, thinking that you've won. That now you can get your way and have Hugo all to yourself." Bianca kept her voice low, almost pleasant. "But you're deluding yourself that by removing me from the picture, you'll make him love you. You're just some governess from a crappy ship, without anything to recommend her but for barely passable drawing skills." She took a step closer, backing me up against a bulkhead. Briefly I wondered if she was about to hit me, but her fists remained at her side. Instead, she chose to bruise and bloody me with more words.

"Go ahead and try to stop this marriage. Hugo and I have history. I knew him before his parents died, and I know him now. Can you say the same?"

I couldn't. And I didn't know if I could compete with Bianca, but I surely knew I wanted to get out of this conversation, so I did my best to disarm her.

"Bianca, I don't know what impression you have of me, but I have no designs on Hugo, and I wish you no ill will. Besides which, I'm leaving tomorrow, so you won't have to worry about me."

"Are you coming back?"

"Yes," I answered, remembering my promise to Hugo.

"Then you're still my problem."

There was no arguing with her, so I used my shorter stature to my advantage, simply ducking under her arm, calling "Good night, Bianca" behind me as I ran away.

nineteen

On my last day aboard the *Rochester* for the foreseeable future, I avoided Hugo like it was my job, worried he would force me to "collect" on my winnings from last night, specifically the decision regarding his marriage. I'd slept unsoundly, tossing against my safety strap, too caught up in questions of what kind of person I wanted to be. My brain buzzed with doubt, worst-case scenarios, and future forecasting, which filtered into my dreams once I finally succumbed to exhaustion. I barely remembered my dreams once I woke, but the feelings remained. Guilt and dread, dread and guilt. I could make the choice selfishly, tell Hugo not to marry Bianca, so nothing would change for the *Rochester*. Go back to evening reading sessions with my captain, my biggest concern being who had attacked Mr. Mason. In fact, it might even be someone from the Ingram party. Another reason in favor of the selfish choice.

Or I could save the *Ingram*, affecting the lives of dozens, sacrificing my own comfort. Ignoring the fact that I didn't think Hugo wanted to marry Bianca at all, that he was relying on me to save him. Save him or save everybody. Mine was a heavy burden.

Talking to the girls the next morning didn't help. They confirmed there were no backup options for the *Ingram*— Bianca had turned them all away, and, given the state of their water-recycling and air systems, they estimated the *Ingram* had maybe two or three months left of sustainable life. It was worth far more as spare parts for the *Rochester*. Marrying Hugo and joining with the *Rochester* was truly their last resort.

I went about my normal day's routine, then prepped Orion on how to follow my lesson plans while I was away, said goodbye to Xiao and Jessa after dinner, and then camped out in my quarters until the last possible moment, avoiding the drawing room and indeed the entire second deck just so I wouldn't run into Hugo. The shuttle would arrive late in the night, really closer to the following morning, and I intended on staying up. To pass the time, I read, something newer this time—an Earth survival fantasy written by Jupiter Morrow, one of the fleet's most popular authors, Orion's favorite book and his parting gift to me.

Indeed, despite the morbid conditions precipitating my travel, I was more than a bit excited to return to Earth orbit and to the rest of the fleet. For the first time since I was a kid, I would be back on the fleet not only with means, but with tech. I could get the fleet news delivered right to my tab—we got it on the *Rochester* on a delay, and on the *Stalwart* only the highlights delivered via message scroll in the mess hall—and with the advance on my salary, I'd be free to purchase my own clothes, accessories, gifts. My plan was to buy some tea and candy on board the *Empire* and send it over to George and my students as a "Hello, I'm still alive and thinking of you!" message.

Close to midnight, after Preity and Lizzy had trickled in—apparently the Ingram party had insisted on an early night—and we had said our goodbyes, I went to the transport bay to wait. Sergei was already here, it seemed, but a note tacked to the loading door told me he was taking a few hours' respite and rest. Just like last time, I fashioned my bag into a makeshift seat, reminding myself to purchase a newer, nicer case during my trip. There was no way I'd be able to fit any gifts I'd purchase to bring back in this one along with my current loads, comprising just my three favorite dresses and both my tabs. But after an hour of sitting in the sad, gray metal box and realizing I could be looking at another two to three hours before we took off, I reconsidered my plan to wait blindly. I left my bag and crept quietly past the drawing room and Hugo's study to my favorite view. The bridge was silent and dark, and a much better place to wait, seeing as I could camp out in the captain's chair and would be alerted by the tab screens when Sergei returned to the transport bay. Only the captain's chair was occupied. By the captain.

"What are you doing here at this hour?" I jumped back, my heart taking off into a gallop. He started at the sound of my voice, broken out of what appeared to be a contemplative stupor.

"I could ask you the same question," he said, swiveling his chair around. I was unused to this angle, me towering over him. The act of towering was itself a new one.

"I came to sit somewhere with a better view while I wait for Sergei to be ready."

"You got sick of the monotony of the outer transport bay?"

"How did you know I was—" I caught sight of the surveillance feed pulled up on his tab. "Were you spying on me?"

Hugo shrugged it off. "I was debating whether I should go down to see you off. And whether I should call on you to make a decision on your winning hand."

"You're not actually insisting on holding me to your wager, then?" I hoped a bit of skepticism on my part would prove the whole thing was some elaborate joke.

"Very much so," he replied, finally standing. Now he towered over me, so close I could feel his body heat. "Last night I wished to test your poker face, and now perhaps I can test your heart."

I took a step back, trying to escape his eyes, which inspired a weakness in me I was determined to fight against. It was in moments like this, just him and me in the darkness, that I imagined we might have a future. It was foolish of me. "Don't you think it cruel to leave the fate of an entire ship in my hands?"

"Don't think about the *Ingram*, then. Think about yourself."

I had thought about myself in the past twenty-four hours. Thought about the type of person I wanted to be. The type of person I could live with being. "I think you should marry Bianca," I said, all in one breath and before I could second-guess myself. Hugo's face fell. "Merging with the *Ingram* is really the right thing to do," I continued, avoiding his gaze, telling the rest of my thoughts to my shoes. "But in all honesty, I don't think you should listen to what I say. I think you should follow your own heart. Make this decision for yourself. Speaking plainly, I find it a bit childish that you tried to force me to make the decision for you in the first place." When I finally allowed myself to look at him again, I found Hugo affecting something close to a smile.

"You, Stella, are my favorite bold girl."

"There's competition for that title, then?"

"Jessa remains in contention, but you always manage to be honest with me when I most need to hear it." Hugo took a step closer, closing the space between us. "You're just a bit fearless, aren't you?"

"Or impulsive," I offered with an awkward chuckle, unsure of how to navigate his proximity. *Insolent.* That had been Aunt Reed's favorite moniker for me.

All thoughts of my aunt, and indeed natural instincts like breathing, left me as I found myself in the crush of Hugo's embrace. It was a full-body hug, warm and solid, his voice vibrating through me like I was a tuning fork.

"Never change," he said into my hair. "And remember your promise to return. I'm holding you to it."

He was holding me, still, tight. Then a warning tone sounded, signaling someone moving about in the transport bay, and the moment ended.

"Your shuttle's ready," Hugo said as he pulled away, leaving me cold. "Safe travels." His hand still touched mine, fingers encircling my wrist. I was sure my pulse was thready under his fingers. I nodded and pulled myself away before I lost the nerve to go.

"I'll write to you if my aunt's illness is prolonged. I'll have to send additional lesson plans for Jessa if that's the case. And speaking of Jessa, maybe spend some more time with her while I'm away?" Hugo opened his mouth to defend himself, then must have thought about the last time he saw her. I'd kept count. It was more than three days ago. I continued to deliver the bold honesty he allegedly enjoyed from me. "And maybe lay off the drinking a bit. Jessa doesn't care for it when you drink."

I turned at the entrance to the bridge and waved, not catching Hugo's expression, his face obscured by shadows.

Sergei greeted me in the transport bay. "I knew I'd come to collect you sooner or later," he said, beckoning me forward. I handed over my bag, which he stowed as I shook my head at him.

"I'm coming back. Not running away."

"Uh-huh." He closed the shuttle door behind me and gestured to my old seat. "Strap yourself in, and we'll be on our way."

As soon as I sat down, securing myself in and then

reclining, the promise of sleep settled over me like a warm blanket. As the engines kicked off and I felt us propel out into space, the adrenaline faded, leaving me to my thoughts. I repeated my last conversation with Hugo on a loop in my mind. He'd compared me to his sister—again—but that hug hadn't felt sisterly at all. Did brothers hold their sisters so tight, hand on their lower back, whispering in their ear?

But it didn't matter what it was or wasn't. I'd advised Hugo to marry Bianca, to honor his arrangement with the *Ingram*, and though I'd pushed that choice back on him, I had faith he'd do the right thing. I repeated once again, *When Hugo and Bianca get married, I will leave.*

I needed to move on.

But first, I slept. How many hours, I couldn't tell. When I woke, Sergei was enjoying his own repose, so I read for a while, ate a bit, peered out the portal glass at the black skies. When finally he woke, I was in a new and strange state of mind. Emotionally spent, my wilder feelings confined to a box, which I closed and hid away at the back of my mind.

"Sergei, who was the last person you ferried from the *Rochester*? Before me. You said others had left."

"Finally asking the right questions, are we?" He invited me to join him in the cockpit. I settled in for an exchange of gossip among the stars. Sergei delivered. "The previous captain, Phillip, had a valet, barely lasted six months past the… transition."

I guessed that was code for "after Hugo's parents died and he moved to the moon."

"There were others. I cannot say what their purpose on board was, and they did not like to talk. But I did manage to get out of them that they were no longer needed. Then there were several governesses before you. At least three, come and gone. Last person was a medical officer. Attacked in the night and in a very bad state. Far too afraid to tell tales."

Attacked. Like Mason had been. "You have no idea who or what attacked him?" I asked. "Could it have been a cat?"

Sergei shook his head. "No cat has claws that big. Or the grasp of weapons. Something hit him. Repeatedly. Speculation was the young captain cannot handle his drink."

"No," I said. "He wouldn't be moved to violence like that."

"It's just one theory," Sergei hedged. "You must be curious, no?"

I was, but I didn't want to reveal too much to Sergei, who clearly liked to tell tales. I didn't want him telling his next passenger my theories about Hugo and the *Rochester*. That someone had tried to kill Hugo, twice. Then Mason. I was sure it was all connected; I just couldn't see how, or why.

The trip passed as quickly as three days in a tiny metal box possibly could, though at least this time I was equipped with reading material. I'd powered through three Jupiter Morrow books by the time Sergei announced we were approaching the *Empire*. As we docked, a feeling of dread started to wend its way up my spine, which didn't dissipate once Sergei opened the door and we descended into the blindingly white transport bay. It was like I was here yesterday, boarding the orphan transport for the *Stalwart*. Nothing had changed. Everything was white, bright, and sterile.

"Send me a message when you are ready for pickup," Sergei said, handing me my bag. "Though I would not blame you if you decide not to return."

"I'm going back," I said with more force than intended.

Sergei shrugged. "I don't see why you ever left this ship, if you've got family here." He turned in a circle, taking in the room. "It's swanky. And this is only the transport bay."

"Bye, Sergei," I said, waving him off as I turned to leave.

I knew exactly why I'd left. I was about to go see her for the first time in six years.

twenty

As I passed through the brightly lit corridors of the *Empire*, it was impossible not to think of death. The *Empire* had always telegraphed the morbid for me, from my parents' death to my uncle's untimely demise shortly thereafter. Then the outbreak of the Kebbler virus sent me to the *Stalwart*. The *Empire* was perpetually cloaked in death in my mind. And in my aunt's quarters, the sense of it was palpable. The sharp tang of medical waste hit my nose first, followed by a heaviness in the air, stale and too warm, like hot breath. And my cousin's expression as the door swung open: grim.

"Finally, you're here," Charlotte said, ushering me inside. "I think she's been holding on just for you." She did not seem pleased by this fact; indeed, Charlotte had never enjoyed the attention I garnered. Never mind that it was entirely negative, but still I overshadowed her, as did her brother, the household favorite. Between adoration for Charles and hatred for me, her mother had little left for Charlotte, who was quiet and unimposing by nature.

"Your message was short on details," I said, treading familiar territory. Down the short hall to the living and dining quarters, which branched off into a series of bedrooms. "What's wrong with her?"

"Cancer," she said, stopping in front of a familiar door. The door to the red room. "It's just like you left it."

So it was still terrifying? I dropped my bag by the door and demurred. "Can I see her first? There will be time to unpack later." I wanted to avoid the red room if possible.

Charlotte shrugged. "Sure. Suit yourself." She crossed over instead to another all-too-familiar door. Aunt Reed's room. I stared at it, frosted, white, and gleaming. Hesitated, until Charlotte reached past my shoulder and hit the button for me. The door slid open, soft as a whisper. I inched over the threshold, poking my head around the door.

The first thing I was struck by was how small she seemed. Aunt Reed had never been statuesque or physically imposing, though she loomed large in my memory. Now she was tiny, skin shiny with sweat and eyes ringed with dark circles.

"Stella, is that you?" she croaked, squinting in my direction and beckoning me closer with a bony arm. I approached, sitting on the edge of the bed, close enough to catch the cloyingly sweet smell of a perfume attempting to cover up the scent of recent sick. Her hair was greasy, stringy; her lips chapped. But she was still fundamentally my aunt. She scowled up at me. "You took your time getting here, didn't you? Insolent, as always."

"My posting is a bit far away from the fleet, Aunt. I apologize."

"That's right. I heard you got a fancy job."

"Indeed," I said, falling easily back into the formality she required. "It's a small private ship where I teach a young girl."

Aunt Reed shook her head weakly against her pillow. "Imagine you, teaching some little girl. To be difficult, I'm sure of it."

"Aunt, why am I here? Why did you call for me? You clearly maintain your dislike of me."

Called out, she set her mouth in a straight line. "Only you would speak to a dying woman in such a way, Stella Ainsley, but touché." Suddenly she rose, half a foot off the pillow, a hacking cough breaking the conversation. She shook, clearly in pain, and without thought, I steadied a hand on her back, supporting her. I fetched her a pouch of water from the bedside table when she asked. She sucked it down greedily but stopped quickly, pushing it back into my hand. "Don't give it to me next time. We'll run out of rations."

"You're on water rations?" A lot must have changed on board since last I lived here. Aunt Reed smiled bitterly as she settled back down onto the pillows.

"We've been relegated to the dregs of society since all the money's gone, but the water rations are shipwide."

I kept a straight face, did not pry, though I desperately wished to know the story. I'd get it out of Charlotte later.

"To answer your question," she continued, her voice hoarse but strong, "I asked you here to make amends. You are the only one left alive for me to gain absolution from." She sighed deeply, seeming to sink into her pillows. "But I will have to wait to die tomorrow, for I am too exhausted to hash it out with you right now. Good night, Stella."

My cue to leave was unmistakable, so I did, though not without some confusion as to the time. It was still morning.

I found Charlotte in the living room, reading. "How is she?" she asked, looking up from her tab.

"Cantankerous," I replied a bit glibly, then sat in the love seat across from her. "And tired. She's resting."

"She does that a lot now."

"How long has she been ill?"

Charlotte closed her tab, apparently giving up on her book. "She was diagnosed a year ago."

"A year?" I said. "Why didn't anyone tell me?"

She looked confused. "Why would we tell you? Mama only started to care a few weeks ago when it got really bad. Before that, you never came up."

Of course not. Charlotte didn't look particularly affected or guilty. I dispensed with any guilt I might feel about prying into their circumstances. "Aunt Reed said something about the money being gone. What did she mean?"

Charlotte rolled her eyes. "Charles spent all our money on booze, women, and high-stakes games. Then he died."

I was taken aback, both by the news and by the matter-of-fact way she said it. He'd been awful to me as a child, but it was strange to think he was gone. We were all still so young.

"Charles died? When did that happen?"

"Six months ago. Which was when they cut off the drugs from Mother. And here we are. The final countdown." I noticed dark circles under Charlotte's eyes. Exhausted.

"Can they do that?" I asked. "Just take away her medication?"

"Apparently. We're no better than a common food ship now, it would seem. Left to die in our own good time."

I took the knock in stride. "And the water's being rationed now?"

"For the last two years."

As Charlotte sank back against the couch cushions, threw her head back, and closed her eyes, I reflected on how much had changed. My aunt was penniless, defenseless, and dying. My elder cousin, who used to torment me, was dead. The glorious *Empire,* reduced to water rationing. The medical rationing for the poor was nothing new, unfortunately.

An unholy sound, like a sputtering engine, came out of Charlotte as she slipped into a doze. I was on my own, the Reed household determined to sleep. My eyes darted to the door to the red room. My old room. I had to go in there at some point. Why not unpack now, connect my tab to the network? I hauled myself up and trudged over, grabbing my bag and hitting the button to open the door.

"Lights on," I said as I stepped over the dark threshold, to no effect. I'd forgotten what it was like to be back in an analog environment. I felt for the light switch on the wall and pressed it on, only to be bathed in eerie red light. How the red room got its name: long ago the lights had malfunctioned, so now they only ever registered red, the emergency-lighting system painting the room in perpetual anger. Of course it had become my room, the least-valued member of the Reed household, because heaven forbid either Charles or Charlotte had to have shared. I felt a pang of sadness; pity. Charles was dead. Nothing was as it had been.

I threw my bag on the bed, taking out my dresses and underclothes, setting them up in the wardrobe. I retrieved both my tabs, setting my drawing one aside while I powered up the other. Immediately, it pinged to the network, home screen lighting up with notifications. I had messages—four, in fact. Who would have sent me four messages in three days? I tapped the icon. George. And I realized it had been almost a week since his oldest message. *Whoops.*

The first and second message were nothing special—the usual from George. Movie recaps and general platitudes. More detail about how it was going with Joy than I wanted to hear. The third was a compilation of messages from the kids.

But the fourth was ominous. I read it twice.

Dear Stella,

You were always the Earth science expert, instead of me. Do you think it's safe to go back there? Jon's really got me thinking about it lately. He told me not to write to you. Said to be careful what I say. If I didn't know any better, I'd say he was jealous.

I hope you're okay. It's odd I haven't heard from you.
Joy is great, but I miss you. If I have to go down to Earth
and face who knows what, I'd want you to be there.
I miss you.
George

It was out of character for him. Paranoid. Emotional. And Jon had told him not to write. Did Jon know what I knew, about Mason reading our messages? I was sure it wasn't because he was jealous. My eyes began to strain—a symptom of the red room—and I gave up trying to read. I could still faintly hear Charlotte snoring in the living room. I did my best to convince my body I was tired, crawling under the covers, not even bothering to undress, and tried to nap.

I slept longer than expected, waking to the rich smell of curry, which set me immediately salivating. Curry meant it was Thursday, and substantive food meant it was dinnertime. I found Charlotte setting two plates and sets of utensils on the dining table, a tureen of steaming brown sauce and vegetables next to a container of rice.

"It's lucky you checked in with the port authority before coming here," Charlotte said, "or they would have sent only enough for one." That she would not have shared her meal was clear.

"What about Aunt Reed?" I asked.

"She hasn't been fit for solid food for two months. And it's a good thing, as we can only afford so many rations. I take it you paid for yourself?"

I nodded. "I earn a good salary on board the *Rochester.*" We sat down, Charlotte at the head of the table, me to her left side. Charlotte sat where her mother used to, eyes flicking to each empty chair in turn, then to me.

"Who would have thought that I'd end up an orphan, just like you?" She threw it out there, a passing comment before she went ahead and started serving herself. I pointedly did not draw attention to the fact that her mother wasn't dead yet.

"What are your plans?" I asked before going to town on my curry and rice. If they were truly bankrupt, the *Empire* wouldn't let Charlotte simply hang out on board for the rest of her life. You either worked or had enough money not to.

"I'll inherit our quarters, of course," Charlotte started. "Mama didn't have time before she got sick to arrange a match for me, but I've had my eye on one of the tea workers aboard." She paused a beat, looking me hard in the eyes. "Don't you dare breathe a word of that to her. It'll kill her straightaway if she knows I'd deign to marry a field hand."

I nodded dumbly, looking past the threat to the more pressing, underlying question. "Why are there tea workers on board the *Empire*? The *Mumbai* is the only tea ship in the fleet."

Charlotte waved me off, nonchalant. "Oh, we started growing our own a few years ago, imported some workers from the *Mumbai*. Saves us fuel and import fees."

The *Empire* had imported workers from the *Mumbai* to

grow their own tea. Charlotte continued talking, oblivious to my no-doubt-concerned expression.

"He doesn't earn a substantial salary, but it should be enough, with my owning our quarters outright and all. Worst case, I figure out how to hold down a job." She wrinkled her nose at that. "You can meet him, if you like. There's a dance tonight."

A rasping cry sounded from Aunt Reed's room. "Charlotte, where is my dinner!"

Charlotte pushed back from the table with a sigh and retreated to care for her mother, leaving me to finish my meal.

I didn't have an appropriate outfit for dancing, so reluctantly Charlotte lent me something of hers, bemoaning loudly that we were the same size and thus she felt obligated. We left her mother in the care of a shift nurse and made our way toward the heart of the ship, to the old cultural center I remembered well. But I'd never been old enough to attend any of the dances held here, and found the *Empire*'s idea of a night of frivolity quite other from that on the *Stalwart*. There was no DJ mixing digi-tunes on a tab, but a chamber orchestra playing. Everyone was doing dances they all seemed to know the steps to, so I sat firmly on the sidelines while Charlotte flirted and danced with her tea farmer, Abhishek, or Abe for short. A boy named Edward took an interest in me and kept prattling on about different types of tea-cultivation methods. I could have been a tree, and he still would have talked on and on. I was bored out of my gourd, but I did glean some more useful information: the *Empire* was growing not only tea but fruit. They had only one small orchard, but nonetheless. It meant that Jon was onto something. It seemed the *Stalwart* was being phased out.

I hated that I couldn't write to him, not with Mason reading. I'd been back on the fleet for only a day, but I felt off-kilter. Treading water while I waited for Aunt Reed to die. I shook away the mere morbidity of the thought, grabbing Edward's hand and demanding he teach me the next dance. Over the next hour, I pranced around in a circle, making a fool of myself and a mess of bruises of Edward's feet, but it was, in some vague measure, a bit of fun. It was an unexpected emotion for the trip, and the only thing that made returning to the red room that night bearable.

Over the next week, I helped Charlotte care for Aunt Reed, who often slept. When she was awake and lucid, she insisted I sit and talk with her, apparently her version of doing penance. Aunt Reed talked about everything and nothing, sharing idle *Empire* gossip and, when I could cajole her into it, telling me more about my mother. They'd grown up together, not exactly friends, but close, by way of family friendship. The derision in my aunt's voice was clear as she relayed the particulars of my parents' marriage.

"Love conquers all," she sneered before a hacking cough overtook her. She recovered to finish off with "And look how well it turned out for her."

It wasn't the first time I'd heard her thesis on how stupid my mother was to leave the comforts of the upper decks of the *Empire* for the lower, all for love, only to die eight years later. I didn't take the bait, refusing to reward her with my protestations.

When I wasn't bound to the family quarters, I availed myself of one of the *Empire*'s shiniest features: the library. Unlike the one aboard the *Rochester,* this was a living, breathing archive, housing works by all the fleet's literary stars, plus a museum of classics—real-life books—under glass. I used to find them eminently impressive, now less so since I'd held so many in my hands. But the archive was what I sought. It contained not just books, but news. I searched for key terms pertaining to the *Rochester* and Hugo, and I drank up every article I could find.

His mother had been sick. His father the toiling scientist. Rumors of experimental drugs. Psychosis. Murder.

Further back, there were fluff pieces about the *Rochester* hosting elaborate parties, even producing a Klaviermeister— Hugo's grandfather. Some permutation of Fairfax—a hundred years back, at least—had pioneered a flu vaccine that saved half the fleet.

The Fairfaxes were high society, integrated into the fleet, key citizens. Then it all changed. The parties stopped; the gossip items turned to speculation about the Fairfaxes becoming hermits. Then murder and self-imposed exile. It painted a puzzling picture. It told me Hugo's history but gave me no real clue as to what was going on now. I had only half the equation.

I knew Aunt Reed was about to die when she started apologizing to me. She wheezed, struggling for breath, but her grip was surprisingly strong. Her fingers dug into my forearm as she locked eyes with me, insistent.

"I did wrong by you, Stella Ainsley. You should hate me, yet you came at my request. You sit by my bedside." Her lip curled. "Your goodness is annoying."

Aunt Reed was still the master of the one-two punch. And she wasn't done.

"I promised my husband I would love you as my own child, but I could not. You were too much like his sister, and he preferred you to his own children. I hated you for it. I'm sure this cancer is my punishment."

I could have protested, reassured her no one got cancer as a punishment, that there was no way my uncle loved me more than his own children, but it seemed unimportant now. My aunt was exercising her right to confession, and the best I could do was listen. She went on, listing both her grievances against me—I ate so much food! Required so much attention!—and her sins. The coldness. Withholding affection. Sending me away.

"Aunt Reed," I urged her as she went on endlessly, working herself up into a frenzy, "please do not worry yourself any further. You were cruel to me, you sent me away, but I am fine. I forgive you."

She sank into the pillows, spent. It was apparently what she needed to hear. Forgiveness. I meant every word I said. I would find my place in the world. Somewhere. There was no need to hold a grudge.

She died two days later. I did not cry, though I absorbed a sea of tears from Charlotte. I attended my fourth funeral, the pomp and circumstance unchanged over the years, in which Charlotte managed a tidy little speech between sobs, shared with the five people who bothered to show up but who had never visited while my aunt was sick. Then I held Charlotte's hand as we gazed through a hexagonal-shaped window, watching Aunt Reed's body—tastefully enclosed in a shroud—vented out into space.

The next day, chaos, and Charlotte wailing for a whole new reason.

"Those bastards!" She slammed her tablet down on the dining table. "They know we don't have any money left, and yet they are requiring I travel to the *Olympus* to file some stupid forms!"

I picked up the tab and read the message myself. To legally complete the transfer of her mother's quarters to Charlotte, she would have to travel to the *Olympus* in person within seven days, or else she would forfeit it. It was crude yet effective: what better way to strip the poor and destitute of their inheritances than to require a trip they could not possibly finance? The valuable real estate would revert to the *Empire*, and they could do with it as they saw fit. Luckily I was in a unique position to help. "I'll pay for the shuttle. I have an advance on my salary, and I know a guy who will take you there for a reasonable rate." I didn't know what Sergei's rates were, since the *Rochester* had always paid, but I figured I'd twist his arm a bit.

"You'd do that?" Charlotte sniffed.

"Of course I would," I replied. "And I'll go with you."

It was uncanny how quickly Sergei could be hailed when you weren't located by the moon. By breakfast the next day, we were on our way to the *Olympus*. It orbited within our cluster, so the journey was short, but the security detail on board was not. The *Olympus* checked our identification papers twice; then officers interrogated Charlotte and me for a half-hour about the purpose of our visit, unsatisfied the first three times we showed them the message Charlotte had received. Finally, we were released to visit the Population and Control Department, two identical keytabs in hand. The security office had already keyed in our destination, pulling up a map of the *Olympus* with a big red dot signifying where we were. Soon we arrived, using the keytab to open a bulkhead door, which lead to a cramped waiting room.

"Who are you here to see?" a bored-looking man asked from behind a cluttered desk.

Charlotte handed over the keytab, which now flashed our clearance stamp. "Mr. Reynolds," she said in a small voice, almost like she was scared.

"Have a seat," the man directed us. "He'll be right with you."

We had a very different definition of "right with you," which I would have classified as "forthwith; very soon." The government drone, however, meant "at some nebulous time in the future." We waited ten minutes, then twenty.

At the forty-minute mark, two miraculous things occurred. First, Mr. Reynolds finally appeared, beckoning us to follow. Then, as we were trailing behind him, making our way down a narrow, dimly lit corridor, I caught a familiar face heading in our direction. I did a double-take, stopping in my tracks.

"Jon?"

"Stella!" He jogged to me, grinning wide, and then enveloped me into a hug. I went stiff at the unexpected intimacy, but thankfully we parted quickly. I looked to see Charlotte stopped ten feet ahead, expression gobsmacked. A cute boy hugging cousin Stella—scandalous! Farther off, Captain Karlson stood, equally bemused.

"Um, go on without me," I told Charlotte, who obliged with no fuss. Captain Karlson let Jon know he'd wait in the lobby, leaving us alone.

"What are you doing here?" I asked.

"I could ask you the same thing. I thought you might end up on the *Empire*, but I never expected to see you here."

"How did you know I might go to the *Empire*?"

"Your cousin contacted the *Stalwart* about your aunt a few weeks ago. I took the call, but advised her to write to you herself. I didn't want to be the one to break the news."

"Oh. Well, Charlotte had to come to sign some papers. So here I am."

When Jon leaned in close, I was afraid he was going to hug me again or, worse, kiss me. But his arms remained at his side, his voice low. "I finally convinced my uncle. We came here to ask for a ship, to send a group down to Earth."

"You can't. It's too dangerous."

"Do we have another choice? They've been systematically moving all our crops onto other ships. Something's going to happen. I just don't know what."

I thought of Mason, telling me in his oily voice that my friends should worry less about vegetables. "Be careful about writing anything in messages. They're reading them."

"Of course they are." Jon sighed. "But how do you know?"

I did my best to explain, and with the way Jon was looking at me, it must have sounded mad.

"You're living on a ship with a potential murderer. You can't go back there."

"I have to go back. I promised." I bit into the last word, let its weight wash over me. How much was my word worth if the price of it was my own heartbreak? I longed to see Hugo again, just one more time, but could I really bear to see him married to someone else?

"A promise is a stupid reason to put yourself in danger."

"You didn't find anything before, when I asked you to look into the crew."

"Doesn't mean there isn't anything to find." The steel edge melted away, leaving an expression I'd never seen on him: weariness. "I know you don't want to come back to the *Stalwart*; probably wise, given our predicament. They're phasing us out, but won't give us a ship that's able to deorbit safely. But couldn't you live with your cousin now? You could apply for a permanent visa, since you're here anyway. My uncle would vouch for you."

It was tempting. I couldn't pretend I hadn't thought about it. Charlotte wasn't my favorite person, but she wasn't as whiny as I'd remembered her being when we were children. We'd both grown up a lot. She was about to come into a four-bedroom unit, and if I could secure a job on board, she might let me move in.

I felt a pang at the thought of leaving the *Rochester* and Hugo behind for good, like someone twisting a wrench in between my ribs.

"I'm going back," I said. I needed a proper goodbye. "But I'm going to just flat-out ask what's going on. If they fire me, I'll make the request to move to the *Empire.*"

"Firing you is a best-case scenario," Jon said darkly.

"They're not going to kill me." I rolled my eyes and punched him on the shoulder. Jon was becoming far too paranoid for his own good.

"You're still here?" Charlotte was back; either her meeting had been short or Jon and I had been talking too long. We headed back toward the lobby, collecting Captain Karlson and making our way en masse to the shuttle bay.

I trailed a few steps behind, my brain running over all the best- and worst-case scenarios for my return. The best brought a grin to my face and a blush to my cheeks, while the worst ran my blood cold and had me glimpsing Hanada down the *Olympus*'s corridor, fuchsia hair flashing in the corner of my eye. Jon's paranoia was rubbing off on me. I looked again, and she was gone.

twenty-one

Sergei laughed as I climbed aboard his ship the next day. "You really want to go back?"

I gave him the same speech I'd given Jon and Charlotte the day before. I'd been gone weeks, I missed everyone, etc. I kept the uncertainty to myself: how long could I stay before the wedding? Where I would go afterward? Would seeing Hugo again twist a dagger in my heart? And then there was the matter of the attacks.

Sergei distracted me with fleet gossip. Apparently, the *Empire* was not alone in growing food supplies. The *Saint Petersburg* was harvesting wheat. The *Lady Liberty* had corn. Sergei had ferried more than a few food workers and inspectors to several private ships, presumably to start their own micro farms. Jon's paranoia was justified; the fleet was rendering the *Stalwart* nonessential. But why wasn't the fleet helping by providing a safe vessel so the *Stalwart*'s inhabitants could go down to Earth? There was no way the *Stalwart* could safely enter Earth's atmosphere without being torn apart. It would need a series of smaller ships, in better condition, if there was any hope of saving everyone. I pushed aside the niggling voice that whispered, *They don't* want *to save everyone.*

To silence the voice, I slept. Finished the Jupiter Morrow back catalog and started on a new author, since I'd loaded up on contemporary books on the *Empire* before I left. Rehearsed what I would say to Hugo when I saw him.

I know you're hiding something.

I wish you and Bianca the best.

I missed you.

As soon as I stepped off Sergei's ship, I felt like I was home. And I hated it. The *Rochester* would not be the first home to cast me aside, but it would hurt the most.

Sergei helped me haul my new trunk into the transport bay, where I realized no one had come to greet me. "Did they respond when you hailed?"

"Of course," he said. "I'm sure they trust you don't require a welcome party. I will wait for Officer Xiao."

I nodded, agreeing with him, but feeling somewhat unloved nonetheless. "You're staying?"

"For a day or so. I require a break after such a long flight. But next time you need me, you know how to get in touch. I'll be waiting."

With a halfhearted wave, I started dragging my trunk along behind me, thankful I'd sprung for one with wheels. I was halfway to the staff quarters when I remembered: I'd won my room back from Bianca during the poker game. It seemed like eons ago, though it was only weeks. Was it real? If I went upstairs, would the bio-lock admit me to my quarters?

To be safe, I continued toward the staff quarters. The rumble of the wheels as they glided along the metal flooring plainly announced my arrival, yet no one came out to greet me.

"Lizzy? Preity?"

Nothing but hollow silence echoed back at me. I tried the sleeping quarters, but no matter how hard I pressed the lock to our room, it didn't open. The crew mess was deserted, rendered eerie in the absence of the detritus of the *Ingram* crew; waistcoats and borrowed tabs strewn on tables and chairs, sneaky flasks of booze tucked away that the junior staff brought in and the seniors pretended not to see (but drank regardless). It was odd how quickly I'd become accustomed to the people in this space. Now everyone was gone.

I even knocked on Hanada's door, but either she wasn't inside or she was ignoring me. One was as likely as the other.

I sat on my trunk, somewhat at a loss, then remembered: I was back on the *Rochester*. My comms piece would work again. I dug it out of my bag, and a minute later Rori's distinct voice, both warm and stiff, sounded a greeting in my ear.

"Rori, where has the Ingram party gone?" I asked.

"They left. Your quarters on Deck Two are ready for you, Stella."

Making the round trip back to the elevator with my heavy trunk proved a workout. I pressed the elevator call button, chest heaving, a sweaty curl dangling stubbornly over my brow, my usual tight bun a mess. I longed for a shower.

The elevator dinged, and I barreled inside. Right into Hugo.

"Oof," he said, and I could feel it reverberate through his chest, through me. My immediate instinct was to jump away, but hands at the small of my back and on my hip stopped me. My world narrowed to the heat where we touched, Hugo like a furnace—or maybe that was me—and my chin tilted up, an action I regretted immediately. We locked eyes, his warm and intense, like the smile playing across his lips. My heart thumped against my ribs, and I did my best not to say anything stupid.

"I'm sorry. I didn't expect anyone to be inside." My words broke the spell; Hugo pulled away and turned serious again.

"No, no, don't apologize." He reached behind me to help with my trunk, raising an eyebrow at its weight. "Is this why you were gone so long? Shopping?"

The doors closed as I stammered out my excuses. "No, see, it took my aunt some time to die, and then my cousin was a mess, and so I found I had to stay longer than I expected. I'm sorry—"

"Stop apologizing," Hugo interrupted. "I'm glad you're back. And I like your hair like this. Loose and a bit wild." He tucked a lock of it behind my ear, and my heart plummeted into my shoes. We were in a tiny box, a breath apart, and he smelled good, and—*ding!* We arrived at Deck Two and the doors opened, letting out all the magic in doing so.

Hugo handled my trunk the rest of the familiar way to our rooms as I trailed behind, hiding my mortified expression. The ship was quiet, the way it used to be, another reminder that the Ingram party was gone. We reached my door—I tested the bio-lock just to be sure this wasn't some cruel joke—and I felt a rush of happiness as it slid open, revealing familiar details, but with one marked difference.

"Are those my drawings on the walls?" I gasped, stepping over the threshold to view them more closely. He'd transferred to canvas some of my greatest hits—a watercolor of the Taj Mahal, an abstract representation of the space outside our windows, a lively scene from the drawing room. And on the wall across from the bed, there was a triptych of portraits: Jessa, Hugo, and me.

"How did you get these?" I hovered up close to them, running disbelieving fingers over rough canvas, and blushing fiercely at my portrait. I'd never felt it was good enough to share, so seeing it here, and knowing Hugo had spent time alone with it… I might as well have been naked.

"I had Orion hack your drawing tab before you left."

I should have been upset at the violation of my privacy, but at the moment, all I cared about was that Hugo had taken the time to do it. That he had thought about making my room that much more mine. I pressed my lips together in a tight smile to stop myself from letting out an undignified noise. "Thank you," I managed, taking my trunk over from him. And then there I was, standing, Hugo just staring at me, like he was waiting for some response, some question from me. Instead, I changed the subject. "I don't even know what time it is. I'm absolutely starving."

"It's nearly dinnertime, so you're in luck," Hugo replied, and if he was disappointed, he didn't let on. "Eat up, and I'll see you in my study after." It was like I'd never left. Like the Ingrams had never been here. Back to our old routine.

At dinner, I was subjected to more hugs in one go than I'd collectively experienced in my whole life.

"It was awful without you. Please don't go away again." It was a challenge extricating myself from hug number four from Jessa. I smiled, ruffling her hair, and tried to answer. The reassuring phrases I knew I was meant to say turned to ash on my tongue, leaving me speechless.

"I'm sure Stella is as glad to be back as you are to see her. I'm glad you're back myself."

Bless Xiao, ever the diplomat. I tried to capture her eye, to thank her, but instead caught an uneasy look between her and Poole. A conversation passed in a glance. They were as aware as I was what Hugo's marriage to Bianca would mean. No promises to stay could be made.

"When are the Ingrams coming back?" I asked, failing miserably at sounding casual. I spooned a double helping of mashed potatoes onto my plate to hide my panic.

"Whenever Princess Bianca feels like it, I would imagine," Poole said.

"Hopefully never," Jessa mumbled into her plate.

"Tell us about your trip, Stella." Orion changed the subject before Jessa could get on a roll. "We'd love to hear what the *Empire* is like."

I obliged, but I lost my chance to get more gossip about the Ingrams and the impending wedding. I'd have to ask Hugo himself.

An hour later, duty carried me to the study, but dread kept me weighted in front of the door. I paced back and forth, pressed my ear to the door to confirm Hugo was inside. I didn't hear anything, but that didn't mean much. Just as I was contemplating going to bed and putting off this conversation forever, Hugo shouted through the door to come in. Cursing that I'd given myself away, I obliged.

Déjà vu enveloped me like a fog: Hugo in his chair; light languorously low, projecting shadows onto the wood-paneled walls. I inhaled the musty smell of books and whiskey, then released a slow, deep breath before taking a seat across from Hugo. My old chair, but a new me.

"I owe you an apology."

"Oh?" I braced myself, schooling my features so I could take the worst.

"I wanted to make the new decorations for your room a surprise, but I realize they came at the expense of your privacy. I'm sorry."

"That's okay. I mean, technically you bought me the drawing tab, so it kind of belongs to you anyway."

Hugo frowned, the shadows exaggerating it into a glower.

"That's no excuse. It was a gift, given freely. I don't own any part of you."

"Then thank you. I appreciate it."

Hugo relaxed back into his chair, as if a considerable burden had been lifted.

"You know, it was Jessa who scolded me about it. You've taught her well."

"I can't take full credit. She was a good kid when I got here."

"Tell me all about your trip."

I relayed my semi-rehearsed platitudes about my aunt's cancer, her passing, helping Charlotte tie up loose ends.

"That's it?"

"Were you expecting a dramatic reenactment?"

"I was expecting honesty. From what I know about your relationship with your family, I figure it wasn't all smooth sailing."

I felt a tug in my stomach, something like longing swelling in my chest. I wanted to share with him, tell him all my deepest feelings. But then defiance whipped up from my core. Hugo seemed to wish to fall back into our old routine, once again skirting the line between employer and employee, friends and something more—though the latter was mostly in my head. Yet he was keeping secrets from me, had put me through terrible social torture all those weeks the Ingrams were here. He was going to marry Bianca. I owed him nothing.

"What about you? Why did the Ingram party leave so suddenly?"

It caught him off-guard. He leaned forward, the dim light casting half his face in shadow. "Surely you know?"

I didn't know, and I didn't like that he was teasing me again. I left my chair for the window, where I wouldn't have to look him in the eye as he humiliated me.

"I know they need to prepare for the wedding, but I don't understand why everyone left. The junior staff should have stayed, at least. I'd like to know when they're coming back, when the wedding is." I turned my back to him, so only the stars would see my disappointment.

"I'm not marrying Bianca."

The breath left my lungs. My vision swam, inky-black universe and dying stars swirling together like a stew.

"I'm sorry; I think I misunderstood you. When are you marrying Bianca?"

"I'm not. Marrying Bianca."

I heard him correctly that time, my head clear.

"Why not?" I rounded on his chair to find that he had stood, as if to lord over me.

"Because I don't love her."

"But I told you to marry her. That it was the right thing to do."

"Right for whom? For me? For you? For this ship?" Hugo punctuated each word with a step, slinking like a cat until he'd boxed me in against the windows.

"For them!" I stopped him in his tracks, hand to his chest. "They'll die without us."

"That's why I couldn't do it," Hugo said, eyes glued to my

hand on his chest, like I'd burned him. "You'd sacrifice your own happiness for the sake of another's. You're incredible."

"It's nothing. Anyone would do the same." I stole back my hand but didn't budge from where I was. I wanted to make him uncomfortable with my closeness, box him in and call him out.

"No, they wouldn't. You are good to a fault. You saw only two solutions, and you chose the one that would hurt you the most, because you thought it was the right thing to do." He laughed at a joke I must have missed. "I wish you'd just asked me for a third option. It would have been a lot simpler."

"I don't understand."

"The Ingrams will be fine. I've made arrangements with the *Lady Liberty* to take them on board."

The weight of two dozen lives lifted off my shoulders.

"So, nothing has to change? I can stay on the *Rochester*?" I sounded as meek as I felt, relief wending its way up my spine. It was the best news I could have hoped for.

"Not if you don't want to," Hugo said. For the briefest moment, I lost my mind and senses to elation, throwing my arms around him in a hug I quickly regretted. I was too forward, too close, too—then Hugo responded, and my panic took on a new form. He was *hugging me back*.

"Don't you want to know why I don't love Bianca?" he said into my hair.

"Because you met her?" I said into the rough fabric of his coat, sure he couldn't hear me. He could, and he laughed.

"That's why I love you, Stella. You have a good heart, but

also a sharp tongue. The perfect combination." He pulled away, while I stood frozen, repeating his words in my mind. *That's why I love you. Like a sister,* he'd probably meant to finish. Right? But his expression, his eyes, were not brotherly at all.

"You've finally dispensed with your poker face," he said, leaning down for some inexplicable reason.

And then he kissed me.

twenty-two

His lips were chapped, rough, but I didn't care. I was far more focused on my own unmitigated panic. I'd never been kissed, not properly, and the last time I'd tried to kiss someone—George—I'd performed abysmally. I knew one thing. If I didn't kiss him back, Hugo would stop, and I did not want that to happen. My entire body was celebrating, every inch of me on fire, beating wildly, shouting with joy. I raised myself up on my tiptoes and returned pressure in kind, parting my lips just so, like I'd seen at many a movie night. And—oh! Hugo pulled me in closer, strong hand at the small of my back, and introduced his tongue into the mix.

Now my body went tight like a harp string, my mind in analytical overdrive. I didn't pull back, but I didn't do anything either. Hugo was trying to do… something with his tongue, and I let him, but that was about it. This was foreign, and I wasn't sure I liked it. He must have sensed my reticence, because finally he pulled back, and I hated how relieved I felt. I'd gone from ecstasy to discomfort in the space of seconds, and I hated that I felt that way. Hugo had kissed me! He loved me!

And now he was looking at me expectantly, nervous and questioning. The panic came back.

"Thank you!" I chirped out, the first and only thing that came into my head. Then I bolted, dodging around the chairs and slamming my hand against the exit button, not stopping until I got to my quarters. It was the coward's response, but one that felt wholly natural. I collapsed on my bed, breathing deep to slow my galloping heartbeat.

Had I just hallucinated that? Boys like Hugo didn't fall in love with girls like me.

Love. My brain stumbled over the concept. He couldn't possibly... I must have misunderstood his words, and maybe he'd been feverish when he'd kissed me—

My comms pinged. Incoming message from Captain Hugo Fairfax. *Frex.* I pushed down my humiliation, currently manifesting as a full-body blush, and answered. We may have just crossed all sorts of lines, but Hugo was still my boss. I couldn't ignore a direct hail.

"Hi."

"Hey."

Silence like a yawning chasm stretched between us. We were off to a great start.

"Listen, I'm sorry—"

"I shouldn't have—"

We stumbled over each other, laughed, then plunged back into awkward, inert nothingness. I stared across the room to the triptych, the winking eyes and sly smile I'd given Hugo unfitting for the awkward boy hanging in my ear. It was time for me to be the "bold girl" Hugo was always calling me with that maddening grin.

"I've never been kissed like that."

"And I've never kissed anyone like that."

"Liar." My tone was playful but earnest. That was not the kiss of a novice, even if its recipient was.

Silence again for a moment then. "Mechanically, maybe, but the feeling behind it…"

I laughed, then caught myself. "I don't mind that you've kissed other people. It's just weird that you want to kiss me."

A pause.

"Stella, you're going to have to let me in so I can kiss you again."

"You're outside?"

He knocked lightly on my door to prove it. I leaped up and across the room with embarrassingly desperate speed. Then, suddenly vain, I dashed into the bathroom to check my reflection, even though Hugo had just seen me exactly as I was. Still, I decided to make one change. I pulled my hair out of its bun, letting a tangle of locks cascade over my shoulders.

I opened the door, breathless. "Hi," I offered uselessly, unable to suppress a smile.

"Hi," Hugo answered, smile tugging equally hard at his lips. He leaned against the door frame expectantly, waiting for me to make the next move. But I found myself frozen, too many questions hanging in the air.

"I'm still half convinced I'll wake up tomorrow and you'll have run away."

"You're one to talk," he shot back. "Running off in the middle of the night to help ailing aunts."

"Last time you ran off, you came back with Bianca Ingram." I arched a brow. "What was that about?"

Hugo grimaced, a satisfying mien of guilt passing over his features. "I was confused. And, um, I sort of wanted to make you jealous. See if you liked me as much as I liked you."

I narrowed my eyes to slits. "That is incredibly stupid."

"I've realized that now, yes."

"You owe Bianca an apology. You led her on."

I found myself crushed in a hug, Hugo's warm timbre reverberating against my neck. "This is why I love you. You're far kinder than I am."

I wriggled out of his grasp, made uncomfortable by the unmitigated praise. "I'm not a saint, so don't make me into one. I just can imagine if she feels a fraction of the way I did that she's probably miserable. I think she really wanted to marry you. She turned down all her other suitors, you know."

"Did you become friends when I wasn't looking?"

"Junior staff talks."

"About me?"

"Often."

"Did you defend me?"

"Sometimes."

A cloud passed over Hugo's face, both of us thinking about Hugo's darker corners. The drinking, gambling, keeping the *Rochester*'s secrets. I thought of these things, at least. Hugo did not dwell on them, the storm passing quickly, the sly upturn of his lips back, eyes staring without pretense at me, my hair, my body, my lips. I knew what he wanted.

I wanted it too.

But I wanted answers more.

"How do I know this is real?"

He cupped his hands around mine, insistent but gentle. "I know that I'm terrible at feelings. I've not had the best role models. I thought for a long time I was better alone, but then you came along. And I don't think that anymore."

I leaned into him, tipping my face up to his, taking the initiative this time. The kiss was likely chaste by Hugo's standards, but it was the first that I controlled—the pressure, the length, where hands went. And it was bliss.

"I'm glad you came back," Hugo husked against my lips as we pulled apart. Our foreheads touched, limbs hopelessly entangled.

"I promised."

"Didn't mean you would."

I kissed him again. "I always keep my promises."

"I'm figuring that out." He pulled away, breaking our embrace, leaving me cold. "I'll see you tomorrow."

"Why tomorrow?"

"Because I can't stay any longer tonight without doing something I'd regret."

The admission practically burned my cheeks off, but it certainly did its job. I said good night, though I was sure I wouldn't fall asleep anytime soon. I was wide awake, my brain running through a dozen scenarios of what the next day, then weeks, months, years might bring, my body thrumming from the adrenaline. When I did finally sleep, I dreamed of Hugo.

I floated through the next day, heart in constant threat of beating out of my chest. It was a feat not to burst into song in front of everyone, herald the news. Somebody loved me.

That somebody stubbornly stayed out of sight all day. I looked for him around corners, in the dining room, while I was teaching Jessa, like his declaration last night magically meant he'd change his routine. I was acting the fool, and I knew it. A fool for love.

I practically flew to the study after dinner, though just as I was about to lay my hand on the OPEN button, I hesitated. What if I walked inside to find the old Hugo? Mysterious and friendly, blowing hot and cold. With a deep breath, I went in, preparing myself for the worst.

Hugo turned from his spot in the middle of the room where he must have been pacing, a dopey grin overtaking his features. He bounded over to me, pulling me into a hug, which morphed into a kiss. We kissed our way backwards, an awkward tango over to Hugo's chair, where I ended up straddling his lap. After a minute or two, I finally managed to get a few words in edgewise.

"What happens now? Same as before, but with more kissing?"

Hugo took a break from exploring the expanse of my neck to look quizzically up at me. "Is that what you want?"

"To be a secret? Not really, no."

"Good. I wasn't planning on keeping you a secret anyhow."

"Oh, really? What kind of plans did you have in mind?" I teased.

"I'll show you." Nudging me off his lap and standing, he slid his fingers through mine, then tugged. "Come with me."

I tripped along behind him, following without protest, if a bit confused. Our destination was the bridge, where he deposited me before the bank of windows and screens with a breathless flourish.

"I want you to have this."

"I don't understand."

Hugo grabbed my hands in his. They were sweaty. He bit his lip, a rare nervous expression passing over his features. "Well, technically I want to *share* it. My ship. Captaining it. As my wife."

I stumbled back, hitting the edge of the captain's chair. "As your what?"

"My wife. I was hoping you'd marry me."

I gave it a second, letting the concept roll around my brain. No, it still sounded wrong.

"You look surprised. I figured it would be obvious."

It most definitely was not. "Why?"

"Well, I was going to marry Bianca."

"She had a ship; it was an arrangement," I protested. "I

have nothing to offer, none of the traditional barters for inter-ship marriages."

"You don't have to offer me anything. A marriage to Bianca would have been a trade deal, one I'd long thought I had no control over. But now I see I have other choices. Better choices. I don't want to marry you because it's a good business arrangement. You're my equal, Stella. All you have to bring is yourself. I love you."

"Say that again," I practically whispered.

"I love you," he obliged, but I shook my head.

"No, the other thing," I insisted.

"What?" Hugo replied with genuine confusion.

"That I'm your equal." It was like music, the crescendo to a symphony. It was something I'd felt, many times before, but to hear it from him?

"You're my equal," Hugo repeated.

Magic.

"Then I will marry you," I said.

This time, when we kissed, I let him try the tongue thing again. And it wasn't half bad.

Breakfast was crowded, every seat at the table occupied for once—me, Xiao, Poole, Orion, Jessa, Hanada, Albert, and the surprise additions of Sergei and Hugo. Hugo was at the head of the table, while I sat to his immediate left; not my usual spot, but he'd insisted I sit close so he could hold my hand under the table. We blinked around the table at one another,

Xiao darting eyes to Hugo, then to me, back to Hugo; Hugo staring intently at Hanada; and everyone unfamiliar with my favorite shuttle captain throwing confused glances his way.

"Sergei, are you extending your stay?" I finally asked.

"*Da*, I need some rest, and Iris was kind enough to find me a bed."

I caught Xiao blushing, which made my own cheeks heat. Seemed more than one of us had found romance on board. Hugo saw that as his in.

"Well, I have good news." He paused for effect. My heart thumped so violently in my chest, it threatened to burst out and flop onto the table. "Stella and I are getting married."

Hanada barked a laugh, while Poole sputtered her coffee and Jessa broke into a whoop.

"No more Bianca! Yes!"

Orion, Albert, and Sergei offered hearty congratulations. Xiao just stared, mouth set in a firm line.

"Do you really think that's wise, sir?" She addressed Hugo, avoiding my gaze. My stomach twisted. Hanada piled on.

"Seriously. I mean, you've known each other, what, three months?"

"Four," Hugo corrected tightly.

Had it been? My sense of time was warped. It felt like a year, but Hanada's estimation felt closer to accurate. Three months wasn't a very long time. Or four.

"You're only nineteen, and she's not even eighteen," Xiao kept on.

"My birthday is next month," I offered uselessly.

Hugo squared his shoulders and set his mouth in a hard line. "Age is no matter. I've been captain since I was fourteen. I can make my own decisions."

"You know my objection. My concern." Xiao's reply was clipped.

I shoved a piece of bacon into my mouth, focusing on the crunch of it under my teeth, the bright, salty flavor as it washed over my tongue. Anything to keep from agonizing. Was it that I wasn't good enough for him? That I couldn't offer a ship for scrap like the Ingrams could? Worst of all, Hugo didn't say anything else. Didn't defend me, or himself. He simply got up and left the table. Left me. I stared at my plate to avoid the gazes of everyone remaining. The rush of air at my back and the sound of the door opening once, twice more after Hugo's departure made it clear there'd been an exodus.

Then I felt a hand on my shoulder. It squeezed, the pressure reassuring. "I'm happy for you." It was Orion, who leaned close and kept his voice low. "Don't listen to them. We should all be so lucky, to find someone to love on a ship this small. That's fate right there."

I looked up to see him leaving, and took stock of the other absences. Xiao, Sergei, Albert, and Poole were gone, leaving me with two people for whom I had opposite feelings.

"I'm glad you'll be my sister."

I swiveled my chair around to meet Jessa's open arms, pulling her into a hug. She was right; we would be family. I held her tighter, glad to have another ally, even if she was eleven.

Hanada leaned back in her chair, arms crossed over her

274

chest, clearly playing the long game. Reluctantly I sent Jessa down to her quarters, promising I'd come down in a bit so we could talk more. Hanada would track me down eventually to say her piece, so I might as well face it now. The morning couldn't get worse.

"I understand where you're coming from, you know," she started. "Getting swept up in a ship romance. It's stupid. But understandable.

"Ten years ago, I was just like you. Eighteen, from a succession of cold ships with no affection, landed here on the *Rochester* and thrown into the company of a brooding Fairfax." Hanada was never without some dramatic pretense, yet this was an earnest admission, I could tell, for her. "Phillip was... everything."

"Wait, Hugo's *dad*?"

"Of course," she snapped. Then her fury quickly ebbed as she fell back into her story. "I was his lab assistant. Hired because his son, who would surely follow in his footsteps, was not old enough. We learned all the basic scientific techniques and theory aboard the *Marie Curie*, but Phillip pushed scientific boundaries. Invented new life out of nothing..." She trailed off. Took a sip of tea. Regrouped. "Science is pure. Love is messy. I don't regret it. But I should."

"What's your point, Hanada?" I was out of patience. She appeared impressed.

"You'll need that bite if you stay. But you can still leave. It's fortuitous the shuttle captain is still here."

"His name is Sergei, and I'm not leaving. Are you actually

going to tell me what your problem is, or are you going to keep throwing vagaries at me?"

"It's not my place to tell you anything." She made for the door, but left me with a parting shot. "You should have a frank conversation with your fiancé about what's going on on this ship."

I found distraction in an afternoon of movies with Jessa, who was all too happy to skip lessons for the day. After an uneventful dinner—it seemed everyone decided to eat in their quarters except for Jessa and me—I paced before Hugo's study door, rehearsing what I wanted to say. After five minutes, I still didn't have an eloquent solution.

"Frex," I cursed.

The door slid open, revealing Hugo and a curiously quirked eyebrow.

"Cursing before you've even talked to me. That's bad." He gestured for me to come in and had a drink in my hand before I could protest. This was becoming a bad habit.

"I should have come and found you after this morning. I'm sorry." Hugo sat in his normal chair, and I in mine. We had a routine, like a proper couple. I felt a temporary surge of warmth in my stomach, briefly assuaging my nerves.

"I figured you needed to cool down. That you would want to be alone."

Hugo cringed. "I hate that you think my default is to be alone."

"Isn't it?"

"Yes, but you're the exception."

I felt a brief stab of doubt, the onslaught of feeling setting me off-kilter. Hugo had gone from coy to devoted in the space of a few weeks. How could I know he wouldn't change again a few weeks later?

But I had a feeling my concerns—that Hugo's feelings were not real, that I may have accepted his proposal hastily—were not the same concerns Xiao and Hanada had. Those were still dangling in the air, like a sword above my head.

"I feel like you're not telling me something," I said. "I've thought that for a while, but never said anything, and after this morning… Hanada said some concerning things to me."

"Mari has her own issues when it comes to me."

"What do you mean?"

Hugo seemed to weigh his words carefully. "Mari has her own reasons to dissuade you. I wouldn't listen."

"And what about Xiao? She seems perfectly reasonable, and she, unlike Hanada, seemed to like me. Until now."

"Xiao thinks she's my mother," Hugo said darkly.

"I'm not good enough. Because I have no ship to barter."

"I told you that doesn't matter."

"To you, maybe."

"Stella," he said my name like a prayer, crossing the short space between us, pulling me up from my chair and into his arms, "you can't let them get to you. They have their reasons, but all that matters is I love you. Xiao will come around, I promise. And what Mari thinks doesn't matter."

But what about what *I* thought?

What *did* I think?

When I retired to my quarters for the night, I laid my head on the pillow and willed sleep to capture me quickly, so that I might wake up sooner, to a better, happier day.

My dreams kept me from a sound slumber. Their subjects were nebulous, the settings obscure, but there was something dark, something that pinned me down, sucked the breath from my lungs, tore me from sleep, gasping. The room was pitch-dark but for a single stream of light, dim. And the laugh. It reverberated down the corridor and made the hairs on my arm stand on end.

I jumped up, making for the door, feeling strange, but pushing it aside. I found the source of the light—my door had been left open. Something had been inside my room. My heart skittered against my rib cage as I poked my head into the corridor, which appeared empty. I patted myself down, from chest to knees, checking for damage.

"Lights on just a bit, Rori," I managed with a shaky voice, squinting at the light, meager as it was. My bed, the wardrobe—everything was fine. No fire. Except... there seemed to be something on my pillow. It was dark—was that blood? I crept closer.

It wasn't blood. My hands flew to my head, feeling with useless fingers for what was no longer there. My hair. Someone had cut it all off.

twenty-three

My feet carried me out to Hugo's room before my brain could second-guess it. I pounded on the door until my palms hurt, taking care not to glance in either direction down the corridor. I dared not stare into the black, for fear I might see something lurking in the shadows.

Finally, Hugo answered the door. "Stella, what is it?" he said, then caught sight of my appearance, eyes going wide. "What happened to your hair?"

"Someone broke into my room and cut it while I was sleeping. Just like someone broke into your room and set the bed on fire." My voice started small, then rose, all the mishaps and accidents flooding back, screaming in my mind. "Someone sabotaged the airlock. And attacked Mr. Mason." I pounded my fists against Hugo's chest, pushing him back a foot. "What are you hiding? Tell me!" On my next downswing, Hugo caught my wrists, holding me fast.

"Stella, I'm sorry." He pulled me into a tight embrace, and I could feel him grasp at the remains of my hair with his fingers.

"Don't apologize," I said. "Tell me the truth. Who would do this? And why?"

Hugo peered down at me, eyes searching mine for something—forgiveness? "I never thought she'd hurt you."

"*Who?* Please tell me."

He pulled back, his look turned wild and cold, grabbed my hand, and tugged me into the corridor. "Follow me."

I tripped along behind him, struggling to keep up. Hugo's strides were long and determined; he knew exactly where we were going. Soon enough, I did too. The elevator, normally locked against my use, took us up to Deck One at Hugo's command.

"Once you've seen what is upstairs, you may change your mind about me," he said as we lifted off. "I want you to know that it's okay. I wouldn't blame you."

His ominous words did nothing to calm my anxiety, which rose like the tide as we ascended. The doors dinged open to reveal a perfectly ordinary corridor, except that it dead-ended in a bulkhead with an extra-large door. Hugo's grip on my hand went tighter, his palm sweatier than before; I realized he wasn't fixed fast to me to keep me in his stride, but rather he needed the comfort of my touch. Whatever was behind that door terrified him.

Still, Hugo approached the bulkhead with measured speed, letting go of my hand to open the bio-lock. "Stand behind me," he commanded as the door slid open.

With that kind of warning, I expected something—or someone—to jump out at me, bearing claws. Instead, I found myself stepping into living quarters just like any others on board. Lights dimmed low with the same superfluous elegant features as Hugo's study—wood paneling, tapestries, furniture made of buttery leather—we stepped through the hatch door into a drawing-*cum*-dining space, where a figure dozed in a large, overstuffed lounge chair.

"Lieutenant Poole?"

Poole stirred, blinking first at Hugo, then at me. Her eyes went wide. "What is she doing here? And what happened to her hair?"

It was like the oxygen left the room; I half expected to be vented into space, my lungs burning, tears pricking at my eyes. I started to cry hot, stupid tears. It was only hair. Except it also wasn't. It was as if the world was collapsing out from under me.

"Where is your patient?" Hugo asked, to Poole's confused look.

"Asleep. Where else would she be?"

Hugo inclined his head toward me, to my hair. He flinched at my tears, which I was desperately trying to paw away, but soon my thin sleeve was soaked and my nose started to run too.

"Frex," Poole said, immediately sweeping into the next room. It was dark, but I could make out a bedroom. Then an earsplitting laugh. *The* laugh.

"That's the laugh I heard, over and over!" I moved behind Hugo, burying my face in his shoulder.

"I know," Hugo said darkly. "She thinks it's hilarious, what she does. She's not herself."

"Who?" I asked, peering around Hugo to see Lieutenant Poole frogmarching a figure toward us. The light revealed a woman, a mass of dark curls obscuring her features momentarily, until she violently shook her head, attempting to wrench free of Poole's grasp. And then I saw her eyes, and it was horrifically clear.

"Stella, meet my mother, Cassandra Fairfax," Hugo said, voice drained of all energy. I stepped out from behind him to get a better look, and immediately she went into a frenzy.

"Phillip, get away from her!" Cassandra screeched, nearly breaking out of Lieutenant Poole's grasp. "She's trying to steal you away!"

"She thinks I'm my father," Hugo explained sadly.

"I thought she killed your father," I asked Hugo under my breath, afraid Cassandra would hear me, but she was wholly distracted by Poole, who'd wrestled her into a firm hug and was whispering something into her ear. Cassandra fought against her, attempting to break free.

"She did," Hugo said sadly. "But she doesn't remember sometimes."

"Hugo, I need help," Lieutenant Poole said, grabbing firm hold of Cassandra's arm and leading her over to a chair about ten feet from where Hugo and I now sat. He leaped up, grabbing something white and stiff from a hook on the wall and joining her.

"I'm going to put you in your dress and go fetch you

something nice to help you sleep," Poole said. Only instead of a frock, she and Hugo fit her, gently but firmly, into a coarse white coat that restricted the movement of Cassandra's arms and stuck her fast to the back of the chair. Poole's role on board suddenly snapped into focus. She was a caretaker. No wonder I rarely saw her, and when I did, she was making off with double portions of food. Her affection for her charge was clear; she tucked a strand of wild hair behind her ear and kissed her on the forehead.

"What's wrong with her, exactly?"

"Psychosis," Lieutenant Poole said. "Brought on by an experimental drug unwisely administered without understanding potential side effects." Her distaste was clear.

"He didn't know," Hugo bit back. "He thought it would help, with her panic attacks…"

"He should have known. He was the fancy scientist. She trusted him."

"Nobody knew it would do this to her," Hugo argued, though the fight had clearly gone out of him. He slunk against the pillows and worried his lower lip with his teeth.

"She's the one who tried to kill you?" I asked. "Twice?"

"Since you've been here," he confirmed. "And once before you came. Now that I'm older, I look too much like him. She gets confused."

"And you're hiding her here," I said, putting all the pieces together as I spoke. "Only you, Lieutenant Poole, Officer Hanada, and Officer Xiao know." Now Xiao's ominous comments about our engagement made sense, plus a lot more. "And it's why Mason was here."

Hugo nodded. I didn't need to say the rest out loud. His mother had been a comms officer, which was how she'd hacked the biolock systems on our doors, known how to sabotage the oxygen in the airlock. And she'd attacked me—cut off my hair—because Hugo had said he liked it wild, tumbling down my shoulders, and she thought he was her husband.

There it was—the *Rochester*'s big secret. Hugo's big secret.

"I'll get the sedative from Hanada." Lieutenant Poole stood, lumbering for the exit, leaving Hugo and me to awkward silence broken by the occasional whimper from Cassandra.

"I don't like to drug her," Hugo said once Poole was gone, though he did not look at me, or at his mother. He stared straight ahead at the opposite wall, where I followed his gaze to find an old family portrait. "Most of the time, we can talk her down. She flits in and out of the worst of it. But sometimes medication is essential."

"Like when the Ingrams were visiting," I supplied. It explained why there'd been absolutely no incidents that entire time. Hugo nodded.

"Though Mason meddled enough to draw her out of her stupor." His derision was clear. Something was wrong with the Mason story, but I couldn't put my finger on it. "She doesn't mean to cause harm," Hugo said, getting up and going over to his mother. He knelt in front of her, reaching up to brush her hair out of her face, like he'd done with me. Only this gesture wasn't at all romantic. Hugo was rendered a boy in front of her, and for her part, Cassandra blinked slowly down at him, face contorted with confusion.

"Why do you look so old?" she asked, her entire demeanor changed. "You're only fourteen, Hugo. You shouldn't be in such a hurry to age."

"I don't mean to, Mom," he said.

"Tell your father not to give you so much responsibility, then. Entangling you with that... *girl*, working on that godforsaken virus for the government." Her expression turned stormy, a shade of her previous hysteria. "It's wrong what he's doing. I asked Phillip to stop, but he wouldn't listen. Why won't he listen, Hugo?"

"I know, Mom." Hugo stroked her arm, squeezed her shoulder. "Dad doesn't mean to upset you. And I... I want you to meet a friend of mine." He turned to me, returning to the love seat, squeezing my hand. I felt panic grip my heart. "This is Stella Ainsley."

Cassandra squinted over at me, mouth set into a frown. "That's a dreadful haircut," she said, and I nearly choked on rage, with only Hugo's squeezing my hand to ground me. But she was clearly unwell, had no clue where—or when—she was. She thought Hugo was a young boy and her husband was still alive, and she did not recognize her own handiwork on me. "And where did you come from?"

"Stella came over from the *Stalwart*," Hugo explained calmly. Cassandra's expression darkened.

"That's one of the targets," she said. "You don't want to stay there."

"Stella and I are to be married." Hugo's response was hasty, as if he was trying to steer the conversation away from where

Cassandra wished to take it. The diversion worked. She looked me up and down, the frown seemingly permanent.

"She's not very pretty, is she? And what about Bianca, Hugo? You and she are already betrothed."

"I don't love Bianca; I love Stella," Hugo said, and my heart fluttered despite Cassandra's wound. "And I find her very pretty. And clever, and kind. You shouldn't say such awful things." I squeezed Hugo's hand in thanks and scooted closer.

"You're only fourteen; too young to marry."

"I'm nineteen, mom. You need to remember this time. Dad is gone, and I'm not him. I'm going to marry Stella. You can't try to hurt her again."

Cassandra began to violently shake her head back and forth, muttering a litany of noes. Her moment of lucidity passed; she gulped for air, cried, thrashed against her restraints. "He was a murderer!" she shrieked. "He made murderers of us all!"

Lieutenant Poole reappeared with Hanada in tow, the latter carrying a small metal case from which she extracted a syringe.

"Not her," Cassandra growled, pulling against her restraints. Hanada was uncharacteristically silent, no biting retort passing her lips. Indeed, she appeared contrite as she administered the dose.

"Don't you see she's trying to steal you away?" Cassandra pleaded with Hugo, who grabbed ahold of my hand, palm clammy, as if to anchor himself to me.

"Mom, please. I'm not Dad."

Cassandra was not convinced. She continued to shout accusations at us, the drug slow to take effect. Hugo's hand tensed in mine; he squeezed to the point that it started to hurt. I feared he'd come undone if we stayed much longer, so I took the initiative, dragging Hugo to his feet, out the door, back to the elevator. I had to take his right hand in mine, press it to the bio-lock as he stood numb, peering back in the direction of the screams. I pushed him into the elevator, hit the button for Deck Two, and nudged him gently along until we reached his study.

"Here, drink this," I commanded, pushing a glass of liquor into his hands. Hugo did not second-guess me, gulping down half the glass in one go. I took a sip myself, relishing the way the liquid burned down my throat, like bitter ashes.

"How are you feeling?" I asked once Hugo had finished the glass. He seemed less shaken. I, on the other hand, felt my pulse quicken, and sweat prickled on my brow.

"I should ask you the same thing."

"I'm fine. It's only hair." I made sure to reinstate my poker face and braced myself for the conversation to come. "What did your mother mean, Hugo? About your father working on a virus and the *Stalwart* being a target?"

Hugo's eyes flashed with surprise and an underlying panic. "She's not well. She doesn't know what she's talking about. You heard her. She thinks I'm my dad." He was hedging. He was *lying*. Tears burned in my eyes; I blinked them back, willing myself not to fall apart.

"Hugo, please tell me your family wasn't responsible for the Kebbler virus."

He looked away, to the window, as if the black expanse would absolve him. "I can't. Now you know."

"It killed so many children," I choked out, letting the tears slip freely down my cheeks.

"Now you know why my mother killed my father. You know all my secrets."

Not quite. "Mason came here to prove that your mother was still alive. That you disobeyed a fleet order of execution, right?" He nodded. "Then why did he leave? It was a month ago, and nothing's happened."

Hugo flinched.

"Something *has* happened?"

He grabbed my hands, grasped them so tightly, it hurt. Wild eyes burned into mine. "I didn't know. You must believe me. Mari's been doing off-the-books experimentation for years, concocting new and deadlier viruses. And Mason knew."

"I don't understand."

"Mason is from the Population and Control Department. Population control is his job. He came here for the virus…"

I extracted my hands from his and looked at Hugo, who looked like his father, a man who had doomed thousands to death not that many years ago.

"Hugo, what did you do?" I practically whispered.

"Everything wrong."

"So that's it?" I said, taking a step back, positioning myself closer to the door. "You just hand over a virus that will ravage the poor of the fleet? And I'm guessing you have a vaccine that will save the rich?"

No reply. Just waves of rage and guilt from the hunch of his shoulders, the way he refused to look at me.

"It's not too late. Just don't give Mason what he wants. We'll figure out another solution."

"It *is* too late," Hugo said to the crystal in his hand. "Mason already has what he needs."

twenty-four

His words were a lead weight in my stomach, and a shot of adrenaline to the heart.

I ran.

To my quarters, where the door was still open from the earlier assault, where I cordoned myself off to think. Mason had the virus, and I was sure the *Stalwart* was a target again. Everything made sense—other ships taking over food production gradually during the last several years. A safeguard in the event the *Stalwart* suffered a major catastrophe, whether that meant reentry to Earth or a deadly virus wiping out most of the population. I had to warn them, warn George, but Mason was likely still monitoring my communication. And besides, what good would warning them do? You can't hide from a virus, and running wasn't an option either. The *Stalwart* was a sitting duck.

I yawned despite the adrenaline, but a glance over at my bed, to the brown hair still on my pillow, soured any wish I had to sleep. Instead, I went into the bathroom.

"Rori, where can I find a pair of scissors on board?" I asked, determined to salvage my new look, distract myself from the horror gripping my heart. My broken heart. I just needed to even out some of the egregious pieces. Cassandra hadn't cut with an eye for symmetry.

"You can find scissors in the kitchen, Stella."

I stole away below deck, my feet bare to save me from making noise that might wake Albert, whose quarters were directly next door. The kitchen was dark, full of lumbering shapes that set my imagination running. Were I younger, I would have conjured up monsters from the shadowy bulk of a refrigerator unit.

"Lights on," I commanded, illuminating the room. And revealing a man crouched in the corner, fork poised before his lips. "Sergei!" I shrieked, a little more loudly than I liked. "What are you doing here? In the dark, no less!"

"Just having a little nosh," he said, his voice a higher pitch than usual. I narrowed my eyes, taking in a half-dressed state and a pair of slippers I recognized. Xiao's. Suspicions confirmed.

"It's good you're still here," I said. "I need you to take me away. Immediately."

"What about your wedded bliss?" His expression turned suspicious.

"That doesn't matter right now. I need to get to the

Stalwart as soon as possible." I spied a pair of scissors resting in a knife block and snatched them up. "And how are you with cutting hair?"

"Better than whoever got you started."

I didn't dignify his wry remark with a response, but handed them over. As Sergei snipped away, I talked myself into my new plan. He would take me to the *Stalwart,* where I could warn George, Jon, Jatinder. Then I'd have to go to the *Empire* for Charlotte. She'd be a target now as one of the poor of the ship, though maybe not if the *Empire* was smart enough to spare the tea farmers. Why sabotage their new bumper crop? The warnings might be futile, but they might not. Charlotte, at least, could likely quarantine herself in her quarters, avoid anyone who got sick.

"All set," Sergei said with one last snip of the scissors. "And if you'll give me an hour, we can depart. If you are sure."

"I'm sure," I said, taking the scissors and returning them to their rightful place. "I'll see you in the transport bay."

My new trunk proved invaluable, as, true to my intention, it fit all my worldly possessions. Seeing everything, every bit of clothing, my tabs, the ties for my hair, my old friend Earl Grey, packed neatly into one space made real my ultimate decision. I wasn't coming back. My happiness couldn't come at the expense of lives. I wouldn't condone murder just because I loved the murderer. I stole one last reminder of him, the only thing in my room that was not mine to take—

the triptych. I would write Jessa later, a letter to explain my sudden departure. I needed a few days to come up with some reasoning she might understand, a lie I could be happy with.

I retraced my steps from only three days before, but this time I made my way alone to the aft end of the ship with my trunk. There were no flirtations, no kind words or teasing, only the hollow sound of the ship in the early hours of the morning. But when I got to the transport bay, Hugo was there, blocking the way. My breath caught in my throat.

"You're leaving," he said, barely a question.

"Yes."

"Please don't go. Stay here; stay with me." Clammy hands grabbed mine, my trunk rocking back with a clunk onto its base. "Please." His tone was hushed, but his eyes were ablaze. I stumbled over the sadness, the desperation I found in them. My thoughts started tumbling over in my head: how many steps it was back to my room. How long it might take to unpack. The things I could live with.

But then there were all the things with which I could not live.

"No," I choked out, extracting my hands from his grip. "I'm sorry."

"I don't want to do this alone. Not anymore. Not again." Hugo's eyes shimmered, as if he were going to cry, but no tears fell. I managed no such strength, hot tears running down my cheeks, splashing salty onto my lips.

"That's what happens when you choose yourself over everyone else," I said, wiping angrily at my cheeks. "I can't. People are going to die. A lot of people."

"I know. If I could stop it, I would," he said. Finally, Hugo stepped aside, leaving the door unblocked, his expression resigned.

"Will I see you again?"

I hesitated; considered lying. But I didn't. "No."

"And you always keep your promises."

What else could I say? That I loved him? I'd miss him? The truth wasn't always the best remedy. I grabbed my trunk.

"Wait. Don't leave yet. Please. Wait here, just a minute. I have something for you."

I was tempted to ignore him, to steal away, hop on Sergei's ship and take off before he could stop us and give me some gift that might make me change my mind. Instead, I waited.

Hugo reappeared maybe five minutes later, a small, rigid black bag in hand. Something inside rattled, like glass clinking against glass. "It's the last of the vaccine supply," Hugo said, forcing the handle into my hand. He moved to touch me, maybe squeeze my shoulder, but instead I felt a sharp pinch in my forearm.

"Ow!" I looked down to see a needle sticking out of my arm, Hugo just finishing up depressing the handle.

"I'm sorry; I had to," he said. "If I didn't make you take it, you'd give yours up for someone else." He withdrew the needle and stepped back with a sad smile tugging at his lips. "That's the kind of person you are."

I hated him for his love. It ripped its claws into my chest and squeezed the breath from my body, drawing my tears once more. This time, there was no dignity in my crying. I could hardly control my breath, nor the anguished sounds that spilled from my lips. Hugo pulled me into a crushing hug, and I let him, my pride in a puddle on the floor. He buried his face in my hair, and I burrowed into the warmth of his chest. I inhaled a shaky breath, holding the air in my lungs, as if to capture him in my sense memory, exactly like this. Solid and warm and mine. I tilted my chin up, let him kiss me. Just once. Chaste. Then I pulled away.

"Hugo, I—" I tripped over what I wanted to say, words that would ultimately both soothe and hurt him. After a deep breath, I opted for the harsh truth. "You did it to protect your mother, right? Giving Mason what he wanted. I understand how much you love her, but she wouldn't want this, Hugo. Her life for everyone else's. You have to know that. It's not worth the price."

His jaw was tight, eyes now guarded. He offered a terse nod, and that was it. It was over.

I gave my own nod and turned around, marching with resolute steps toward Sergei's shuttle. Every step was heavy, as if someone had turned the gravity up a few notches, some part of me reluctant to leave. I released a deep sigh as Sergei took my trunk and the vaccines from my hands.

"Is he still there?"

"*Da.*"

"How does he look?"

I received no reply, but his face said it all. Not good. I refused to glance back, lest I lose my nerve.

"Let's get out of here," I said, pausing on the steps up to the shuttle just briefly to hear the *whoosh* of the outer bay door as it shuttered. I pictured Hugo behind the glass, watching me disappear through the metal door. Saying something to the glass, something I would never hear but would appreciate anyway. Something more satisfying than that nod.

I strapped myself into the passenger seat, vaccine bag clutched tight against my breast. And as the shuttle took off and I felt us rocket away from the *Rochester* for the last time, I knew in my heart that Hugo hadn't stayed at the window to watch. He'd left. The space behind the window was cold and empty and gray, like the space where my heart used to be. I closed my eyes and allowed myself to weep.

"Stella, we have problem." It had been nearly two days, and I'd spent much of them knocked out, Sergei's sleeping draft my only solace. I chose to numb myself from the reality of my situation; if I thought too much about it, regret washed over me like lead.

Sergei frowned down at his tab screen, then up at me. "*Stalwart* does not simply receive visitors. You have no visa."

"What?" I climbed into the copilot seat and read the message for myself. The *Stalwart* was suspicious of who we were, why Sergei was requesting permission to land only temporarily. I'd planned to be on board for only a day or so; then we'd head to the *Empire*. Now everything was in jeopardy. I looked out the window at Earth and the fleet, slowly but surely growing larger in our view. I'd need to figure this out fast; we were almost there.

"Tell the *Stalwart* I'm coming back. Permanently," I said, making a split-second decision. "They'll take me back if I can work."

"Do you really think that wise?" Sergei's expression made clear that he did not. "We can go to *Empire* instead. Much nicer place to be stuck."

I shook my head. "I can't abandon my friends there. The children. They need these vaccines."

"And what about your cousin?"

"You can still go to the *Empire*, can't you? Just to make a delivery of the vaccine?" Sergei nodded. "Then that's what we'll do. I'll go to the *Stalwart,* and you to the *Empire*. And then..." And then I'd be back on the *Stalwart* forever. Or at least until all their systems failed and we plummeted back to Earth. Whichever came first. "Let me vaccinate you now."

"Like I told you before, I am fine. I've survived many viruses before this one. Do not waste your precious vaccine on me."

"Humor me, Sergei," I said. I was not getting off this ship without giving him a dose. "And confirm with the *Stalwart* I can come back. Permanently."

Sergei looked at me as if I were mad, and perhaps I was. The right thing to do often sounded crazy.

Either the *Stalwart* had changed or I had; I suspected the latter. The transport bay seemed smaller than last I'd seen it; the finishing duller. The *Stalwart* had never been a nice ship, but the *Rochester* had clearly spoiled me, as I found myself wrinkling my nose in distaste at features that never irked me before. And perhaps the heavy sense of foreboding I felt was because I would never again leave the hulking carcass of this ship.

Sergei helped me unload my trunk, patting me on the back as his version of a farewell hug. "Good luck. I am sad to have carried you away from the *Rochester* under such circumstances."

"Just take care of yourself. And give my best to Charlotte. Tell her I'll write her once I'm settled."

"Stella Ainsley and her tiny hands are back!"

I groaned, and Sergei quirked a brow. "You know him?" He pointed to Jatinder, who was making his way over with an obnoxious grin on his face.

"Unfortunately," I said. "Bye, Sergei." I gave him a real hug, then waved him off before turning to face Jatinder. "They sent you to collect me?"

"I volunteered. Kind of. It was either me or Karlson, and from the level of excitement he displayed at your being back, I thought I should step up before he could."

Good old Jatinder, I thought, fighting a smile. Being back wouldn't be all bad. "So, you didn't replace me, then?"

"Oh, we did." Jatinder continued his chivalrous streak, hauling up my trunk. "But there's sickness going around, and you're already qualified, so the captain gave us clearance to bring you back on the team."

My stomach turned. The virus was already here, and the

Stalwart was hedging its bets. We turned right outside the transport bay, so I guessed he was taking me to my quarters first.

"Listen, Jatinder, about that—" I started, clutching the vaccine bag tight. But we were interrupted before I could explain any further.

"Stella!"

My reaction was visceral, the sound of George's voice eroding my world-weary armor in a flash second—my heart pounded, my body went warm, and hastily I handed off the vaccine bag to Jatinder so George could crush me in a hug. He was enthusiastic, lifting me straight off the ground. I was flooded with happiness, but of a different character than before. Any romantic feelings I'd had for George were gone, leaving only pure, platonic love. I grasped him tighter.

"I can't believe you're back," he said, then set me down and gave me a proper once-over, starting and ending back up at my hair. "What happened?"

"I cut it," I said, purposely a bit obtuse. While my hair certainly garnered notice, George was most likely inquiring as to the reason for my return. He would have to wait for it. "Did Jon tell you about the message thing? I didn't want you to think I just stopped writing."

He swept me into another hug. "I was worried. But now you're here!"

Jatinder took me down to Ward Z, orange lights flickering intermittently as ever before, but he turned right where I expected left. We weren't heading to my old quarters. "They gave your room to the newbie. Sorry about that." Jatinder stopped in front of a door labeled Z053. He waved a code card in front of the lock, opening the door to reveal my new home. "It's still a single, but it's basically a closet," Jatinder said, handing me the card. "Welcome back!"

I stepped inside, commanding "Lights on" out of reflex, but nothing happened. Right; I wasn't on the *Rochester* anymore. Jatinder scoffed, turning on the light manually.

Indeed, it was a closet, only wide enough for a bed and one foot of maneuvering space, the bed lofted above a set of drawers, and there was no window. I sighed, surveying my space as Jatinder rolled my trunk up next to the dresser; if I moved an inch, I'd bump into him.

"See you later, kid."

He left before I could think to ask him the time, which, without Rori in my ear, I was hard-pressed to find unless I went up to the main decks. I settled into my new space, folding most of my dresses into the bottom dresser drawer, where they'd surely collect dust. I balanced the triptych on top so that I might see it every morning and night as I crawled in and out of bed, Hugo and Jessa reminding me of all I left behind. And I placed the bag of vaccines next to it, to remember why I left.

twenty-five

To: Ocampo, Karmina (*Lady Liberty*)
From: Clarke, Joy (*Stalwart*)
Subject: URGENT news tip

Dear Ms. Ocampo,

Despite the moniker of this account, I am not Joy Clarke. I am a resident of the *Stalwart*, but I am unable to communicate with you via my own account because it is being monitored by the government. They don't want me to disclose what I am about to tell you.

There is a new virus that has been manufactured and released into the fleet. Several people on board my ship are already sick. Like the Kebbler virus seven years ago, this one has been purposely released by our government in order to cull the population and conserve resources.

In short: our government is murdering us. In particular, poor and less "useful" ships will be the target. The rich will receive vaccinations to ensure they are spared.

Please get this story out so people can protect themselves. An immediate quarantine is needed, especially on the poorest ships, in order to save lives. People should stop traveling and accepting shipments immediately.

Thank you,
Hermione Granger

To: Clarke, Joy (*Stalwart*)
From: Ocampo, Karmina (*Lady Liberty*)
Subject: URGENT news tip

Dear Ms. "Granger,"

Love the name, from one of my favorite classics. I'll give you the benefit of the doubt and assume this isn't a prank, though I'll admit that was my first thought. Nonetheless, I am a journalist, not a stenographer, and thus am unable to print your tale without being able to corroborate these "facts" myself.

I'm going to need more information: a name, somewhere I can look. A cursory search of fleet medical reports shows no such outbreak at present. Crying Kebbler is very serious business. I'll give you one more chance to give me something I can go off. After that, I'm blocking you.

Best Regards,
Karmina Ocampo
Fleet Tribune

To: Ocampo, Karmina (*Lady Liberty*)
From: Clarke, Joy (*Stalwart*)
Subject: URGENT news tip

Try Tucker Mason. Population and Control Department.
Hermione

To: Clarke, Joy (*Stalwart*)
From: Ocampo, Karmina (*Lady Liberty*)
Subject: Need more information

Hermione, I need more to go on. I looked up Mason but
didn't find anything related to a virus. If I'm going to talk to
him, I need to be able to ask him the right questions, press for
the right information. I feel like you're withholding something
from me. You seem to know a lot about this alleged virus...

To: Ocampo, Karmina (*Lady Liberty*)
From: Clarke, Joy (*Stalwart*)
Subject: Need more information

Check the travel logs to the *Olympus* within the last month.
Look for the name Hanada. Would have had medical cargo
with her. Check traffic from there to other ships, particularly
ones like the *Empire*. They would be distributing vaccines to
the wealthy and skipping everyone else. The virus presents
like a mild flu for the first few days, then escalates. They burn
up with fever, and their organs just... liquefy.

We have seventeen cases here already. Three have died.
We're running out of time, so please investigate and go to
print as soon as you can! The *Stalwart* has already enacted
quarantine procedures. Everyone else needs to, too.

EXCLUSIVE: SENIOR CABINET MEMBER MAY HAVE BROUGHT DEADLY VIRUS INTO FLEET

by Karmina Ocampo

Fleet Tribune Staff

A top government official could be linked to the outbreak of a new virus that so far has claimed the lives of twenty-eight citizens fleetwide and infected scores of others, according to top-secret documents obtained by the *Fleet Tribune*.

Cargo records show that Secretary of Resources Joseph Ralphs had viral samples delivered to him on *Olympus* approximately one week before cases started to appear on the fleet. The *Tribune* also found Ralphs received a similarly marked shipment within a week of the onset of the Kebbler outbreak, which decimated the population by 20 percent nearly seven years ago. A source with knowledge of both deliveries says the viruses were part of a government-wide plan to control the fleet's burgeoning population and conserve resources.

Director of Population and Control Tucker Mason denied these claims but said Ralphs has been suspended immediately, pending an investigation. Mason also called for an immediate fleetwide quarantine.

The records indicate that both shipments came from *Rochester* virologist Mari Hanada.

LADY LIBERTY OWNER HUGO FAIRFAX IMPLICATED IN HANADA OUTBREAK

by Karmina Ocampo

Fleet Tribune Staff

In the last week since the *Fleet Tribune* broke the story, more than six hundred cases of Hanada virus have been reported fleetwide, with a death count now approaching sixty. The virus is named for Mari Hanada, who created the strain on board the private ship *Rochester*. Sources indicate Hugo Fairfax is more involved in the scandal than previously thought.

Fairfax became captain of the *Rochester* at fourteen after his mother, Cassandra, murdered his father, Phillip, the virologist who created the Kebbler virus. Hugo Fairfax brokered the deal with former Secretary Ralphs to provide the new viral strain, as well as vaccines for the fleet elite.

Both Hanada and Fairfax are being sought on charges of conspiracy to commit murder. The search for them is ongoing.

To: Mason, Tucker (*Olympus*)
From: Ainsley, Stella (*Stalwart*)
Subject: Hi

I don't know what you did to get the *Tribune* to spin your lies, but your reprieve won't last long. Ocampo may have blocked my messages, but I'll find someone else to listen. I'll find proof, and I will take you down.

You won't get away with this.

To: Technical Support (*Olympus*)
From: Mason, Tucker (*Olympus*)
Subject: Communications embargo

Please block all nonessential communication traffic to and from the *Stalwart* until the end of quarantine. Hold all incoming and outgoing messages for my review.

twenty-six

My back burned under the solar array, intense heat soaking into the black fabric that was meant to keep me cool but was in fact powerless against the onslaught. But the crops took precedence over my comfort, and food needed light to grow. Beside me, issued a groan and a curse. Jon stood from his crouch, stretching tall until his back gave a resounding crack. At least I wasn't alone in my misery.

"Please tell me the quarantine is ending soon," I said, sighing as I stood for the first time in an hour. We threw down our tools and retreated to a patch of shade below a steel walkway. George and Joy followed our lead.

"My uncle says two more weeks, at least. There are still a few dozen cases in sick bay, and he doesn't want to risk it."

"If I'd known being vaccinated meant I'd have to take field duty, I would have passed," Joy said, inspecting her hopelessly dirt-caked fingernails.

We all glared at her with varying levels of contempt, George's being the gentlest. People were dying. *Stalwart* had lost fewer than we might have without my warnings—and limited supply of vaccines—but any loss was too much. The death count was hovering just under one hundred, one-sixth of the ship's population gone in the month the virus had raged through the fleet. Better than a third, like it had been last time. But it was one hundred too many.

Feelings flooded me, blurring my vision. My knees buckled, but Jon caught me, saved me from getting a face full of dirt.

"You're overheated," he said, but I knew it was my guilt. I suffered its pangs daily, that I couldn't save everyone. That I had dared to choose who to save, like I was God. It turned my stomach.

"Drink this." He shoved a water pouch into my hands, followed by an apple from a nearby barrel. "Think of it as a frex-you apple."

Our consolation prize for being stuck in a quarantine after our government tried to murder us: we kept all our harvest for ourselves now.

I turned at the sound of a juicy crunch. George was availing himself of a snack as well. Soon we were all chomping on apples, counting down until we had to get back out into the fields. Our shift was another two hours.

"We need to mobilize as soon as the quarantine ends," Jon said, getting keyed up like he always did. "The *Stalwart*'s built-in reentry pod can only safely carry two hundred down to Earth, so we need to find another ship and go down in smaller groups. Maybe the media would help."

"Are you going to use my account to leak information again?" Joy did not sound pleased, and she looked scared. We'd had to use her messaging account to get the word to the press about the virus, as she was the only one not being monitored. She worried the *Olympus* would retaliate against her. I figured they'd already tried to kill us once. Why worry?

Perhaps I had become a bit jaded.

"Don't worry, hon, we won't make you do that again," George reassured her, much to Jon's consternation.

"You can't promise that," he said. "We may all have to do things we don't want to, if we're going to save ourselves."

"Maybe I don't want to go down to some frozen planet to die!" Joy stomped away, George following to comfort her.

"You should go easy on her," I said. "She's not a natural rebel."

"Neither were you, until more recently." Jon nudged my shoulder playfully. It was strange to think he'd become my closest friend since my return. George just wasn't the same, now that he was George-and-Joy.

"Yeah, well, I went through some stuff."

Was *still* going through some stuff, technically. Every day I thought of Hugo, about the horrible things I read in the news before they cut the *Stalwart*'s communications. My heart ached and my blood boiled, longing and fury warring for dominance. I couldn't decide whether I hated Hugo. At least once a day, I certainly did. But the rest of the time...

"You ever going to tell me exactly what went down?" Jon asked.

"Nope."

"Fair enough."

"I am worried about the crew of the *Rochester*," I said finally. "After everything that happened, with Hugo—I mean, Captain Fairfax—and Hanada being dragged through the press... I know they don't owe me a response, but still. Not one of them has replied, even the crew members who liked me." That not even Jessa had replied to my apology letter hurt, even though she owed me nothing. My letter was full of pretty lies, anyway.

"Maybe the *Olympus* intercepted them and they didn't go through?"

"Why do that? I didn't write anything of substance. Just inanities. 'How are you doing? Hope you're okay. Sorry I left.'"

"You were responsible for telling the whole fleet that their government was trying to murder them. Well, some of them," he corrected, like the scope of the murder plot mattered. "A lot of people lost their jobs. More than one ship is seriously considering deorbiting, taking their resources with them. Blocking your messages is the least they could do to hurt you."

"Maybe."

Or maybe everyone on the *Rochester* hated me.

"Look, if it makes you feel better, I'll ask my uncle to look into it. They haven't revoked his network access. Yet."

"Thanks. I appreciate it."

There was a high-pitched *pop*. Then darkness.

"Frexing power outage." I felt the rush of air as Jon jumped to his feet. "I'll go see what the damage is."

I screwed my eyes shut, counted to ten, then opened them, finally able to make out some dark shapes in the black. I got to my feet. "Shouldn't I go with you?"

"That's what apprentices are for. You should take it easy today."

Right. It was my birthday. I'd forgotten.

"Oh, wait for me at dinner. I have a surprise for you."

Jon must have had eyes like a cat, because he jogged off, unfazed by the darkness. I, on the other hand, had to feel my way carefully along the edge of the fields to find the metal stairway up to the exit.

"George? Joy?" I called out, but got no reply. I sat at the top of the stairs, savoring the solitude.

I was eighteen. Now officially an adult, though I'd carried the burden of adulthood for some time. Adults had to make terrible decisions with no good outcomes, all the responsibility falling on their shoulders. And the blame.

Still, I should try to enjoy the day. George was surprising me with a cake at dinner. Joy was terrible at keeping secrets.

With the new bounty, there was enough apple cake for everyone on our dinner shift, making me the new best friend of approximately one hundred people. It was fortuitous the cake had been baked before the power outage, which took a good two hours to fix and meant dinner was mostly crudités.

At least it was fresh. I'd pulled these carrots from the soil with my own hands. They gave a satisfying crunch as I bit into them.

"I'm done, Stella." Arden pushed her tab across the table to me. School was canceled for the duration of quarantine, but I did mini-lessons for her and a few other cleared children at mealtimes. I reviewed her writing assignment between bites, getting the distinct feeling I was being watched. I looked up to find her eyes big and glued to me.

"Are you going to get married?"

Her question was like a shock of cold water. I hadn't told anyone about Hugo. That I had been, if briefly, engaged.

"Why do you ask that?"

"Because you're eighteen now. Isn't that what happens?"

"Not for everyone."

"Oh." She seemed disappointed.

"Arden?" I pried, gesturing for her to elaborate.

"It's just, if you were looking to get married, I thought you might marry my dad. So we could be family."

My heart ached. She reminded me so much of Jessa.

"I'm sure your dad is still grieving for your mom, right?" She nodded. "We can be like family, just without the marriage part, if that's okay."

Arden nodded vigorously. "I'm so glad you came back. I missed you."

I smiled, but it was bittersweet. Jessa had wanted to be my family too. And I'd walked out on her. I shoved cake into my mouth and chewed with purpose, a distraction so I wouldn't cry.

"Maybe you could marry him." She pointed behind me, and I turned to look. It was Jon, looking freshly showered and finely dressed. To my horror, I felt my heart speed up just a bit. But I didn't have any real *feelings* for him. He just looked kind of good. Damp blond hair curled around his ears, and he grinned when he saw me, bounding over.

"Hey! Happy birthday. I hope you saved me a piece of cake."

I pushed a spare slice over to my right as he took the seat beside me. To my chagrin, he smelled good, like fresh-cut oats.

"You showered." I stated the obvious.

"Yep. Skipped my water rations yesterday so I could shower tonight."

"Special occasion?"

He stared at me expectantly.

"My birthday?" I felt my whole body flush. This was so not what I needed. Jon was unabashed.

"I'll eat quickly so we can get to your surprise."

True to his word, ten minutes later, he left me struggling to keep up with him as he ran ahead, up two flights of stairs and aft. The double doors *whoosh*ed open to reveal the observation deck in all its glory: wall-to-wall windows in a room it took two minutes to walk the length of, even at a brisk pace. And it was empty.

"There's no one else here," I stated the obvious.

"I guess so," he said, failing completely to feign surprise. At my look, he fessed up. "I, um, called in some favors."

I made my way to the windows. They offered the best view of Earth and the rest of the ships trailing behind us. I couldn't decide which view I preferred. The endless expanse of space I could view from my bedroom window aboard the *Rochester,* conversely terrifying and wonderful, a reminder of how small I was, and how infinite everything else. Or this, a tableau of life, circling, waiting for the opportunity to set foot on solid ground again. Ground that might be deadly white, the air cold enough to stop your heart. I squinted down at the surface below, looking for patterns that might inspire hope. Jon spotted them first.

"See there?" He pointed, off to the far left. The most promising bit, the one that had been driving his Earthbound campaign for years, was coming into view. There, the relentless white receded, revealing a small mass of browns, blues, and greens in the middle. "That's where we think the *Crusader* went down. It holds the most promise for sustaining life."

"Do we know which continent it is?"

"Nope," he said, grinning down at the planet, a little too gleeful for my liking. He gazed down like it was his pet, and they were about to embark on a grand adventure together.

"We have no idea if Earth can support life," I said. "If the ice age isn't over, we'll have no chance."

"We have no chance up here," he countered. "Eventually the life-support systems will fail beyond repair. Human beings have survived ice ages on Earth before."

"Not many of them."

"We've been up here for the worst of it. We'll be fine.

Anyway, I have more surprises." He jogged off into a dark corner, leaving me confused, returning a moment later with a dark glass bottle and two glasses. "I got this from Jatinder and stashed it up here." Jon poured a generous measure into each glass, handing one to me. My first instinct was to decline. I'd gotten stupid drunk on the stuff the night of the memorial. But it was my birthday, dammit.

"Happy birthday," he said as we clinked glasses. Then the music started.

At first I thought I was imagining it, that I had gotten unceremoniously drunk faster than anticipated. Then I saw the tab in Jon's hand, realizing he'd turned it on. It was light, something classical played on a piano. Romantic.

"Is this a date?" I asked, wary.

"No?"

"Jon." My tone carried a warning.

"I thought about inviting George, but figured he would insist on bringing Joy, and that would be uncomfortable. It's just you and me, and I was hoping… but it doesn't have to be if you don't want it to be."

I groaned. "Jon, I just… can't."

"I know. I had hoped what happened on the *Rochester* wasn't too serious, but clearly it was."

"What are you talking about?" I couldn't keep the panic from creeping into my voice.

"Just, with what you said. And what you didn't say. I figured you and Hugo Fairfax must have had something. I read between the lines."

I turned away, watched the ships in the near distance dance in orbit. "Does anyone else know?"

"No. Most people don't pay as much attention to you as I do."

That earned him a look, which I realized might have been his intention. He got me to turn around. *Jerk.*

"Do you want to tell me what happened?"

"No?" I slumped against the glass. Slid down until I was sitting, the chill at my back oddly comforting. Jon sat too, sure to keep a few feet of distance. At this point, I trusted Jon more than anyone. An odd sensation.

"I was engaged," I said finally. "To Hugo." An invisible weight lifted from my shoulders. Someone else knew my secret now.

"And you left. Because of the virus?"

I nodded. Jon didn't say anything at first, his silence sparking my worst fears. Finally, he nodded and said the two words I hadn't known I needed to hear: "I understand." And then, barely missing a beat: "Now, do you want to search for constellations or play 'guess the continent'?"

I smiled, thankful not to have to hash it out in excruciating detail. "How about a little of both?" Following his lead, I searched the skies for familiar patterns and proceeded to make the most of my birthday.

twenty-seven

Quarantine ended a week later with little fanfare. Everyone was exhausted, or mourning, and eager to get back to our pre-sickness duties without fuss. I would not miss the heat at my back, the soreness of my muscles from repetitive action. Field duty was not for me. The *Stalwart* returned to its normal rhythms, and I to mine, but with one major difference. Captain Karlson permitted me to teach as my primary occupation on board; no more regular engineering shifts for me. And the residents became more and more enamored of the idea of going down to Earth. Never mind that Jon and his uncle still hadn't figured out how we'd safely get there. But everyone had pretty much accepted that we had to. The fleet had written us off.

"Will we die if we go down there?" Arden brought the day's lesson to a dead halt. Twenty blanched faces with big, curious eyes zeroed in on me.

"No," I said, more firmly than I believed. They were too young to know the risks, the statistical analysis the crew had been doing, gauging our odds. "It may be cold, but we'll be fine."

"My mom said we'll freeze up instantly," Jefferson said.

"No one can say that for sure." I sighed. "Every day that passes, the Earth gets warmer. And we're not going down right away. Don't worry. Now, on to today's chapter!"

I pulled up my tablet and opened up where we'd left off. This was our new routine: Earth classics Monday, Wednesday, and Friday; art on Tuesdays and Thursdays. I loved seeing the kids' eyes light up as we read books they'd never even imagined, my cache taken from the *Rochester* archives coming in handy.

I asked Jefferson to read, a small punishment for terrifying us all, but then of course he read like a pro. He beamed when I complimented him, and I forgot my annoyance. They were good kids, and I was lucky to be teaching them.

I was happy here. I was. But it felt hollow. My life was a facsimile of the one I'd had on board the *Rochester*. Similar rhythms, but the wrong beats. A missing melody.

Missing him.

When our hour was up, they begged me to keep reading, but I knew Destiny was waiting in the wings with their Farming Essentials lesson. Reading was a pleasure, an escape, but Destiny's class was practical. Soon, these kids would be responsible for growing and sustaining the food that could mean the difference between life and death for our colony on Earth. I caught myself and my pronoun use. *Our.* I was already, at least subconsciously, committed to going with Jon and everyone else. Still, a part of me hesitated, yearned to use my family connections on board the *Empire* to stay. In my heart, I knew what held me back, but I was loath to admit it.

If I left behind the stars, I was leaving behind Hugo.

I was in the middle of chastising myself for the thought, for my stupidity at thinking about him, reasoning with myself how maybe I could go back, when I ran headlong into Jon in the hallway.

"I was looking for you. Someone is here to see you." When I looked around in confusion, he continued. "No, like, someone came here to see you. In a ship. They're in the cargo bay. Says they're your driver."

I didn't bother with pleasantries; I simply took off, rushing to the cargo bay as quick as my feet would allow until my suspicion was confirmed.

"Stella, my girl," Sergei greeted me with a bone-crushing, back-slapping hug, which I received gladly.

"I'm so glad you're safe," I said into the scratchy fabric of his jacket, then pulled away to search his face. I found it looking almost... guilty? "What are you doing here?"

"I'm here to deliver a message."

To my great surprise, he extracted from his coat a set of folded papers. It was so terribly antiquated, I laughed.

"Is that a letter?" He nodded, solemn despite my smile, which promptly slid from my lips. "Is everything okay?"

He hesitated, then nodded. "*Da*, I am sure everything is fine. I promised to deliver this into your hands as soon as quarantine ended, so here I am." Finally, he handed me the sheaf of papers. "I have some business to attend to with the captain, so I will leave you to read." Sergei grabbed my shoulder and gave it a squeeze before he left.

I unfolded the bundle, and after reading the first few lines, I felt like I might pass out. It was from Hugo.

"Stella, you okay?" Jon jogged up to me, and hastily I slapped the papers together and shoved them into a pocket.

"You followed me down here." I stated the obvious.

"Yeah, I was worried… Did I see you putting paper into your pocket?" He craned his neck, eyeing the exact pocket where the letter was hiding.

"You are too nosy for your own good, Jonathan Karlson," I chastised him with a sigh, extracting the papers. "It's a letter. From Hugo."

Jon allowed himself only momentary surprise. Then he nodded, as if I'd relayed a mission command. "You'll want to find somewhere private to read it, then."

I could have kissed him, were the circumstances different. Jon was a good one.

Gratefully, I let him usher me away to a nearby storage room he unlocked with a private key code.

"I'll leave you to, um…" he trailed off, offering a smile before he closed the door, leaving me to read Hugo's letter among great towering piles of discarded tools and supply crates. I sat on the cleanest-looking box I could find, running shaking fingers over the crisp paper before unfolding it with a rushed exhale of breath.

My dearest Stella,

I am sure I am the last person you want to hear from, but I hope you will read on and give me a chance to explain. This was the soonest I could get word to you without Mason, or anyone else, being able to read it, and what I have to say is just for you. I can live with everyone else believing me a murderer, but not you. Your opinion of me is paramount.

I swear to you I did not know what Mari was doing, that she was developing new viruses in her spare time for fun. She's always been an odd sort of person, and wholly dedicated to science and advancement of human knowledge, but I never imagined she'd inherited my father's penchant for coaxing deadly viruses into existence. Unlike him, however, I don't believe she intended to cause harm. Mason threatened her parents, just as he threatened mine.

Yet does it matter what the intention was, the circumstances of Mari handing the strain over, of my not trying harder to stop it? We're implicated in a terrible thing, and no reasoning can make up for all those who died.

But I need you to know that I wasn't aware of what had happened until after Mari had handed over the virus and the vaccines to Mason. I don't know why I let you believe that I had done it. Perhaps a part of me didn't believe that I deserved your love. It happened on my ship, and I am my father's son. It was good that you got away from me, really. You could never be free of my family's curse if you stayed.

Please be happy. Find someone else to love. And above all, stay away from Mason. He remains dangerous.

I love you, always.

Hugo

My heart thumped in my chest, there was a rushing in my ears, and desperately I read the letter over again and again. My poor Hugo. Mason had concocted a story for the press, tying him to Hanada by association. And even her... of course Mason had blackmailed her. He was vile.

I paced the storage room, thoughts tumbling over and over as if caught in a metal drum. I had to find Hugo. What an enormous, idiotic martyr he was being. I didn't care if he was in hiding; I had to go to him. Sergei delivered the letter, so he had to know where Hugo was.

I burst out of the room, startling Jon, who was waiting in the corridor. "You have to take me to your uncle. He's meeting with Sergei. I must speak with him."

Jon didn't need to be told twice. I nipped at his heels, his stride much longer than mine, up two levels and all the way forward, to a part of the ship I'd never been permitted to see before. Jon gave an unmarked door a special knock and, upon hearing a gruff reply, opened it for me.

"Sergei!" I rushed in, catching the captain off-guard. He rose from his desk, and I was struck, like always, by his uncanny resemblance to his nephew, but pushed the thought aside to focus on my mission. I barreled up to Sergei, who was sitting across from the captain. "Where is Hugo? He gave you the letter. Please, you have to take me to him."

"Whoa, whoa, hold on just a moment, Miss Ainsley," Captain Karlson said, sitting back down. "What is the meaning of this?"

I didn't have time to explain it to him, nor did I want to.

"Sergei," I repeated, more forcefully this time, ignoring the captain.

"Stella, it isn't safe to take you there," was all he said, his gaze steadily avoiding mine. I searched the captain's quarters, realizing they doubled as both an office and a living space, finally finding a second chair in a corner near the door. Placing it next to Sergei's, I sat, bringing us on the same level, so he couldn't miss me.

"So that means you know where he is. Quarantine is over, and I got the vaccine. I'll be fine."

"Miss Ainsley, I'm afraid you don't understand." This time the captain spoke. I was surprised to see him get up, walk over to a sideboard, and pour out a cup of steaming tea, which he brought over to me. "Drink that," he said lightly but firmly. Despite my furor, I did. I'd sincerely missed tea.

"There's a problem," the captain said after his own long draw of tea. "Sergei here just informed me that you are being charged with treason. The government wishes to extradite you to the *Olympus* for trial for leaking the news about the virus."

"What?" I said to a twin shout from outside the door,

muffled through the metal. Then the door cracked open, and Jon came rushing in.

"That is bullshit. She's not the one who sent it to the press." Jon defended me well, though we both knew it was a mere technicality that the messages had come from Joy's account. Jon and I had sent them. The captain knew it too.

"Stella was the only person to leave the *Rochester,* and shortly thereafter, the whole fleet knew about the virus and how it was being used. They're saying you incited panic, which is a treasonous act."

"I've been here for almost two months. Why did they wait to charge me?"

"I think they were hoping you wouldn't make it through," Captain Karlson replied.

"So you're sending me away?" I asked.

The captain frowned. "Of course not. They'll have to lay siege to this ship if they want you."

"This is why it's not safe for me to take you, Stella," Sergei chimed in. "The news is not yet public, but soon your face will be splashed across every feed in the fleet."

I digested this information, which gave new definition to the idea of being trapped. It also removed any choice I might have had in the matter—I was going down to Earth, as soon as we found a way. It was no longer safe for me anywhere on the fleet.

I would never see Hugo again.

No, that was unacceptable. I'd spent the last two months with my heart shattered into a million pieces, unable to reconcile my feelings with what I thought Hugo had done. I needed to go to him, now that I knew the truth.

"Then my window is short, isn't it? Until the news is public. Now is the only time you can take me to him. Sergei, is he close?"

He looked like he didn't want to tell me, but finally he acquiesced. "I came from the *Lady Liberty*. It's a short trip."

"I'll go with you," Jon jumped in excitedly. "It wouldn't be that hard to get a visa for someone who isn't Stella, and two of us going will lessen any suspicion. We can get you a cover identity."

"And what reason should I give for these two people to take a vacation aboard the *Lady Liberty*?" The captain was clearly skeptical.

"Jobs," Sergei said, the mischievous glint I was accustomed to seeing back in his eyes. "There are many postings to replace the dead." He paused briefly, out of respect, bowing his head.

"Yes, that's it." Jon clapped his hands together excitedly. "Say it's me and, I don't know, Joy taking an informational meeting with their engineering corps. And it'll give me a chance to ask around, try to find us a ship that can manage reentry. Kill two birds with one stone."

The captain nodded. "I have a contact I was hoping to meet with in person. I hadn't had time since the quarantine ended, but this would work."

I couldn't believe this was happening. "I'm ready to go."

"Tomorrow morning," the captain said. "I'll have the visas by then. You'll be on a twenty-four-hour countdown clock."

"Jane Elliot," Sergei greeted me the next morning with a nod as Jon and I stepped onto his shuttle. My alias was plain, but it would do. I was taking on the identity of one of our fieldworkers who had already been on a shortlist for a job interview.

The trip was short, pushing close to an hour only because we ended up in a holding pattern before we were permitted to dock. It gave me time to get the *Lady Liberty* in my sights, take her in, this famous ship that Hugo owned. She was wholly unlike any other vessel in the fleet, more space station than ship, multiple resident wings circling a central vertical column, capped on top by a domelike structure. We docked in the middle, where immediately the hustle and bustle of the packed American ship became apparent. The transport bay was full of ships, packages, and crew; beyond the doors came the echo of activity. No one paid us much mind, nor did anyone hear as I prompted Sergei and Jon to set the twenty-four-hour countdowns on the closed-circuit comms we'd borrowed from Captain Karlson. Then Jon and I left Sergei behind as we proceeded to customs screening.

Customs was quiet, unsurprisingly, given it was seven a.m., but the scarcity of people only meant the agent on duty paid extra care and attention to the two of us.

"You're twenty-eight," he said, looking down his nose at me and alternately scrutinizing the tab in front of him. The captain had altered Jane Elliot's travel file to bear my picture, but being no hacker, he left the rest of her files untouched. I sat, trying not to squirm, affecting my best calm and normal face, hoping the customs officer didn't look any further past my visa file. Or rather, Jane's visa file.

"I've always looked young," I answered. "Had to cut my hair short just so people would take me seriously." Hopefully Jon hadn't been lying about it making me look older. I was banking on it.

"And you're here about a job?" he continued, seeming no less skeptical than before.

"We both are," Jon chimed in. "I'm sure you've heard the *Stalwart* is on its last legs. We're not crazy enough to go down to Earth, but we can't just transfer to any other ship. We need to get hired."

The customs officer became engrossed in his tab unit, flicking and swiping his finger between documents, making a series of noncommittal sounds as he evaluated one piece of information against another. "You're twenty and interviewing with the engineering corps, and she's twenty-eight and looking for fieldwork?"

"The captain made special arrangements," Jon jumped in, smooth as ever. "I'm his nephew, and she…" He hesitated, clearly grasping for a good lie. "Well, she's pregnant, you see." I would have made an involuntary noise, but Jon grabbed my hand just in time and squeezed hard enough to stop me from reacting. "Please don't put that in your file, though. It's a very delicate situation, but I'm sure you can understand why our captain doesn't want to send some poor, defenseless baby down to that freezing deathtrap. A job transfer is her only hope."

Jon's histrionics worked, softening up our interrogator just enough. The firm line of his mouth wavered, and he looked at me with sympathy. "My partner and I are having a baby soon. I understand completely." Then he wrinkled his nose, made a few taps onto his tab screen, and let us go. As soon as we were clear, I punched Jon in the arm so hard, he hissed pain through his teeth.

"Pregnant? What on earth were you thinking? I obviously don't look pregnant."

He shrugged me off. "He'll just assume you're in the early stages. And moreover, I've just handed us a perfect backup story. Now if he wasn't convinced that you're twenty-eight, or indeed Jane Elliot at all, he'll just assume you're some poor, pregnant teenager who lied to save her unborn child. Instead of, you know, a revolutionary who's wanted for treason."

"I'm not a revolutionary," I grumbled as we made our way toward the central elevator bank. His logic for the double cover was annoyingly good. But now I was saddled with the knowledge that someone had found it one hundred percent convincing that I was currently with child.

The elevator arrived and we stepped inside, my eyes searching the buttons for my destination. Each residential level was named for a famous American, and my eyes scanned past Roosevelt, Lincoln, Hamilton to find my target: Gates Level, where the captain had confirmed Officer Xiao and the crew were. I moved to press the button, only to find

Jon's hand on my arm, stopping me. "We have to go to our interviews first. They're scheduled for eight." He pressed the button for the Roosevelt level.

"Seriously? We're going through with the whole ruse?" My whole body buzzed with anticipation for my reunion with Hugo.

"Of course. You'll still have plenty of time for your reunion." We zipped down, until the doors opened and Jon pointed me in a leftward direction. "We'll meet back here in an hour. Good luck!"

We ended up meeting up more like two hours later. My interview with what I came to find out was termed the Life and Sustenance Department took forever, first because the overly friendly interviewer insisted on talking about life aboard our respective ships, exchanging fleet trivia, and then because she was inordinately fascinated in all I had to share about soybeans. I spent nearly forty minutes mining my memory for everything I'd learned in school and doing my best not to make it obvious I hadn't tilled the soil in aid of soybean production in my life. She couldn't have been interested in apples or carrots? By the time I found Jon back at the elevator bank, I was exhausted.

"How did it go?" I asked.

"Nailed it." He punched the elevator button with gusto. "I saw no point in blowing the interview, even if it's just a cover."

This time, he let me choose the Gates Level and up, up, up we went, the ride feeling like forever. It was likely only about two, three minutes, but it demonstrated the scale of the *Lady Liberty*. We followed a sign that denoted one of six corridors, branching out from the elevator bank like spokes, as the one that would lead me to my quarry. After walking what felt like a long stretch down a white, glowing hallway, we came to a door marked Ward K. Unlike on the *Stalwart*, where wards simply labeled a corridor of rooms, on the *Lady Liberty*, each ward was a fully functioning microcosm, like a tiny city-state in space. When we pressed the door-release button and stepped inside, we found ourselves in the middle of a bustling town square, a central hub of stores, restaurants, and leisure destinations.

"By the moon, they have a bar!" Jon exclaimed with some wonder, and I had to grab him by the arm to stop him from charging off in search of a drink.

"And a library stand," I observed, eyeing the tab station with a pang of jealousy. It was so easy to get books, food, drink, entertainment here. All the luxuries of life in one place. No wonder Hugo had told me not to worry about the Ingrams ending up here. It was some consolation prize.

I did a turn, assessing where the residential wings would be, wondering how I was supposed to find Xiao. Sergei had just said Ward K, Gates Level, and nothing else. I caught sight of a wall-mounted tab screen behind us, its big blue letters blinking INFORMATION. A few taps brought up a map. The map led me to a resident index, and Xiao was the only name in the x listing, making her a quick find. Her quarters were down a corridor to our right. I practically took off at a sprint, not bothering to see if Jon was keeping up.

Every door had a bright tab screen with the inhabitants' names emblazoned on it, and they whipped past my peripheral vision like dancing candlelight, until I found the one that said XIAO. And FAIRFAX, CARMICHAEL, and POOLE. A shiver ran through me. I touched a finger to the tab screen, bringing up a screen of options, choosing the CALL ON THIS HOUSEHOLD button.

"You can go fast when you want to, despite those short legs." Jon finally caught up.

And then the door opened.

"Stella?" a voice shrieked, and then I found myself tackle-hugged with surprising force. Jessa hadn't changed one bit. "I'm so glad you found us! I have so much to tell you!" She grabbed me by the hand and practically dragged me inside. Their quarters were like those on board the *Empire,* where we walked straight into a living room. I could see the room branch off into two corridors, where presumably everyone's bedrooms were. The hair at the back of my neck prickled at the thought that Hugo was in one of those rooms.

"Is Xiao here?" I asked before Jessa could launch into a story. I would likely get a more cogent telling of how they'd ended up on the *Lady Liberty* from one of the adults. Jessa nodded, putting a finger to her ear and hailing Xiao on comms. A moment later, Xiao appeared, eyes going wide at the sight of me.

"I didn't think you'd actually come," she said by way of greeting, followed by a firm handshake—the equivalent of a warm hug, coming from Xiao. "It's good to see you, Stella, though I have to admit I was surprised to receive the hail from your *Stalwart* captain on your behalf."

"I was worried when I didn't hear from you. From any of you."

Xiao and I locked eyes, hers stormy, which then flicked over to Jessa. "Jessa, you should go to your room."

"Why? Because you're going to talk about *him?*" Jessa's tone was cutting, bitter. Beyond her years. I took it back. She wasn't exactly the girl I'd left. Jessa *had* changed. Now I was itching to know why.

"Uh, I'm just Stella's chaperone," Jon cut in like Jessa had been referring to him, making a total idiot of himself. He was trying to lighten a mood that wasn't lifting.

"Who are you?" Jessa narrowed her eyes at him.

"I'm from the *Stalwart*. Name's Jon. Karlson."

I couldn't believe it. He squirmed under her exacting gaze. Jon Karlson was being felled by an eleven-year-old.

"You eaten breakfast?" When Jon shook his head, Jessa inclined her head toward a door on the opposite wall. "Come on. Today there's soy bacon."

"Xiao, what happened?" I asked as soon as they were gone. She sat on the couch across from me and sighed.

"Things did not go well after you left." She paused, laughed to herself. "That's an understatement, actually."

"It's all my fault. If I hadn't leaked everything to the press—"

"No, Stella, don't feel guilty," she interrupted. "You did the right thing. No, the spiral started before that. As soon as you left."

"What do you mean?"

"I don't know how to tell you this. I suppose it's best to just... say it straight."

Her demeanor, her words rattled me; I braced myself for impact.

"Cassandra Fairfax is dead," she started. "She set her room on fire. Which I suppose is essentially the same thing."

"Did the fire damage the ship? Is that why you all moved here?"

"Not exactly," she said.

I heard a sound in the corridor behind me; a shuffling sound, then retreat. I whipped around but found only shadows. Hugo. It had to be.

"Can I see him?" I asked with my voice low enough that I wouldn't be overheard.

Xiao looked puzzled. She turned to look where I'd heard the noise. "Captain Fairfax isn't here, Stella. I think it's Lieutenant Poole who is hiding from you."

"But he's on the *Lady Liberty*, right? Sergei gave me his letter, and I came right away."

Xiao looked distinctly uncomfortable. She avoided my gaze. "No, Stella. Captain Fairfax, Hugo, he—well. He went down to Earth. He's gone."

twenty-eight

It was as if the ice covering Earth had hopped into the skies and gripped my heart. "Why would Hugo go down to Earth?"

"Well." Xiao lowered her voice. "Mason made him go. It was either exile to Earth or a public trial and a death sentence. Either way, Mason didn't want the full story getting out. The only reason the rest of us are living free is Hugo bargained for our protection in exchange for going. Jessa unfortunately is too young for the full truth, so she thinks he left her willingly."

A million questions ran through my head; I was panicked. Hugo could be dead. I could have been existing, breathing, running around the fleet this whole time, while Hugo was down on Earth, suffering, freezing, starving. "When did he go? How long ago? Was the *Rochester* even built for safe reentry?"

"We parted ways a week ago."

"And the ship?"

"Should have made it safely. She was better equipped than this vessel, at least."

"Have you heard from her? The ship, I mean. Gotten a ping, confirming he landed safely?"

Xiao looked at me like I was asking her if the moon was made of cheese. "There's no mechanism for that. And the captain made the decision last-minute enough that there was no time to reprogram Rori to do such a thing. To ping a system up here. She wasn't built for that."

"Why not?" My voice was thick, impending tears tightening my throat. "Do you at least know where he planned to land? The *Stalwart* is trying to find a ship, sending a party down. We can look for him."

"I don't, no. We've been in limbo up here. We can only guess. And hope."

"You were his First Officer! How could you not know?" I regretted my outburst as soon as I saw Xiao's reaction. Hurt, mixed with pity.

"Stella, I'm sorry. We're all upset and worried. There was no stopping him once he'd made up his mind."

I nodded, like I had accepted what she was telling me, though my blood thrummed through my veins, my mind grasping at straws for something they wouldn't have thought of; a way to contact Hugo. A way to save him.

Xiao started talking, but not to me. She seemed to be telling Jessa it was okay to come back into the living room. Talking over comms.

"You still have comms," I said. "Aren't those run through Rori?"

"No, but it's similar," Xiao said after ending the call. "The system on board the *Lady Liberty* is called Lori, but our comms are on a closed system—we can communicate only with each other."

LORI. Of course. "The two systems have to be related, given the name," I said. "Can they talk to each other?"

"We'd have to ask Orion," Xiao conceded. "He's on the bridge."

I was out of my seat before she finished speaking. "Jon! Get out here." He appeared within seconds, like he'd been waiting for my call. "Will you take us to him?" I asked Xiao.

She hesitated. "The captain is going to think we're way out of line, but yes, I will."

I was already at the door, challenging Xiao and Jon to keep up with me. Jon waited until we'd left Ward K behind before asking any questions.

"Why are we going to the bridge?"

Xiao pointedly sped up, moving ahead of us, ostensibly to call the elevator. I chose my words carefully.

"Hugo's not on the *Lady Liberty*. He went down to Earth. By himself."

Jon hissed air through his teeth. He got it. Going down to Earth alone was beyond dangerous.

"I'm hoping the AI on board the *Lady Liberty* can be networked to communicate with the one from the *Rochester*, since both were built by the same company. I need to figure out where he landed."

"You want to go after him." It wasn't a question.

"I have to," was all I said. We reached the elevator bank, joining Xiao. Jon didn't ask any other questions.

The ride was short, the Gates Level being just one down from the top. Xiao sweet-talked our way onto the bridge, using to her advantage the fact that Jessa now owned the *Lady Liberty*. I got a clearer picture of Xiao's role on board—she was acting as Jessa's guardian and proxy in managing Fairfax interests until Jessa came of age. I quickly located Orion and charged over to his station. I allowed brief greetings, a hug, before I launched into my directive.

"Do you think you could reprogram Lori to search for pings from Rori down on Earth?" I asked, keeping my voice low so the whole bridge wouldn't know our aims. Xiao and Jon stepped aside, creating a one-sided visual shield so Orion and I could talk and be less likely to draw notice.

Orion's eyes darted around, and then he leaned in closer to me. "You want me to hack into the AI?"

I nodded. "Like you did before. Hugo said you hacked into my drawing tablet."

"Not exactly," he said. "That was more like... I convinced Rori to do it for me. She's a sophisticated AI. You don't hack her."

"Okay, then convince Lori to search for Rori's pings."

He shook his head. "Lori is a different story. They have the same base programming, but at some point, the *Lady Liberty* reined her in. She has far less latitude, and to reprogram her would require serious skill."

"Can you do it?"

Orion squirmed, clearly uncomfortable. "Yes," he finally acquiesced, and quickly followed up: "But if I get caught, I'll be arrested. Likely charged with insurrection or mutiny."

"We won't let that happen," I reassured him, even though doing so was far beyond my means. I improvised. "Jessa owns the *Lady Liberty*. She can protect you. This is our only hope for finding Hugo alive." A ping sounded in my ear. It was my comm device reminding me that Jon and I had to return to the *Stalwart* in no more than eighteen hours. "The thing is, I need you to do it in the next eighteen hours."

"No way." Orion was emphatic. "A reprogramming hack like you're asking will take days, maybe even weeks. And that's if I forgo my normal job, and don't get caught."

"Can you... unleash her, then? Undo whatever limitation they put on her, then convince Lori to reprogram herself?"

He seemed to chew on that. "That might work, though if I'm caught, it'll be even worse than a simple reprogramming hack. If Lori evolves in the... wrong direction, she could kill everyone on board. A self-aware AI is not something to play around with."

"If she's anything like Rori, it'll be fine."

He didn't look convinced, but nonetheless he nodded. "I'll do my best. One question, though. Why eighteen hours?"

"Because she's wanted for treason and is here on a false visa," Jon said before I could, breaking the illusion that Orion and I were talking privately.

"We need to leave the bridge immediately," Xiao said.

One look at Xiao's expression, and I didn't have to be told

twice. I hugged Orion one last time, wishing him "Godspeed" before heading back to the elevators. Xiao held her tongue until one arrived, but then the gloves came off.

"How could you not have told me? You've taken an enormous risk coming here, Stella!"

"I had to come. Hugo had Sergei deliver a letter. He was saying goodbye." I swallowed hard and balled my hands into fists, digging my nails into the palms to stop tears from welling up. Xiao shot me a look full of pity, her anger having receded.

As we stepped into Ward K's hub, I was immediately accosted by a high-pitched squeal.

"Is that Stella Ainsley? It is!"

It was Bianca Ingram. Of course.

"Give me strength," I heard Xiao mutter under her breath, reminding me why I liked her so much. Any tension between us dissipated as we united in annoyance against Bianca. She flitted toward us, hands full of parcels, in a dress as exquisite as ever—blue with creamy chiffon accoutrements and needlessly impractical shoes, as always. Preity trailed behind her, barely suppressing a smile—her, I was genuinely pleased to see, and I threw her a small wave. Bianca handed off her packages and pulled me into an awkward hug.

"Good to see you." I put on my best smile, hoping to please her so that she wouldn't say my true name again, or loudly.

"What brings you here? I saw you weren't part of the *Rochester* party that moved here. I was told you went back to the *Stalwart*."

"I'm just visiting. With my friend, Jon."

Seeing only her beauty and knowing nothing of her personality, Jon enthusiastically offered his hand in introduction, along with his most flirtatious grin. To my surprise, Bianca did not sneer or look down her nose at him, despite his being from the *Stalwart* and being my friend clearly telegraphing his status. She blushed and gladly received his attentions.

"You must have dinner with us this evening, then. We can catch up. Xiao, you're welcome as well, though we've just seen you the other night. The more, the merrier."

Xiao politely declined, citing paperwork she needed to do, though I suspected her real entertainment for the evening would involve Sergei. I wasn't so lucky. Bianca wouldn't take no for an answer, and Jon was no help, enthusiastically receiving the invitation. I just had to keep up the charade for a couple of hours until Orion cracked Lori.

We reported to the Ingrams' quarters at five p.m.

"See that you don't get taken in," I warned Jon as we stood before their door, my finger poised over the tab screen to ring the bell. "They can be very charming, showy, but I assure you, they are all snakes."

Jon shrugged me off. "Bianca seems perfectly fine."

"Don't mistake beauty for goodness," I said, then pressed the tab button, and we waited. Lizzy opened the door, greeting me enthusiastically, then led us to the dining room. I introduced Jon as the nephew of the *Stalwart* captain, hoping to elevate his status enough that he might be treated with some respect, and it certainly seemed to impress Captain Ingram, who monopolized him in conversation for the first quarter of dinner.

This left me to Bianca and Lucy, who grilled me on my movements since we'd last seen one another. Then, thankfully, I was able to deflect the spotlight over to them with one well-asked question about their migration to the *Lady Liberty* and their feelings about their new home, which set the whole party off, enthusiastically comparing their old life to their new. The Ingram children seemed to have adjusted better than their parents; Bianca and Lucy loved the amenities—the endless parade of parties to attend, goods to procure—while Braxton didn't have to say a word for it to be clear that he enjoyed the unfettered access to both young women and booze. Justine was as sullen as ever, likely given the happiness of her husband. The captain disliked his lack of power on board, going on at length about how misguided it was for the *Lady Liberty* to discount his lifetime of experience. I bit my tongue, not pointing out to any of them how privileged they were to have been granted passage aboard this ship with no expectation that any of them would have to work.

Most pointedly, despite the reason for our acquaintance, no one mentioned the *Rochester,* or Hugo, or the monumental events that had happened on the fleet since we last saw one another. It was the elephant in the room. Once we'd eaten, I mentally prepared my excuses to leave. I didn't want to get pulled into any poker games, or worse, a musical evening, courtesy of the Ingram sisters. Bianca caught me off-guard with other plans.

"Now, Jon, you must stay and play games with Lucy, Braxton, and Justine—they love playing their settler game, but it bores me to tears. And Stella, I must steal you away for a walk."

She'd grabbed me by the arm and whisked me out into the corridor before I could protest. We headed in the direction of the hub, Bianca's arm linked in mine, uncomfortable given our height difference, but her grip was iron.

"Your friend Jon is lovely. Are you sweet on him?" she asked, drawing a snort of laughter from me.

"Definitely not," I said. "Though for some reason, he's, uh, sweet on me."

We took a turn left before the hub, down a narrow corridor, forcing our arms apart so we could walk single file.

"You don't give yourself enough credit. Why do you think it weird that he would like you?" Bianca's voice drifted back to me. Maybe it was because I couldn't see her face that I could dissociate from the fact that I was having a heart-to-heart with Bianca Ingram, but I gave her an honest reply.

"Because I am ordinary. My face is, at least. There is a beauty standard that I do not fit. My shape, my features, my behavior. No one was ever interested before. Not until—" I stopped myself before I could say his name. But Bianca was not stupid. We came to the end of the corridor and were met with the stars. It was a promenade with windows all along one side so we could see out into space. Now I could not escape the knowing quirk of her lips.

"Until Hugo," she completed my statement for me. Then she grabbed my arm again and pulled me back into formation. We began to stroll, the stars to our left side. "I was seethingly jealous of you, you know. I didn't get it at all. You're not as plain as you think, Stella; you're honestly quite pretty, but that wasn't it. I mean, you're a governess." Her tone dripped derisively, like always. "But I realized that that wasn't the point. Your status was irrelevant, and apparently mine was too. Hugo likes bold, and your flavor of it far more than mine. Give yourself more credit."

I was left speechless, unsure if I was being paid a compliment or an insult. Bianca didn't wait for my response anyhow.

"You know, if I'm honest, it all worked out for the better. I'm happy here. I'm no longer being trotted around the fleet like I'm some prize cow. It doesn't really matter who I marry at this point. It's nice."

"Did you love Hugo?" I dared to ask. She seemed to think about it a minute.

"Like a brother, I think," she finally said. "Though I like him more than I like Braxton, so there's that. I would have been happy married to him. But not as a consolation prize, so ultimately he made the right choice. I'm just surprised that you gave him up."

Ah, now we were getting to it. Bianca was fishing for gossip. I halted our stroll, wresting my arm from hers so I could face her. I needed to be able to read her expression, determine whether she meant to manipulate me. But I found her inquisitive eyes free of scheming, and I'd played enough poker with her to call her bluff. She wanted to know why I'd left him.

"At the time, I thought I had to," I said.

Bianca's expression darkened. She could hardly have missed the news. "I'm worried about him," she said. "He didn't come here with the rest of the crew, and no one will tell me where he's gone."

"That's why I came here," I admitted. "To find him."

"And did you?"

"No," I said. "He deorbited. By himself."

"That stupid idiot," Bianca said, leaning against one of the windows, suddenly weary. "He was always prone to dramatics." She let out a sigh. "So, what are we going to do?"

"We?"

"Yes, I imagine you have some sort of plan brewing, and I'm not going to sit idly by while my oldest friend dies. He saved my family. I owe him." Bianca obviously meant business. She crossed her arms over her chest and looked at me, clearly awaiting a full appraisal of my plans.

"Well, if I can find out where he landed, the plan is to go after him. The *Stalwart* is already planning a mission, but we don't have a ship."

She grabbed hold of my arm, this time to drag me back in the direction we'd come. "You can take the *Ingram*. She's just sitting in storage, of no use to anyone."

"No offense intended, but wasn't the whole point of your marrying Hugo that your ship was no longer in good working condition?"

"She had her issues, but should manage reentry perfectly well." We'd entered the narrow corridor again, her nonchalance echoing behind her, as if to reinforce her resolve. "I'll settle it with Father tonight, and you can take her in the morning. I'm assuming you have a pilot?"

I had Sergei, but no idea if he'd agree to pilot someone else's ship away from the *Lady Liberty*. Down to Earth. I'd figure it out later.

"Hey, Bianca, wait." We stopped outside the door to her quarters. I wanted to say something before we went inside and everything exploded in a flurry. "Thank you. You're unexpectedly… I don't know."

"Do go on," she said, eyebrow artfully quirked. "I have a feeling you might be heading toward a compliment."

"Just, thank you." I pulled her into a hug, a genuinely felt one this time. "You're more decent than I thought." She snorted into my hair, and we both laughed.

We had a ship, someone to pilot it back to the *Stalwart* (Xiao could be persuasive; Sergei stood no chance otherwise); we needed only Orion to come through with the coordinates for the *Rochester*. It was late in the night, my time allowed aboard the *Lady Liberty* rapidly counting down. Jon dozed on the couch, oblivious. Well, at least for the moment. I'd bent his ear for hours, obsessing over the possibilities of the day's outcomes, plans for our next steps, and on and on, before he gave up and drifted off. I couldn't sleep; I paced restlessly in the living room, waiting for Orion to come back with good news.

I checked the time. One in the morning. *Ticktock.*

At some point, against my better wishes, I fell asleep. I awoke to a pinging in my ears; one hour to our deadline. I shook Jon awake, even as he pawed at his ears to turn off the alarm.

"Jon, wake up," I ordered.

"Did he find it?" he mumbled, sitting up, rubbing at his eyes.

"No," I answered, attempting fruitlessly to keep the despair from my tone. "He's not back yet."

"We have to leave in an hour."

I nodded, mood grim.

We sat, side by side on the couch, and I stared at the door, willing Orion to appear. When he did, a micro tab stick held aloft between two fingers, I blinked slowly, sure I was imagining it. Then he spoke.

"I've done it," Orion said, stumbling as he came toward us. He was clearly exhausted. "I can't exactly tell you how, but Lori did as I asked, and she started talking to Rori. Who's operational, which means the *Rochester* safely landed and maintains her power source."

Relief, followed closely by an explosion of hope, flooded my body as I leaped up from the couch. I grabbed the tab stick, clutching it to my chest as if it were a holy relic. "The location is on here?"

"Lori is on there. At least, a piece of her is. You'll need her to interface with Rori in real time. Just plug that into your ship, and she should take over. She should also enable you to communicate with us once you land, let us know you're all right."

"Thanks, Orion," I said, pulling him into a hug. "We'll let you know when it's safe for you to come down and join us." Orion only shook his head at me.

"I prefer it up here, thank you very much. And, um, I'm kind of seeing someone. His name is Sebastian. I'd like to see where it's going before I do something drastic like crash-land on a planet."

His response dimmed my shine just a bit. "Then I'll never see you again?"

"You'll hear from me, if Lori Junior works the way I hope she will." He hugged me again. "Godspeed, Stella, and now I am going to go sleep for the next year."

I waved him goodbye, though I did not allow myself to expend too much sorrow on his behalf. I would be saying far too many permanent goodbyes in the near future, indeed in the next hour, than I could stand. I had to stay strong, or else I'd be useless on the journey ahead.

"Did he find him?" Xiao appeared, wrapping herself up in a dressing gown. I'd never seen her so casual, though her expression was nothing but serious.

I gave her the happy news, and once more implored her to come with us, to bring Jessa.

"We don't know if it's safe down there. And there would be

no one left to see to the Fairfax interests," Xiao said, repeating the excuse she had given earlier in the day. I didn't press her further; no, I fully intended to work my persuasive powers on Sergei instead. Thus, when it came time to say goodbye, I told myself it was not for all time. It made our parting easier. Nothing about my last moments with Jessa was easy, on the other hand. She cried, pleaded with me to stay. Xiao pulled Jessa back so I could leave, which I did with a heavy heart.

Sergei loaded us eagerly onto his shuttle, which he then flew around to the very bottom of the *Lady Liberty*, where the *Ingram* was docked. Using the remote password Captain Ingram had provided, we turned her on, docked Sergei's vessel inside, then flew her back to the *Stalwart*. While she was smaller than the *Rochester* and not half as splendid, the *Ingram* still ranked high on the list of ships I'd visited. We could fit a decent-sized landing party inside, at least a hundred people, and Sergei affirmed she was in fine working condition to make for a safe reentry. I used that as my opening as we came to a stop alongside the *Stalwart*. Jon would pilot the *Ingram* the short distance into the loading dock, while Sergei went off again with his own shuttle.

"Sergei, please come with us. Pilot her down."

He demurred. "I am trained in basic flight, keeping a ship airborne, not crashing her down."

"I don't think anyone on the fleet is actually trained in reentry," Jon jumped in. "Our plan was to wing it. For *me* to wing it, more specifically. You'd know more about captaining a ship than I would." I was glad to have him on my side.

"You could convince Xiao to come," I said. "Make a new life down there."

Sergei narrowed his eyes at me. "You're bold, Miss Ainsley."

"That's what they all tell me." I threw him a smile. "We need at least two days to prepare the landing party," I said. As Jon was buckling himself into the captain's chair, I pulled Sergei close, practically begged. "Please consider it. Talk to Xiao. She no longer has any ship to run, and you're a man of honor. You've seen the state of the fleet and what her government will do as it continues to decline. Make a new start with us."

"Enough talking now so you can get back to the *Stalwart*," he deflected. "But I'll think about it." With a half-smile, he headed aft to his shuttle, leaving me with a glimmer of hope.

We came to a stop inside the *Stalwart* loading bay to find it in complete darkness.

"The power must have gone out again," I said as we descended the stairs.

"None of her outside lights were out, though." Jon's tone was wary. He grabbed my hand as we walked careful steps toward the corridor.

"Stop right there," a voice rang out as the lights stormed back to life. I threw a hand over my eyes at the brightness, then squinted toward the voice until I could make out the face ten feet in front of us. Mason. Jon gripped my hand tighter, hurting my fingers.

"Thank you for your little trip, Miss Ainsley," Mason said.

"It gave us confirmation that you were alive, and cause to come and get you."

My eyes flicked to Captain Karlson, standing behind him, expression grim. Behind them were two massive figures wearing security jackets, one holding a pair of handcuffs.

"You can't take her!" Jon shouted, breaking away from me and going for Mason. His uncle intervened before he could do any damage.

"Indeed I can. She's been charged with treason for betraying government secrets and inducing panic."

"You're the one who should be charged with treason. You're a murderer," Jon spat.

"Yes, well, as I'm the one controlling the narrative, it will be Miss Ainsley who will serve as an example."

Their exchange became nothing but a roaring in my ears, noise filling the space between my thoughts. The sentence for treason was death. My vision went white at the edges, and the world tilted on its axis.

I was going to die.

twenty-nine

Jon caught me before I hit the ground. As he helped me back to my feet, I caught sight of Mason's smug expression, and suddenly I felt the full-body flush of embarrassment. Nearly fainting when I should be strong. Defiant. I would go bravely to my death—

A sob broke from my chest, tears springing to my eyes. *Or not.*

Jon crushed me in a hug, and I heard the captain's gruff voice behind me.

"She's only a child, Mr. Mason. You've kept your job by the skin of your teeth and achieved your purge of many hundreds. Leave her be."

"No," he said, simple as that. I felt the heat of the two security guards at my side, then the icy grip of a handcuff as it encircled my wrist. They tore me away from Jon, wrenching my arms behind my back to complete the metal link. Everything progressed in slow motion. Mason slunk over, and with a snap of his fingers, they began to haul me away. I dragged my feet to slow their progress back to their shuttle, until the bigger of the two security guards hauled me up in her arms like a baby. The last thing I saw before they threw me inside their transport was Jon whispering furiously to his uncle.

And that was it. The last I'd ever see of them. Heavy tears trailed down my cheeks as they strapped me into my chair. My wrists dug painfully into the small of my back, arm sockets aching from the strain. I willed my breath steady, my tears to slow and dry. I would not offer them anything else of myself. I waited for the engines to start, determined to depart with dignity.

We sat for five minutes before I sensed something was wrong.

"Frex you, Karlson!" I heard Mason shout from the cockpit. Then a quieter but no less aggressive, "Yes, of course I want somewhere to keep her while you frexing fix it. Better fix it quickly or I'll bring you up on charges of obstruction. And see to it that I have sufficiently fine quarters to sleep in."

"What's happening?" I dared ask the male security guard, who came back to unstrap me. He made reluctant eye contact, flinching. I couldn't miss the pity in his expression.

"Power's gone out in the airlocks, so we can't leave yet."

"Frex this trash bucket and its frexing malfunctions." Mason tore through the hold, past me, and down the stairs.

As the guard hauled me back into the dark transport bay and frogmarched me past the captain, his expression unreadable behind his flashlight beam, hope sparked in my stomach. Perhaps my friends had bought me time.

It came as some surprise that the *Stalwart* had a brig on board. By the looks of it, she hadn't seen company in many decades. The metal bled with water damage, and the door creaked out a protest as the male guard pried it open. Most antiquated of all, it locked with a physical key! No way my friends could hack their way in and get me out. I watched from my perch on a rusted metal bed as he pocketed it and took a seat across from me for first watch.

"Aren't you tired?" I asked. He glared.

"We're taking it in shifts."

"What's your name?"

More glaring. But he acquiesced. "Callum. Now be quiet."

"I'm Stella. I'm eighteen." I knew I was being manipulative, trying to appeal to his humanity. But fear rendered me shameless.

"Quiet." He turned away and would not look at me.

Silence became my companion over the next hours. I could not sleep on the moldy thing they called a mattress; I was too keyed up to sleep, even if it had been in pristine condition. The female guard came to relieve Callum, and I asked the time. They were on six-hour shifts. He handed off the key, and as she sat down, I caught a glimpse of a gun at her waist. It shot holes through the hope I'd been clinging to. If my friends attempted rescue, she wouldn't go down without a fight.

If they attempted rescue.

I was starting to feel stupid at the hope of it. That my friends in engineering had purposely shut power to the transport bay to buy me time. Time for what? They couldn't overpower the guard without someone getting hurt, and I couldn't bear anyone dying on my behalf. The lights flickered off, the guard's curse piercing the darkness. Another blackout to prove the happenstance of the first. The flicker of hope died out, and my body forced sleep upon me.

I awoke to light and the return of Callum. At least twelve hours gone, then.

"They still haven't fixed the landing bay?"

"Apparently not."

At least he answered me.

"It's good you're up." He moved to the door, picking up an ancient comms phone and speaking into it. "Send them down." He turned to me, returning to his chair. "Your captain lobbied on your behalf for a last kindness, given the delay."

Moments later, I understood the nature of this kindness. My friends had come to say goodbye. Jatinder, Navid, Joy, George, Jon, each one approached my cell in turn, apologies for my situation and regrets tumbling past their lips. I held it together for the first three, but I lost it with George, who started crying immediately, setting me off.

"I'm so mad at you, Stel. Doing the right thing and saving everyone at your own expense. I only just got you back."

"I didn't save everyone." I licked salty moisture from my lips.

"Damn near enough. Why did you have to go off-ship like that? You should have stayed here with me."

"I had to go," I said. "It's hard to explain…"

"Because you've been keeping things from me."

Was he really choosing now to fight with me?

"And it's my fault," he quickly said, cutting me off in my anger. "I pulled away. Got too wrapped up in my own stuff. I'm sorry."

"No, no, I'm glad you're happy. With Joy. Don't let go of that. Love is—" I cut myself off. There was nowhere to go that wouldn't feel saccharine and wholly unlike me. "I went because I had to find out what happened to Hugo. Fairfax. I love him."

And now I'd die for it. I choked on anguish, the tears welling up fresh.

"We'll tell the children you went down to Earth, so they don't know what happened," he said, grasping at my fingers through the bars. "I love you, Stella."

I nodded, pushing him away. "I love you, too. *Empire* orphans forever."

"*Empire* orphans forever."

And then he was gone. Jon handed me a handkerchief through the bars, a move so practical that I had to laugh.

"Thank you," I said, dabbing at my cheeks.

"I'll want that back, you know," he said.

"You're terrible at goodbyes."

"Yep. I'm too angry about all of this to be sentimental. You'll thank me later for not weighing you down with another emotional goodbye. See? You've already stopped crying."

"Would that there weren't bars between us right now. I'd hit you," I managed with a laugh. "But seriously," I brought my voice low, "give me a proper goodbye. One last moment of honesty. No jokes."

He met me close to the bars, kissing my fingers that gripped tight to the metal.

"You are extraordinary, Stella. We won't let them win. Remember that."

"Will you look for him? Down there? For me?"

"I will. Now dry your eyes." He left me wholly unsatisfied, waving on his way out the door.

"You should have ended with the ginger," Callum said. I glared at him until he turned away.

The guard shift changed once more, putting us at eighteen hours. I couldn't sleep. I kept staring at the door, expecting Mason to storm in at any minute, announcing that the airlock was fixed and we would be departing shortly. With each minute and hour that passed by, my insides knotted tighter. I blinked back images of Hugo, imagined so vividly that he was present, that I could hear his voice in my ear, whispering that he loved me.

I shook away the delusion, closing my eyes, thankful for the black. I could not manage any more of Hugo's face.

I jarred awake at a series of sharp snaps in my ear, blinking my eyes into focus to find the female guard hovering close. It was dark again, like there'd been another power cut.

"Get up. We have to go. Now."

She hauled me up by my arms, pulling me out of my cell. My body was seized with fear; I stumbled, but her firm grip of my arm kept me upright.

"Follow me closely, and keep up the pace," she said, creeping along the pitch-black corridor toward the stairs.

"Aren't you going to handcuff me?"

She stopped at the juncture between two passageways, shaking her head. "That'll slow us down. You're being rescued, if that's not clear."

My stomach swooped with tentative elation. "You're letting me go?" She wasn't even the nice guard. "I don't even know your name."

"Do you need to know my name for me to rescue you? Because we're wasting time."

"No, sorry, I—I'm just in shock." I hurried along after her, taking the stairs two at a time.

"It's Meredith," she said as we arrived breathless at the loading bay a few minutes later. All primary lighting was off, but a collection of emergency lamps lit the space in an eerie glow. I could see figures hustling bags into the *Ingram*'s hold. Two of them rushed up to us, voices hushed.

"Oh, thank God, Stel." George engulfed me in a hug, and

as soon as he released me, I smacked him in the shoulder.

"You let me blubber like that when you knew I was being rescued!"

"I didn't know," George said. "Jon only just told me."

"I wasn't sure it was going to work out," Jon said, nodding at Meredith. "Though I owe George here for tipping me off that Meredith looked familiar, from the orphan transport. Gave me an idea."

"Thanks for the spot," Meredith said. "And frex Mason." She jogged off to the *Ingram*.

"What is going on?" I rounded on Jon.

"We don't have much time. We're faking another blackout so Mason doesn't suspect." He grabbed me by the arm and steered me toward the ship. "I did what I could to move up the timeline, gathering a landing party. I managed to fill almost every seat. We're leaving for Earth, now. It's the only way to save you."

"Do we even have a pilot? I told Sergei forty-eight hours, not twenty-four. He won't know—"

"I got ahold of him," Jon interrupted. "He's here. And he brought some surprises for you. But that comes later. We have to get you on board."

Elation coursed through me, making me bounce on my toes. Everything would be okay. I grabbed George by the hand, tugging him along, but he made himself an anchor, stopping me short.

"I'm not going. I'm sorry."

"What do you mean? You have to go. We're all going..." My voice sounded small, like a child's.

"I just can't," he said. "Joy doesn't want to, and I love her. I just didn't know how to tell you. I'm only here to make sure you're all right." He kissed me softly on the cheek. I was sure he came away with salt on his lips from my tears. "Jon told me you may be able to communicate with us up here. So we'll talk. This isn't goodbye. Not really."

"Stella, come on." I felt myself being pulled away by Jon, but I didn't want to go. I was frozen to the spot, feet holding fast, and my other arm fixed by the hand still grasping George's.

"Don't forget me," I said.

"I won't—"

"STOP AT ONCE!"

Mason's rage filled the loading bay, the harsh backlight casting him in shadows like a hulking monster. Jon yanked my arm so hard now that he nearly wrenched it from its socket. I dropped George's hand, stumbling back.

"Stop NOW!" Mason screamed as he barreled toward me, coming into the light. "This is mutiny! You have all committed treason! And you—" He brandished a gun, pointing it straight at my chest. "You are not going anywhere. I am authorized to carry out your execution, and so I will."

Before I could register what the click I heard meant, George dove, and Jon pulled, and the shot rang out so loud and bright, I had to close my eyes, wincing against the ringing in my ears. I fell hard against the ground, shoulder and hip radiating sharp pain, George landing on top of me.

"Stella, are you okay?" Jon rushed over, trying to help me stand.

"I'm fine," I said, checking my body for wounds and finding none. "George, are you—"

He wasn't. His blood seeped black onto the floor beneath us; I could feel its wetness soaking through my clothes. He groaned, but did not speak.

"No, no, NO." I gasped for breath, pressing futile hands to his midsection to stem the flow of blood. He was barely conscious. It was a bull's-eye shot.

"Stella, we have to go." Jon tugged my arm, but I wrested it away. I had to help George. Seeing now that I was unharmed, Mason leveled his gun again.

"Oh, no, you don't—" Captain Karlson tackled Mason from the side, shouting at us to go.

Frantically I scooted back, Jon pulling me to my feet. My sobs punctuated the pounding of my feet as we ran the short stretch to the *Ingram*'s open hold, Jon climbing up inside, reaching down for my hand, pulling me in. I landed in a heap on the floor, clinging to the grooves, filling them with tears, as Jon manually shut the door, calling on comms for Sergei to leave immediately. The engines sprang to life, and we pulled away, leaving my oldest and truest friend dead in our wake.

thirty

"Stella?" Jon's voice was soft but firm in my ear. "You have to get up. There's only a few minutes to get strapped in for deorbit. You'll die if you stay in here."

"George is dead." I sobbed uselessly.

"Most likely, yes, and I'm sorry. But we can't lose you, too. Come on." He hauled me onto my feet, leading me into a labyrinth of trunks and crates that had been stacked on top of one another and strapped to the floor. I felt a kick as we departed the *Stalwart* and made our way into open space.

I tripped along behind Jon, until he led us to a room aft and below that looked as if its sole purpose was to provide safety and comfort during reentry. A few dozen faces swiveled at our entrance, peering up at us from high-backed seats into which they were strapped. I recognized a few from the *Stalwart*, but no one I was close to. Half the seats faced away, so I wouldn't get a full sense of the party until we landed. Jon had mentioned Sergei brought surprises. But I was full up on those for the moment.

Jon had to lead me like a child over to a free seat, and he took care to strap me in. We both ignored that he got blood on his hands and had to wipe it away on his trouser leg. He sat across from me, eyes creased with worry and fixed to my face. Sergei's voice came over the address system, light and airy like we were taking off for a pleasure cruise, surreal in my grief.

"Hello, everyone! Prepare for immediate departure, and strap in tight. From what I have learned about this model in the last five minutes, we are equipped with a parachute slowing system, so do not be alarmed should we experience a sudden jerk about halfway down."

A murmur of concern went through the room. "Don't worry, everyone. Sergei is the best pilot I know," Jon said, clearly the group leader and voice of authority. "Trust me, you want him piloting more than me."

"And if he hadn't shown up?" a woman sitting next to Jon asked. I realized with a start that it was the security guard, Meredith.

"You'd probably be praying harder," Jon joked.

And then, suddenly, I was pushed back in my seat by the gentle pressure of acceleration. My stomach did a little flip, and I had to shove down my grief and confusion, for there was only speed and pressure and the exhilarating terror of reentry. We moved faster, harder. We broke atmosphere, and the moment was reduced to nothing but heat, pressure, panic.

The extreme forces of gravity pressed my body down and back simultaneously, while the friction produced as we hit drag and slowed boiled the air. I sucked in gulps of hot, soupy air and kept my eyes closed; I didn't want to know if we encountered an issue, see the ship burn too bright, break apart. The darkness behind my eyelids provided my only solace, as the angry roar in my ears, the insistent weight of gravity, provided none.

Someone was screaming. Someone else crying. I heard Jon spit a curse, and just like that, I was laughing. It was, frankly, rather hilarious that we were hurtling to Earth with nothing but a thin layer of metal and faith in some heat-shielding between us and certain death. Anyway, the laughing kept me from full-scale panic.

Suddenly we jerked backwards, then slowed. The parachute had deployed. The worst of it was over. All around me, I heard sighs of relief, and the screaming finally stopped. I cracked open one eye, then the other, and didn't perceive anything on fire or ripped open. We seemed to coast forever; I tried counting the seconds, but the numbers crept too high, into more minutes than I wished to mark.

The ground came quickly and hard, our harnesses holding us fast as we bounced once, twice, the whole ship shuddering as it dragged to a stop. Then we were pitched into darkness. The heavy breathing of those around me, coupled with the thudding of my own heart, played a soundtrack to the dark. The song lasted only about a minute. As the lights flickered back on, the low glow of emergency lights hummed in rhythm as we snapped out of our harnesses.

We waited for the captain to check in on comms, but no such update came.

"I'm going to go check on Sergei," a familiar voice said, one row over. *Xiao!* I felt a flare of happiness, but tamped it down quickly. Now it was imperative to assess, and act. Reunion could come later. My grief would wait too.

"Jon, can you go with her? I'll get everyone out." I gave Jon an assuring nod. I could handle myself now.

We parted ways accordingly, a hundred weary souls following along behind me like ducklings. The *Ingram*'s emergency lights were red, casting everything in a sanguine tone, and as I keyed in the open-airlock command on the tab-screen console, it looked as if my hand was bathed in blood. Peering through the glass of the outer bay window, I watched the airlock doors open to reveal something I had never seen before: natural light. We'd gone from night up above to day down below.

We walked gingerly through the hold, careful not to trip over the few boxes that had come untethered during the flight, and I *tasted cold*. I stood on the precipice of the open hold door and the outside, closing my eyes, breathing in deeply. I tried to put my finger on it, but it was indescribable. I didn't yet have the vocabulary for this place.

There was a six- to eight-foot drop down to the ground—another foreign concept—but luckily one of the taller boys alighted first, then caught me when I jumped. The ground was solid but not too hard. There was a springiness to it; I crouched down and touched my fingers to it. The soil was damp. Not frozen. Several of the fieldworkers were making similar investigations, already getting to work in determining whether we could farm.

Despite the thinness of my clothes, I was not too chilled: the moisture-wicking fabric insulated my arms and legs; only my ears and nose were in want of something to cover them. And yet, the discomfort was only enough that I felt mild annoyance. A surge of joy provided momentary warmth: it was not too cold. This was survivable.

I walked away from the shadow of the *Ingram*, and the human ducklings who seemed to cling fast to my steps, until it no longer loomed large behind me. I ran my fingers through tall stalks of grass, doing a turn to survey my surroundings. On our right was a copse of trees, scraggly and thin, and all around was the unruly grass, alternately green with patches gold and brown. In the distance, mountains. I stood in awe of them, more magnificent than anything I'd ever imagined, let alone rendered with my stylus: towering like gods cloaked in purple and white.

"Stella!" Jon's voice rang through the field, and I whipped around to see him jogging toward me. "He's alive," he panted as he came to a stop, catching his breath.

"Who, Hugo? You found him?" Frantically I peered in the direction Jon had come from, back to the ship, expecting him to appear any moment.

"No, George," Jon corrected. "Lori connected with the *Stalwart* as soon as we landed. My uncle messaged right away."

"Really?" Everything slowed down, my senses blurring,

grief turning to happiness in an instant. "He's going to be okay?"

"My uncle says it's not pretty, but they were able to stop the bleeding. He's in surgery now."

I pulled Jon into a hug, crying happy tears into his shoulder. I heard him sniffle a few times too, the big old softy.

"Can you believe this place?" he asked as we pulled apart. Then he glanced down at me, brow furrowing. "You're covered in blood."

My eyes flicked down to my skirts, but it appeared black-on-black to me. Then I noticed my hands, stained dark red, nearly brown.

"Come on." He grabbed my hand, pulling me through the grass. The reeds thinned to reveal a stream of burbling, glistening, glorious water. I crouched on the bank, threading my fingers through the stream, watching the icy water wash away red. I pulled off my dress, thankful for my bodysuit, and drenched it in the gentle current.

Jon crouched upstream from me, drinking water from cupped hands, alternately swearing and grinning. "This place is incredible," he said.

"Please don't say 'I told you so.'" I rose from my crouch, wringing out my dress, but determining it too wet to wear again. It was strange without an overdress. I felt naked.

"All right, then, I'll just think it."

I didn't dignify his stupid joke with laughter. Jon frowned at me in my suit, a blush rising to my cheeks, and surprised me by removing his jacket.

"Here," he said, passing it to me. "I don't want you to be cold."

"What about you?" I considered refusing, but it was too tempting to cover up.

"It's a short walk back to the ship. I'll live."

It was good enough for me. As we neared the *Ingram*, I saw Xiao walking over to us, two coats and a tab screen in hand. She wasn't alone.

"Hello, Stella." Her voice struck ice through my veins. Hanada.

"What is *she* doing here?" I asked, balling my hands into fists at my side.

Xiao launched into peacemaker mode immediately. "Mari was in hiding with us on the *Lady Liberty*, and I promised Hugo that I would take care of her. Ensure her safety. So we brought her along."

"What about Jessa? You left her behind, but brought… *her?*"

"Jessa is safely and happily in the care of Orion and Grace," Xiao explained, laying a comforting hand on my arm, squeezing gently. "I made Orion promise to arrange for her to come down once we know it's safe." I felt myself begin to calm, just enough.

"What was reported in the news about me was not entirely accurate," Hanada piped up, tone infuriatingly even. "After your experiences with Mason, I'd think you'd be willing to give me the benefit of the doubt."

I knew exactly what had happened. Hugo had explained in his letter. Logically I understood the position she had been in, Mason blackmailing her, threatening harm to her family. But my heart hated her for creating the virus in the first place. Hugo was too forgiving.

But everyone was staring at me, waiting for an answer.

"You're going to have to explain to everyone here, and many of them won't forgive you, no matter how good your reasons were," I said. Hugo would want me to forgive Mari, so I'd have to work on it. And we were going to find him safe and alive. I had to believe that.

Xiao nodded, launching into mission mode. "Mari, get what medical supplies you can from the cargo bay and tend to Sergei. We'll be back soon."

She ran off, leaving me confused.

"Is Sergei okay?"

"He's mildly concussed, but Mari will tend to him. She can earn her keep with her medical know-how." She handed the tab unit to me. "Lori's tracking program is loaded on here, and it says the *Rochester* is a mile away."

I wasn't sure I had the strength to walk a mile, but she didn't have to tell me twice. I gave Jon back his jacket and pulled on the heavier coat Xiao brought, leaving my dress to dry by the ship. "You're not staying with Sergei?" I asked Xiao, whose reply was quick.

"Fussing over a man, who is mildly injured at that, is not in my wheelhouse. I'd rather find Hugo."

We took a brisk pace, Jon serving as navigator with the tab screen aloft in front of him, following a red dot. We trudged on, first five, then ten minutes, until we could see the

Rochester in the near distance. She'd come down where the grass turned to light forest, and as we came closer, my heart started to gallop. The *Rochester* had taken damage. The front was twisted and crumpled; it looked as if the bridge had been gutted. I broke into a run.

"Hugo?" I shouted, nearly tripping over my feet, as they were unused to sprinting across such terrain. I rounded on the ship, whose aft end had suffered its own dings, but nothing that looked catastrophic. The hold door had been forced open several feet, as if some creature had clawed it from its frame. But there were no monsters on Earth, as far as I was aware. Someone—Hugo?—must have used something large and metal to pry it open.

"Be careful." Jon came up behind me, surveying the scene. "I should go up first, then pull you in."

"I'm going to stay out here and keep guard," Xiao said. Much to my surprise, she pulled a stunner gun from her hip. I had not been part of the planning committee that discussed weaponry. What did we think we were going to find? Still, I did not protest, letting Jon make the precarious climb up to the hold door before I followed.

I squeezed through the hole into pitch-black space, sure I was in the transport bay, though it felt wholly unfamiliar to me in the dark, with one side crunched in and debris all around. I scrunched my eyes closed, willing them to adjust, then opened them, thankful to find my own feet represented in dark shades of gray. I could at least navigate myself, and after a scan, I had a beacon: the faintest glow of an electronic light. The ship was not dead.

"Be careful," Jon repeated his warning from behind as I made my way forward. "We know the front took damage. Who knows how bad it is back here?"

I grunted a response and made my way gingerly across the floor, my eyesight thankfully adjusting with every passing moment. There were spare parts strewn everywhere, but nothing that posed real risk. We arrived at the beacon, which turned out to be the backlit lock panel. It still recognized my bio scan.

"Fancy tech," Jon said under his breath as we moved into the outer bay, then past the next door into the ship herself.

"Wait until you meet Rori," I said, thankful to find the ship was running her night-cycle lighting, so we could find our way.

"Hello, Stella. It is nice to see you again," Rori, always listening, piped up. Jon nearly jumped to the ceiling.

"Rori!" I sighed with relief. "It's good to hear your voice."

"I'm glad you found me," she said. "I was surprised to meet Lori; she was rather rude, but I approved of her mission and allowed her to interface with me."

I nearly laughed at the idea of the two AIs having a conflict of personality. "Why are the emergency lights on, Rori? Do you not have full power?"

"My solar panels are drawing adequate power. Thank you for asking. The bulk of our power reserves is being directed to the medical bay and library. My protocol tells me their survival is paramount."

It made sense—you wouldn't want to lose the Library of Congress, and the medical bay held essential medicines and vaccines. I began to call out Hugo's name as we neared his quarters.

"Hugo is not here, Stella," Rori said once I'd ceased shouting.

"What do you mean? Where is he?"

"They took him."

They. The pronoun rolled around my brain. It meant there were other people here. But who? Survivors from another downed ship?

"Who are 'they,' Rori? Where did they take him?"

"I do not know that, Stella. I am sorry."

Jon leaned down, whispering in my ear. "The ship's system just apologized to you, Stella. This is so weird."

"Rori has all sorts of feelings," I said, forging on toward the bridge. It's where Hugo would have been for landing, and the part of the ship that appeared to have taken the most damage. I had to see.

The picture came into sharp focus as we reached the space where a staircase used to be. What was left of the connection between the rest of Deck Two and the bridge, of the stairs down to Jessa's quarters and the kitchens, was a gaping hole, jagged metal pieces, and debris visible if you gazed down into it. Someone had laid a wooden plank across it, establishing a walkway.

Jon went first, annoying in his chivalry, but I didn't complain. The drop made me nervous, and balance had never been my strong suit. Taking tiny, slow steps and accepting a hand from Jon at the end, I made it across, and found my favorite spot on board in ruins. All the tab screens had been shattered or cracked; some exhibited signs of superheating. So did the metal fittings at the windows; they'd melted and been reborn as gnarled appendages twisting in unnatural directions. There'd been a fire here. The heat shields must have failed.

"Rori, was Hugo injured?" I asked, voice rising with panic as I took in the state of things.

"Yes, he was. He would not rouse, so when the strangers came on board, I let them come up to the bridge, and they took him away."

"Did they say anything? Do you have any clue who they were?"

"They did not speak to me; thus I had no reason to converse with them."

"Come on, Stella." Jon tugged my arm back toward the plank. "He's not here. We should go."

We went back the way we'd come as the questions ran over and over in my head: Who had taken Hugo? How badly injured might he have been? What if he was dead? All this time, I'd interpreted the fact that the *Rochester* was on, that Rori was sending out a ping, as the promise that Hugo was alive. The thought that I could have come all this way only to lay flowers on his grave… My legs nearly buckled out from under me, but Jon was there before I could fall.

"We'll find him," he said, intuiting my fears. His reassurance gave me a tiniest flicker of hope, but I was bracing myself for the worst-case scenario nonetheless.

"You didn't find him," Xiao said as we exited; no need for a question.

"Rori said he was injured in the landing, but someone came and got him. We found a plank they used to get to the bridge. But there's good news. The med bay is completely intact, and Rori's been diverting power to keep everything up and running."

"Good." Xiao nodded. "If Hugo's injured, that will come in handy. We should look for tracks, signs of life. There must be a settlement nearby."

"Maybe it's the survivors from the *Crusader*," Jon suggested. "They came down, what, a year ago? If Fairfax's bizarrely sentient computer system chose this as an optimal landing spot, their ship's computer might have as well."

Jon sprang into action, circling the ship, looking for tracks, while Xiao and I went in the opposite direction.

"There's sign of disturbance in the underbrush, heading into the forest," Jon said as we met back at the front of the ship. "But I don't know if now's the most opportune time to proceed." He turned to look behind us; I followed his gaze and clapped eyes on a sight that competed with the mountains for beauty.

"I think that's a sunset," I said. "Or at least the beginnings of one. I read about them in so many books, but I never imagined…" Literature could not begin to touch the reality I beheld before me. But neither Jon nor Xiao had the eyes of an artist; they observed for a moment, then turned back to the matter at hand.

"We'll make camp for the night, then rally a search party in the morning," Jon concluded, already turning and heading back the way we'd come. I lingered, wishing desperately to take off into those woods, though I knew the soundest thing was to start fresh the next day. Strange, because as far as my body was concerned, it was still midday. It would take some time to adjust to the new clock. Xiao tugged on my arm until I moved reluctant feet in the wrong direction. With the sunset at our backs, and despite the coat I wore, a chill set into my spine.

thirty-one

We spent the night on board the *Ingram*, dividing up the sleeping quarters among us, but sleep had eluded me for the most part. Restlessness brought me into the transport bay when the sky was still dark; I sat on the edge of the open doorway and gazed up at my former home. The stars were beginning to disappear, but the moon was still clearly visible. She looked so far away, so lonely without the *Rochester* to keep her company.

I wondered once more at my new home, watching as my breath turned into white puffs upon hitting the cold air. As the light began to flood the landscape ahead, I could make out rustling grass, signs of an animal skittering about. And if I thought the sunset incredible, the sunrise proved equal if not surpassing it in measure. Watching inky blue and dusky purple turn pink, then orange, finally giving way again to the lightest blue was a revelation. It was also a welcome sign that it was time to go.

Jon and Xiao were a given, but I was surprised to see Justine join our search party. I hadn't realized she'd come down with us. When I asked her about it, she sniffed and said in heavily accented English, "After the marriage I have had, I am ready for an adventure." Fair enough. Then I saw Hanada approach. And she had a stunner gun.

"She is not coming," I said.

"Mari knows the med bay better than any of us," Xiao said.

"And she knows how to fire a gun," Jon threw in. *Traitor.* "We need her."

Overruled, I gave in, and in no time at all, we overtook the *Rochester* again. Hanada raided some supplies from the medical bay, and then we pushed onward through the trees.

"What exactly are we looking for?" Justine asked.

"Signs of human beings, likely dragging a body," Jon answered, from the point position. Hanada was the sweep.

"Dragging Hugo," I corrected him. "Body" made it sound like he was dead.

"Who do we think they are?" Justine's voice shook just a bit.

"The leading theory is that we've landed close to the survivors of the *Crusader.*" Jon looked back, offering Justine a reassuring smile. "Don't worry—we assume they're friendly. The guns are just a precaution."

I sided with Justine on this one; after what had happened to George, I didn't care for guns at all. Even those that just stunned. "It doesn't have to be the *Crusader*, does it?" I asked, shifting the subject. "Couldn't it be survivors from that ship that went down three years ago? I think it was *Wuthering Heights*?"

I could see Jon shake his head. "They didn't make it."

"How do you know that?"

"My uncle told me. Said she had communication tech on board and was supposed to hail the *Olympus* once she landed. They didn't hear from her, and she's presumed lost."

"No one's heard from the *Crusader*, either," I said, tamping down the alarm I felt at learning *Wuthering Heights*'s fate.

"She didn't have any comm tech, so we're hoping for the best."

The forest was more like a dense outcropping of trees; in no time, we were through, once again walking in fields of tall grass. It was easier to follow the trail, crumpled and bent stalks guiding our way. We had no timepieces to judge our progress, but I watched the sky; I'd read in enough books that the sun traversed east to west, and at midday would be straight above our heads. The sky grew ever-brighter blue where patches of colors broke through dense cloud cover, and I guessed we'd walked about an hour through the grass when the trail veered right. We followed it a quarter of an hour to a road, the first true sign of human influence, and a thing to behold: worn tracks of dirt instead of metal grating. Here, we found distinct grooves—something with wheels had been through here.

"They have a vehicle of some sort," I said. "A cart, I think."

Jon grinned at the sight of them. "I'm doing my best not to gloat," he said. "I told you guys there was life here. We should have come down ages ago." It put a new spring in his step, and we had to push to keep pace. Two hours later, the rain started.

"By the moon, what is this?" Justine shrieked, attempting in vain to cover her hair.

"Weather," I said, pulling my coat around me and trudging on.

It stopped after an hour, during which time I thought my clothes and hair must have absorbed more water than previously I'd been rationed in a month aboard the *Stalwart*. We stopped by the side of the now-muddy road to check our packs. Our sleep sacks and spare clothes were soaked through as well.

"This is not what I had in mind for an adventure," Justine said.

"We never said it would be dry," Jon cracked.

While I managed a smile, I found myself weighed down by serious thought. We'd walked a third of the day, yet it seemed we were no closer to finding Hugo, and now it was likely the tracks had washed away. I felt a hand touch lightly to my arm. Xiao.

"Don't worry, I'm sure we'll find them soon. I'd wager whoever we're chasing is only a few days' walk away."

A few days? I did my best to hide my consternation, and after another minute's rest, we forged on. I counted steps instead of minutes. Four hundred steps, and the cold and damp set into my bones; a thousand, and my pack of supplies was killing my back. But it took only one step around a bend to turn weariness into excitement.

I could see people.

Four figures loomed on the horizon, maybe half a mile ahead of us on the road—I was getting the hang of judging distance—so I knew if I sprinted, I could reach them in just a few minutes.

"Wait, Stella!" Jon barked before I could get farther than a few feet past him. I stopped and looked back to see him incline his head at Xiao and Hanada, who both placed ready hands on their gun holsters.

"Is that really necessary?" I squinted into the distance. "They don't look any bigger than I am."

"It's a precaution."

"A stupid precaution," I argued. "If they meant us harm, they would have left Hugo for dead, not carted him off, presumably to help him. If they see we have guns, they may assume we're a threat and respond in kind. Have a little faith." I looked to Xiao for backup; she was an officer, but she understood diplomacy, too. After a moment of clear consideration, Xiao relaxed, moving her hand away from the gun. Mari followed suit.

"Let's approach carefully," Xiao said, specifically directing her authority at Jon. He was the tracker and planner of our group, but she had fifteen years as an officer under her belt. "Stella, you take the lead; Jon and Mari fall back."

We began to move in new formation, finding that our potential friends hadn't stopped to argue about their approach and thus had bridged a quarter of the gap between us. I could make out some features. They reminded me of Jatinder,

Navid, and Preity. "Did the *Crusader* have a significant South Asian population?" I asked, quickening my pace.

"I don't think so," Jon said.

"Hello!" I called out when we were finally within hearing distance. But all I got back was confusion. Justine attempted a greeting in French, and Hanada tried Japanese, Korean, and, inexplicably, German.

"*Nín hǎo!*" Xiao tried finally, which immediately elicited a reaction. The four of them turned and started chatting excitedly to one another. "They speak Mandarin," Xiao informed us with considerable amusement. There was no way they came from the *Crusader*—the chief language among the fleet was English. Who were they? And where were we?

Now close enough to have a conversation, Xiao rattled off something, of which I caught nothing but Hugo's name. As a conversation was conducted in rapid-fire Mandarin, I observed the party, affirming my belief that they were not from any fleet ship. Their clothing was roughly hewn but looked sturdily made—they wore bodices made of leather over tawny-colored slacks. Brown, tan, and bleached white were the dominant color scheme, which led me to believe they had no access to the variety of dyes we had on the fleet.

"They have Hugo." Xiao turned to us breathlessly to report the good news. "And he's alive. Injured, but alive. They saw our ship come down and were coming to investigate. They'll take us to him now."

Xiao walked up front with her four new friends, the rest of us following behind, hopelessly shut out of a conversation we couldn't understand. Every few minutes, Xiao relayed the highlights to us in English.

"It's absolutely unbelievable," she said. "They're from here. From Earth. Descended from survivors of the ice age." She turned back to the woman who seemed to be the ringleader, who wore a long, neat braid that stretched halfway down her back and had bright hazel eyes that crinkled at the edges. I placed her at maybe forty. When she spoke, her tone was warm but firm.

Xiao piped up with new information. "They lived in underground shelters carved out of old mining shafts until about sixty years ago. We're heading toward their settlement."

"Where are we, exactly? Do they know what part of the world we're in?" Jon asked.

"More importantly for the present," Justine piped in, "how long until we reach their settlement? I am exhausted."

"It's a few hours' walk, I'm afraid," Xiao replied. "They say they walked all morning, as we did, though they likely set out a bit later. And to answer your question, Jon, they say we're in the country formerly known as India."

Like Hugo's Jungle Book, I thought.

We introduced ourselves, with Xiao acting as interpreter, and they did the same. The leader was Reshma, the other two women named Jia and Adeebah, and the man was Ravi. Xiao asked why they spoke Mandarin and relayed that the shelter their ancestors had taken was Chinese in origin; thus, they had learned that language primarily. I wished I remembered enough of the Hindi Jatinder had taught me to ask if they had retained that language too. But then again, this part of the world had had hundreds of languages. So much culture had been lost.

When I witnessed my second sunset, I was no longer in any position to express awe; I was still damp and my muscles ached, the gravity of Earth and our long journey no match for my space-light bones. By the time we reached Reshma's settlement, Jon was telling any of us who would listen about new plans for endurance training so as to acclimate to our new environment.

The settlement was built right on the main road; first we saw several dozen small houses, which quickly gave way to multi-dwelling units, then businesses and shops, a veritable main street. Residents peered out of windows and stopped on the street, gawking at us as we passed.

Reshma explained that the town was called New Delhi, not the real city of old, but named in honor of it, as we were apparently very close to those ruins. Jon cracked a joke about how it should have been called *New* New Delhi, but I was too tired to laugh. We left the road, going onto a side street, until Reshma stopped in front of a building. Xiao translated the Mandarin written on its front.

"This is the hospital," she said. "Hugo must be here."

The words stopped my breath.

Jon took that as his cue. "Xiao, could you ask them if we could sit down somewhere, maybe dry our things, if there's a fire?"

"And eat something," Justine chimed in. "I am starving."

"I'll go with you, since you'll need a translator," Xiao said. When I protested, pointed out that surely she wanted to reunite with Hugo as badly as I did, she demurred. "I'll have my turn." She said some words to Reshma, indicated me, and from the way Reshma's face softened in pity, I knew Xiao had told her about Hugo's and my relationship. My checks burned at the attention.

Based on the medical bays I'd seen on the fleet, I was expecting shiny metal and a sterile air, but New Delhi's clinic entry hall was lit by candles, and the air was fragrant with spices—cloves and cardamom. But underneath, I could make out the smell of sick and ointments.

"He has suffered burns. And has mostly been sleeping," Xiao translated for Reshma before they led me toward the back of the building and stopped before a plain door. Then Xiao departed, promising to fetch me food. I thanked her and tried to tell her not to worry about it, but she smiled and patted me on the arm, repeating her intentions.

When I opened the door, my stomach dropped; I choked on shock, bile rising in my throat.

He suffered burns. Reshma had said it. I'd seen the damage to the bridge, but I'd not really thought about it, spent any time imagining what that could look like. I stumbled a few steps forward, put my hand to my mouth to stop from crying out. Hugo lay on a bed spread-eagle, large leaves of some kind draped over his chest, abdomen, upper arms. Skin, tender and pink, peeked out from the edges. His right leg was in a cast. A large swath of his cheek, extending to his collarbone, glistened with ointment. The burns were less severe there, but that was a relative statement. I could see yellow, angry blisters bubbling across his skin from the door.

There had been an engine fire on the *Empire* when I was a girl; thankfully my father had been off-shift and was unharmed. But against his instructions, I'd snuck down to the scene of the accident. I wanted to see the bodies. They were angry red and black, charred—some unrecognizable. Hugo was lucky to have escaped that fate. But he would certainly bear many scars. And a painful recovery.

I found myself thankful he was asleep. It afforded him some relief, and me the chance to slip in quietly to a chair by his bedside. I held my breath, touched tentative fingers to an uninjured spot on his shoulder, to his cheek, through his hair. He was real, and he was alive. I licked the salt off my lips, wiped at my eyes.

"Hugo, I'm here. I came all this way to make sure you were all right. And I'm really mad at you for doing something so stupid as running off to Earth by yourself."

He wheezed, breath rattling in his chest, then coughed, stirring. Perhaps to respond to my ill-timed joke.

"I imagined death would feel better."

I frowned, trying to puzzle out his meaning.

"Hugo, you're not dead," I reassured him. I touched the back of my hand to his forehead, which was burning up. His eyes fluttered open, but he did not turn his head or seem to see me.

"I must be dead. You're here, which is impossible. So you

must be a ghost, and I am in purgatory." His breath caught, and he winced, his burns obviously smarting. "That would explain the pain. Atonement."

I didn't know what to do or say—he thought he was imagining me, and how could you convince a person under such a delusion of what is real verses imagined?

I stood, and carefully but firmly kissed him. "I'm real, Hugo, and I'm here. Now stop being so dramatic. Bianca was right." Hugo finally opened his eyes wide, blinked up at me.

"Stella," he breathed, breaking into a smile, then wincing. The burns on the left side of his face impeded physical expressions of joy. I had to settle for words and the light that danced in his eyes. "I don't understand. How are you here?"

"The *Stalwart* sent down a forward party before they settle here. I convinced them to track your ship, turn it into a rescue mission."

"But why would you come after me? You must hate me. What I did."

"I could never hate you." I took his hand, careful not to disturb his arm. "I got your letter, and I understand. Xiao told me about your mother—" I cut myself off. I couldn't bring myself to say it. "Hugo, I'm sorry."

"It was all for nothing," he said, voice barely above a whisper. "I let Mason get away with it, and she still died."

"We stopped the worst of it, though. We went to the news media; there were quarantine procedures put in place."

"Four hundred and fifty-three people died. Those deaths are on me."

"I think you've suffered enough for it." I stroked his cheek, fussed with his hair, pushing sweat-soaked locks off his forehead. "We're starting a new life here. You and me. And Xiao. And, oddly, Justine Ingram." It felt good to joke a bit, to see the corners of Hugo's mouth quirk. "Hanada came too," I said. Hugo winced. "We'll talk about that later."

"What about Jessa?"

"Still safe on the *Lady Liberty*, with Orion and Poole."

"Good." A coughing fit overtook him, shaking his body painfully. He winced, and I couldn't help doing so as well.

"We'll get you pain meds from the *Rochester*," I said. "You'll be okay."

"I have some now, actually." Xiao appeared as if by magic. She joined me at Hugo's bedside, frowning down at his prone figure. "We should get Hanada in here to examine your burns. But in the meantime…"

While Xiao administered a shot of clear fluid into Hugo's vein, I partook of her other offering: dinner. The curry I'd had on board the *Empire* paled in comparison to this; it was rich, aromatic, perfect. I'd not even finished eating before I looked over to find Hugo asleep. Xiao held on to his hand tightly, stroking his hair.

"I've known him his whole life," she said. "I never admitted it before, but he and Jessa are the closest I'll ever come to having my own children." She let out a shuddering breath. "I should have done something, acted like the mother he needed instead of playing the part of the First Officer. I can't help but feel this is all my fault."

I settled a hand on her shoulder, giving it a squeeze. "It's not your fault. Just... focus on the fact that we're here now. We'll start over. That's the most any of us can do."

Reshma came a short time later with a tumble of blankets and a pillow, intuiting that I would not want to leave Hugo's side. I slept fitfully, waking every few hours with a start, rising to check on him, paranoid he would stop breathing. But everything was fine. The pain meds worked like magic, blurring the next few days as Hugo slept through the worst of his recovery, and I held court by his side. We rarely talked, even when he was lucid enough to do so; all we would do is run ourselves in circles, Hugo castigating himself, me repeating over and over that I loved him. I was here. That had to be enough.

I waited until Hugo was better recovered; after a week he was sitting up, and with yet another, he was walking, albeit with the aid of crutches. I took him outside on a brisk Tuesday evening to watch the sunset; we huddled up close on an overturned tree that had been fashioned into a bench, gazing up at the sky. The words I'd said to Xiao echoed like a new mantra. I shared them with Hugo, hoping he'd find the same solace in them as I did.

"I think we should start over," I said. "You and me. Well, all of us. But particularly you and me."

Hugo bristled. "You don't love me anymore."

I rolled my eyes at him, refusing to take his histrionics seriously. "I've told you a hundred times a day for the last two weeks—of course I love you. I came down to Earth for you.

Don't be stupid." I kissed him on the forehead for good measure and wove our fingers together. "But the circumstances of our meeting, our engagement, the people we were—that was our old life. I don't want to pick up where we left off. I want to start over. No parties with Bianca Ingram this time."

That got him to crack a smile.

"We're not defined by who we were up there," I continued, looking up, rendered breathless as always by the cascade of colors giving way to pinpricks of starlight. "Who our parents were, or how they died, what jobs they had, the ships we lived on. We're all equals down here." I squeezed his hand. "Let's start over. Okay?"

He squeezed back. "Okay."

epilogue

We created a settlement by our landing site and began the long process of learning how to survive on Earth, the next weeks and months full of wonder, frustration, compromise, and, gradually, contentment. It was hard to say which presented the greatest challenge—learning to understand and live with weather, or the sudden lack of indoor plumbing. Jon could be heard ranting to anyone who would listen that, if only more engineers would come down, we could fix the abhorrent issue that was the indignity of outhouses. I didn't mind them; in the grand scheme of things, it wouldn't kill us to use simple systems of resource management, so long as our population was small and easily sustained. The New Delhians briefed us on myriad elegant solutions for living off the land, from how to filter clean drinking water to animal-based farming techniques. They lent us horses for plowing fields, cows for milk, chickens for eggs.

We lived inside the *Ingram* on half power until we learned to build houses and while the farmers among us waited for crops to sprout. By that time, Hugo was fully recovered, though he would walk with a limp for the rest of his life, and his scars would always tell a story. I did not care one whit how he looked or walked; I was thankful that he was alive.

Lori and Rori argued for weeks on how to establish video communication links with the fleet, but eventually Xiao and I coaxed them to work together, the two AIs seeming to make each other smarter with every interaction. Three weeks after landing, we could finally not only talk to, but see the *Lady Liberty*, let her know that we were okay and show them Earth was habitable and had been for many decades. Soon enough, the *Stalwart* wasn't the only ship planning reentry. But she was the first, and two months later, she landed in a field two miles from the Fairfax settlement, hundreds joining our community.

I found myself in a classroom again, no longer teaching theories about the Earth as it might be, but facts about how things were. The children adapted more quickly than anyone, Arden and the other *Stalwart* kids taking on farming and building tasks, in addition to their studies, and generally keeping the older teens and adults in our place. If we ever complained, all it took was an incredulous look from a nine-year-old having the time of her life in the fresh air to knock you to your senses. They also picked up our new language with incredible speed. Xiao taught not only the children

Mandarin, but everyone else, too. On weekends, some of the New Delhians would visit us to learn English from Xiao as well. It became a full-time job, and she frequently took breaks on the *Ingram* bridge, talking to Orion up on the *Lady Liberty* and begging him to recruit some more Mandarin speakers to come down.

She got more than just Mandarin speakers: the *Mumbai* deorbited next, then the *Saint Petersburg*. Each ship established its own town, and soon we had our own little Earth-bound economy going. Over the coming years, more would join us. Eventually, we hoped, all.

We received word that Mason had finally been exposed and brought to justice, though not the fleet's old standard of death by airlock. Orion had him confined to the brig on the *Lady Liberty* so he could keep an eye on him. We owed it all to George, who had taken it upon himself to track down Karmina Ocampo at the *Tribune* and made her print the truth. In time, Hugo could forgive himself for the role he played, though it was long after everyone else had done so, including me.

Partnering with the New Delhians and using the *Rochester*'s considerable stores of medicine and medical equipment, we established a hospital halfway between our settlements and theirs. Hanada devoted herself to its running, making herself useful but never outright apologizing. But she devoted herself to the good of us all, conducting research and keeping everyone healthy. I was thankful for her presence most days.

Hugo also made the massive digital library on board

available to all, though with limited electricity and tech, the population had to get their fill in turns. Health and information became Hugo's gift to our new world, a fresh Fairfax legacy to outlive the old one. We destroyed all the viruses. Biological warfare would not be a weapon used again in our lifetime.

We started over, got to know the latest versions of each other. Hugo remained smart, flirtatious, and generous with me, but he'd become more closed off. Harder on himself. He remained stubbornly overprotective of those he cared about, including and especially me. I found I frequently had to put him in his place, remind him I didn't need taking care of. I had changed too.

Even so, Hugo took me on dates: a walk along the river, a starlit picnic among the poppies, a night in New Delhi watching a play neither of us could understand. It was nice, spending time with him outside of a study, doing something other than reading books, though that remained our staple activity. Rori kept the power running to the old study on board the *Rochester* just for us.

Eventually, when it became clear that Hugo's lingering guilt would not ebb away despite pretty words from me, I proposed. We already acted like we were married, and had been ready to take the plunge before, having known each other far less, so why not? Marriage didn't mean a whole lot down on Earth, given we had no lawyers to draw up a marriage contract, nor any central government to enforce its validity, as Xiao and Sergei argued more than once. They had no intention of getting married. But it was a tradition, a holdover from the old ways, and frankly, I wanted to have a party. Still Hugo hesitated. I knew why. Jessa was missing.

I encouraged Hugo to do something his pride and guilt had not allowed him to do over the past year: talk to her. It took me dragging him onto the bridge of the *Ingram*, physically plopping him in the comms station chair, and establishing the call link myself to get him to do it. And once they started talking—after Jessa yelled at Hugo for taking the fall for Mason and not telling her the truth, and Hugo apologized—they both started crying, and all it took was the invitation to get Jessa to agree to join us. She came down on the next ship to deorbit, leaving the *Lady Liberty*—and thus the Fairfax empire—in Orion's hands. And I got Orion to make a promise: that he'd bring the *Lady Liberty*'s passengers, and himself, down to Earth within the next decade.

And so another Tuesday arrived, bringing another sunset, one of thousands to come. The house Hugo, Jessa, and I shared stood at my back, grass and trees and mountains before me, with the skies beyond, and I knew I was home. At last.

acknowledgments

First, to my US publishing team at HMH: It cannot be overstated how in every way you have made all my publishing dreams come true. I have been guided by not one, but two incredible editors. Sarah Landis, thank you for your endless belief in this book, and the way that you just got everything I was trying to do. You were a dream to work with, and I am thankful for our continuing friendship. Cat Onder, thank you for "adopting" me, and shepherding me through the rest of the publishing process, answering my endless questions, and being my tireless advocate at every level.

I could not have asked for a better marketing and publicity team, who have brainstormed bigger and bolder than I ever could have, and championed my book in ways that have honestly made me a bit teary! Lisa DiSarro, Tara Shanahan, Tara Sonin, Rachel Fershleiser, Amanda

Acevedo: you are all rockstars of the highest order.

I am beyond grateful to Titan Books for bringing *Brightly Burning* to the UK. You have blown me away with your excitement, and with the care you've taken to produce a truly gorgeous edition. Thank you especially to my editor, Sam Matthews, for all your guidance through the process, and to Julia Lloyd, for a cover that took my breath away.

Elana, my incredible warrior of an agent, I am thankful every single day that you loved this book and wanted to take me on. You were and are everything I didn't know I needed, and I couldn't do any of this without you. And thank you to Tamar Rydzinski at Laura Dail and Laura West from David Higham for working tirelessly to find *Brightly Burning* a UK home.

Thank you and all the hugs to my longtime CP and friend, Heather Kaczynski, for being with me through every step of this journey and for letting me be with you on yours. You are a brilliant writer and human being, and I feel privileged to call you my friend.

To Elly Blake, the most sweet, positive, and supportive friend. Your enthusiasm kept me going through every draft and your beautiful writing pushed me to be a better writer. Any captivating turn of phrase in this book I owe to you; reading your lush descriptions sparked my own imagination so many times. All my love and gratitude to Natalie Simpson, for speedy and repeated reads when I was convinced everything was terrible. I'm so glad I met you, and can't wait to return the favor. Mary Elizabeth Summer, you always make things better with your wit and insightful comments, whether they be about the book at hand, the industry, or life. Thanks to Emmy Neal for your incisive comments, including and especially how I should kill someone in the third act, and for being a good sport when I told you NO! and then ended up doing it eventually anyway. Yes, he didn't stay dead, but the point is, mea culpa!

To every early reader who gave me something to think about, or just reassured me I didn't suck: Samantha McClanahan, Liz Parker, Kester Grant, Chelsea Sedoti, Sophie Gonzalez, Marize Alphonso, Destiny Cole, Kristine Kim, and Katie Doyle. To my fierce ladies of science, Emily Suvada and Mandy Self, for checking the science part of the sci-fi, helping me to embarrass myself a bit less. Any remaining errors of hand-waveyness are on me!

All my supremely awesome author friends, just for being you: Adrienne Kisner, Emily Duncan, Kevin van Whye, Claire Wenzel, Gretchen Schreiber, Jessie Cluess, Kaitlyn Sage Patterson, Maura Milan, Rebecca Schaeffer, Heather Ezell, Lily Meade, Kat Cho, Adrienne Young, Kristin Dwyer, Emma Theriault, and Rosiee Thor. My fellow Electric 18s: Stay Electric. My California Electrics: I adore you all. Team Elana: I love you all, you pretty writing nerds. My Reddit fam, especially Lilah Vandenburgh for always putting perfectly into a few words what I am trying to say with a paragraph, and to the whole UpvoteYA podcast team.

To Beth Revis, for inspiring me to write space YA in the first place and for not being weirded out by my multiple homages to *Across the Universe* in this book. Your kindness and professional guidance over the years were instrumental. Susan Dennard for treating me like a peer long before I had a book deal and for always offering the best advice. You are a class act, and one of the most talented writers I have the privilege of knowing.

Thank you to the entire AMM fam: My mentees and friends Whitney Wyckoff, Alyssa Colman, India Hill and Lindsey Meredith: You are all destined for great things and I can't wait to be there for them. Special thanks to Whitney for her help with the journalism parts, since I am terribly rusty in that arena, and to Alyssa for the brainstorming sessions. To all the mentors whom I also consider friends: Stay salty.

To WriteGirl, for welcoming me with open arms and unlocking a passion for teen mentorship, which has launched me down so many surprising paths. Never underestimate the power of a girl and her pen. My DragonCon YA Lit Track squad who have been with me on the entire journey: Casey, Mel, Tara, Jenn, Natalie and Bev. Bev especially: I have learned so much from you and think you are the bee's knees.

To my LA family, Patty, Daniel, Holly and Sylvia. Thank you for being my home away from home every holiday and letting me write while you watch football. I owe many words on the page to the NFL package.

Everyone at IMD: Adrienne, Nicole, Elizabeth, Mike, Scott, Katie, Doug, Patrick and Katherine. You are the best work team anyone could ask for. Thanks to Nicole for helping me with my Mandarin (inevitable errors are my own), and special thanks to Adrienne Alwag for always supporting my writer life and my work life.

Anyone I may have erred in forgetting: you are wonderful; I am terrible.

Charlotte Bronte, for creating a heroine who speaks to so many people, myself included. I'm convinced you wrote the first YA novel, and it has brought me so much joy since I was a teenager. I am sure I did not do justice to your beautiful book and characters, but thank you, nonetheless.

And last but never least, my mom, who has always believed in me and encouraged me to be a writer. You still tell people that I wrote a Babysitter's Club "book" when I was eight and it was as good as the published stuff, and I don't believe you, but I love that you think so. I am here because of you, and I love you.

about the author

When she's not writing science fiction and fantasy, Alexa Donne works in international television marketing. A proud Boston University Terrier, she lives in Los Angeles with two fluffy ginger cats named after YA literature characters. Visit her at alexadonne.com, and on Twitter and Instagram at @alexadonne.